Advertising Works 25

Proving the payback on
marketing investment

Case studies from the
IPA Effectiveness Awards 2020

Edited and introduced by
Sue Unerman
Convenor of Judges

First published 2020 by Ascential Events (Europe) Limited (t/a WARC)
33 Kingsway, London WC2B 6UF
Telephone: 0207 467 8100
Email: enquiries@warc.com
www.warc.com

A CIP catalogue record for this book is available from the British Library

ISBN: 978-1-84116-230-0

Typeset by HWA Text and Data Management, London
Printed and bound by CPI Group (UK) Ltd, Croydon, CR0 4YY

Contents

Contents

Sponsors

The success of the 2020 IPA Effectiveness Awards is in no small part down to its sponsors, and the IPA would like to thank the companies listed here for their continuing support.

FACEBOOK

Acknowledgements

Many people worked hard to make the Awards a success, especially the following: Sue Unerman, Convenor of Judges and Harjot Singh, Deputy Convenor of Judges.

At the IPA, the team were: Jana De-Vos, Ed Elworthy, Ava Gill, Carlos Grande, Maria Grey, Tessa Gooding, Kay Heenan, Janet Hull, Roger Ingham, Angelika Libera, Kathryn Patten, Ramandeep Sandhu, Kirsty Walker, Sylvia Wood and Charlie Young.

We also owe a debt of gratitude to:

The IPA Awards Board Members

1980/82 Convenor of Judges, Simon Broadbent (d)
1984/86 Convenor of Judges, Charles Channon (d)
1988/90 Convenor of Judges, Paul Feldwick
1992/94 Convenor of Judges, Chris Baker   Bacon Strategy and Research
1996 Convenor of Judges, Gary Duckworth
1998 Convenor of Judges, Nick Kendall   Broken
2000 Convenor of Judges, Tim Broadbent (d)
2002 Convenor of Judges, Marco Rimini   Mindshare
2004 Convenor of Judges, Alison Hoad
2005 Convenor of Judges, Les Binet   adam&eveDDB
2006 Convenor of Judges, Laurence Green   MullenLowe
2007 Convenor of Judges, Richard Storey   M&C Saatchi
2008 Convenor of Judges, Neil Dawson   Wunderman Thompson
2009 Convenor of Judges, Andy Nairn   Lucky Generals
2010 Convenor of Judges, David Golding   New Commercial Arts
2011 Convenor of Judges, Charlie Snow   Consultant
2012 Convenor of Judges, Marie Oldham   VCCP Media
2014 Convenor of Judges, Lorna Hawtin   TBWA\MCR
2016 Convenor of Judges, Bridget Angear   AMV BBDO
2018 Convenor of Judges, Neil Godber   Wunderman Thompson
2020 Convenor of Judges, Sue Unerman   MediaCom
IPA Director General, Paul Bainsfair
IPA Director of Marketing Strategy, Janet Hull
IPA Head of Marketing Strategy, Kathryn Patten
IPA Marketing Manager, Kay Heenan

The Judges

Sue Unerman
Chief Transformation Officer, MediaCom
Convenor of Judges

Harjot Singh
CSO EMEA & UK, McCann Worldgroup
Deputy Convenor of Judges

CLIENT JUDGING PANEL

Stevie Spring CBE
Chairman, British Council
Chairman of Judges

Conrad Bird
Director of Campaigns and Marketing
Department for International Trade

Benjamin Braun
CMO
Samsung Europe

Cheryl Calverley
CEO
eve sleep

Annabelle Cordelli
VP Global Marketing
Virgin Atlantic and Virgin Holidays

Asmita Dubey
Chief Media Officer, L'Oréal Group
and Chief Digital Officer, Consumer
Products Division, L'Oréal

Catherine Kehoe
Chief Customer Officer
Lloyds Banking Group

Fernando Machado
Global CMO
Restaurant Brands International

Michelle McEttrick
Group Brand Director
Tesco

INDUSTRY JUDGING PANEL

Heather Alderson
Global Planning Partner
adam&eveDDB

Jo Arden
CSO
Publicis • Poke

Neil Barrie
Co-Founder and Managing Partner
TwentyFirstCenturyBrand

Ed Booty
CSO
Publicis Singapore APAC

Michael Chadwick
CSO, APAC
Dentsu

Richard Dunn
Chairman & CSO
Wunderman Thompson

Charlie Ebdy
CSO
OMD UK

Jane Frost CBE
CEO
MRS

Melpo Gkofa
Strategic Consultant
Freelance

Sarah King
Global Head of Brand, Insights Division
Kantar

Douglas McCabe
CEO
Enders Analysis

Brent Nelsen
CSO
Publicis Communications & Leo Burnett
North America

The Judges

Susan Poole
Strategic Consultant
Freelance

Shobha Sairam
VP, CSO, Global
the community

Stuart Sullivan-Martin
Global Head of Strategy
Wavemaker

Kate Waters
Director of Client Strategy and Planning
ITV

Helen Weavers
Strategic Consultant
Real World Planning

Malcolm White
Founder
krow

Amy Winger
Global CSO
VMLY&R

TECHNICAL JUDGING PANEL

Andrew Bertolaso
Senior Partner
Gain Theory

Jane Christian
Managing Partner, Head of Systems
Intelligence
MediaCom

Harry Davies
Head of Measurement and Analytics
Google

Andrew Deykin
Managing Consultant
Data2Decisions

Bill Doris
Insight Executive Director
OMD EMEA

Ian Forrester
SVP, Research & Analytics
Whalar

Jamie Gascoigne
Director
Brightblue Consulting

Verity Gill
Director, Marketing Science EMEA, Agencies
Facebook

Chris Hutchings
Senior Director
MarketCast

Sara Jones
Director
Pearl Metrics

Dr Grace Kite
MD and Economist
Gracious Economics

Nick Milne
Founder & Director
Go Ignite Consulting

Abs Owdud
Operations Insight Controller
NOW TV

Nic Pietersma
Business Director
Ebiquity

Paul Sturgeon
Data and Analytics Consultant
Freelance

Mike Treharne
Head of Insight
Leo Burnett

Francis Walton
Head of Research, Strategy
Publicis Sapient

Zhao Zhang
Lead Data Strategist
Imagination

Introduction

By Sue Unerman
Chief Transformation Officer, MediaCom

As Convenor of the 2020 IPA Effectiveness Awards, I would bet that I have been asked a question that no other Convenor in the history of the Awards has been asked.

'Are you cancelling the Awards?'

In the first quarter of 2020, at the time of the IPA Effectiveness Awards deadlines, the coronavirus pandemic swept through the world. The disruption was unprecedented, and at the time of writing, is ongoing.

Of course, discussions were had about the Awards with agencies, marketers and effectiveness experts, given the huge crisis facing society. Should they be cancelled? Should they be postponed? The answer was a resounding, 'no'. The IPA Effectiveness Awards are more important than ever.

We're in a recession. We need evidence of the contribution that advertising makes to business.

There is a global pandemic. We need longer-term perspective to ensure that we survive. The findings of the FT and IPA report, *The Board–Brand Rift* in 2019, were that while business leaders know instinctively that too much focus on the short term is bad for business, over half of business leaders rate their knowledge of brand building as average to very poor. And that critically, this lack of knowledge has a significant effect on attitudes to the benefits of long- and short-term balance in marketing.

Our industry is renowned for its resilience. So, of course the answer was 'no'. The Awards, which many people have been working on for months or years, went ahead.

There was a slight reduction in the normal number of entries, but this was less than 10% which, given the shock of the circumstances at the time of the deadline for submissions, was both understandable and minimal.

Judging was in virtual rooms rather than in the hallowed halls of the IPA building and we adapted. Judging was vigorous, argumentative and passionate, perhaps even more so than usual (there were tears on one occasion).

For 2020 there were two other key and, in this case, planned adjustments to the judging process.

First, there were more international judges than ever before. The IPA Effectiveness Awards are the most rigorous and respected in the world. They are international in scope, with special prizes for multi-market entries and international entries from businesses based outside of the UK.

Second, for the first time *every* Awards entry went through a significantly extended technical panel made up of experts in data, research and analytics (in the past, only those with econometric appendices did so).

So what have we learnt from 2020's award-winning submissions?

There are several key themes that present themselves.

The importance of an effectiveness culture in the whole business: our Grand Prix winner Tesco evidenced this in an outstanding fashion.

Audi (winner of the special prize for Best Dedication to Effectiveness) and Diageo (winner of the ones for Best Use of Data and Best New Learning) are great exemplars of this too.

In the IPA Reports, *Culture First* and *Building Bridges with Finance*, consultant Fran Cassidy highlighted the importance of language when describing marketing deliverables as business-focused benefits to ensure that the whole culture gets behind effective marketing.

Academic Tim Ambler has suggested marketing should be redefined from an expense and outlay to 'the sourcing and harvesting of cash flow'.

The power of consistency came through in long-term entries from Audi, John Lewis Partnership and Guinness (winner of the Best Multi-Market prize).

The alchemy of effectiveness when creative and media work together is particularly potent in the papers from Audi, Central Coast (winner of the the prize for Best International), Lloyds and Tesco.

Great human insight can pivot effectiveness. A twist in understanding of the role of the brand for Baileys led to its award-winning effectiveness story. A breakthrough in understanding how kids saw themselves drove the SickKids fundraising entry (winner of the prize for Best Contribution to Effectiveness through Technology).

There was significant controversy over the line between a PR stunt and a great tactical communications coup. The judges were divided. If effectiveness is proved, beyond any doubt, does it even matter? KFC's Aussie underdog entry, which scooped the Best Small Budget prize, showed huge returns from earned media value.

There were missing themes too: very little about diversity and inclusion, which is a surprise to me this year. Let's hope that since this is now firmly on the agenda of every business, and that the balanced scorecard is accepted best practice in the boardroom, this will feature next time.

There was also much less on proving the value of purpose than in 2018. Has this fallen off the marketing effectiveness agenda?

The 2020 IPA Effectiveness Awards are inspirational. They show that effectiveness can and should be cemented into the culture of business. Effectiveness cannot and should not be left solely to the strategists and the econometricians any more than creativity should be the sole remit of the creative department; or diversity and inclusion left exclusively to the human resources team.

It is the responsibility of every leader, and every putative leader, to own, to develop, to pioneer and to preach effectiveness in every organisation. Any business that fails to put effectiveness at its heart and through every muscle and sinew is shortchanging its clients, its shareholders, its customers, and its own future.

SPECIAL PRIZES

Grand Prix
Tesco

The Channon Prize for Best New Learning
Diageo portfolio

The Tim Broadbent Prize for Best International
Central Coast

Best Multi-Market
Guinness

Best Small Budget
KFC

Best Use of Data
Diageo portfolio

The President's Prize for Best Contribution to Effectiveness through Technology
SickKids

The Simon Broadbent Prize for Best Dedication to Effectiveness
Audi

Effectiveness Company of the Year
BBH

Effectiveness Network of the Year
MullenLowe Group

SECTION 1

New learning

Great lengths

All that is good about having a long-term strategy

By Jo Arden
CSO, Publicis • Poke

I am writing this chapter for *Advertising Works 25* in the summer of 2020. It is a year of seismic change. This is the fifth month of the UK lockdown as coronavirus continues to cost thousands of lives worldwide and the world has entered what is predicted to be the biggest recession of any of our lives.

The everyday-ness of our lives has been in upheaval since March. Children have largely been out of school. Summer holidays, if they have happened at all, have mostly been spent in the UK. City centres are empty. Basically, thinking about anything in the long term is weird. Adaptability, agility, and responsiveness are the order of the day.

Reading IPA papers that celebrate long-term thinking is like looking back to a different time. But a long-term strategy doesn't mean anything until it sees you through a global pandemic, so it is also an interesting time to be reading these brilliant papers and to think about where we might be when we all meet again for the Awards in a couple of years' time.

Long-term thinking is all about setting up a brand for a future we don't yet know. The long-versus-short is a constant theme in our industry. Indeed, Alison Hoad wrote a terrific essay on this same topic for *Advertising Works 23*. Anyone reading this will surely be well-versed in the discussion and the context which has given rise to short-termism. So it should be noted with disappointment but not surprise that alongside this year's bumper crop of long-term papers, there have not been more papers celebrating four or five years of thinking – maybe authors are saving it for bigger anniversaries.

2020 has certainly been a vintage year and there are five papers in particular which excelled in both their commitment to, and measurement of, long-term thinking over ambitiously long timescales. These are:

- Audi – 40 years
- WaterAid – 16 years
- John Lewis – 10 years
- Aldi – 10 years
- Guinness – 8 years

Each paper is extremely valuable in its own right of course, but it is also interesting to look at some of the themes they share.

Category-defining distinctive ideas

The first thing that strikes me about these papers is that, in their five different categories, they represent work that broke the mould. Whether through message or medium, they were all in one way or another pioneers and have redefined how their brand peers do communications.

It is not new for value retailers to advertise on price or to use humour. But Aldi's unapologetic focusing of humour on the comparative prices of its brand versus big ones (through its campaign, 'Like brands') was a breakthrough. The subtext of 'we all know this brand stuff is nonsense' is brilliantly countercultural for a grocer that was itself trying to build a brand. By being direct about the relationship between price and taste (or lack thereof), Aldi brought the consumer in on the joke and changed the game for price-led advertising.

It's hard to remember a time when the John Lewis Christmas campaign wasn't a cultural phenomenon, but, as its 2020 paper reminds us:

> *'In 2009 the brand had a low profile and was respected but not loved. For many it seemed expensive, aloof and out of touch with the times.'*
> John Lewis IPA Effectiveness Awards paper, 2020

In just ten years, the brand has changed the tone and tempo of the Christmas retail season; in both spend and popular interest it is now the UK's Super Bowl of advertising. There is, of course, debate about the merits of this change. But in terms of advertising spend, excitement and a showcase for British creativity, there is a lot to celebrate.

Guinness' 'Made of more' is a lesson in long-term brand thinking. It is all the more impressive given the impeccable history of Guinness communications ideas – 'Good things come to those who wait' being the best booze strategy ever written in my view. 'Made of more' so convincingly describes the very essence of the product and is so consistently and beautifully expressed that it is surprising it is only eight years old. In a sector which has responded to a changing drinking culture and increased regulation with tacked-on purpose initiatives, 'Made of more' goes so much further. It is a long-term strategy which has paid back consistently and continues to provide a firm foundation for the full spectrum of that brand's communications tasks. Perhaps most importantly right now, it is a thought which is at once fixed and flexible; another characteristic that these long-term papers share.

An idea expansive enough to move with the times

It is a special kind of talent that finds an enduring idea. The mythology behind Audi's 'Vorsprung durch Technik' suggests that a certain degree of luck is involved too, but there is no luck involved in how Audi and BBH have kept that idea current. Successive generations of marketers and agency teams have tapped into what the brand idea means in the context of today's culture. As Audi's paper puts it:

> *'Spiritual answers from within a brand are much more likely to be embraced by the organisation and people out in the world eventually, simply because they are true. Everyone can feel it. As such, we deliberately never really defined the brand too tightly. The brand onions made our eyes water. We knew what it stood for and let the guardians make the right calls to flex to the times.'*
> Audi IPA Effectiveness Awards paper, 2020

Such a liberated approach to idea definition has allowed Audi to move from an also-ran to a category leader in a relatively short time and to stay there for over 40 years.

Similarly, whilst the central strategy of John Lewis' Christmas campaigns remains the same year after year (i.e. 'John Lewis is the home of thoughtful gifting'), each campaign taps into the mood and energy of that year. From the beautifully conceived and crafted film to the activation, partnerships and promotions that sit around it, there is a clear thread which weaves through a decade of volatility and change. John Lewis at Christmas is that brand at its purest and with the recent (August 2020) scrapping of its 95-year-old price promise, 'Never knowingly undersold', it is an investment which will be the point of consistency as the brand enters a new decade.

WaterAid talks with impressive honesty about the changes it made to how its strategy was delivered over the 16 years its paper covers. In building a new communications model, it iterated channels and content in response to new learning. From switching out TV for press, to changing the timelines over which it made an ask to donors; in keeping the overall mission clear, it was able to experiment with how best to get there.

Playing it long … and short

This year's entries featured a number that had a laser-like focus on brand building, and were actively opposed to short-term activation or tactical initiatives (or at least this opposition was emphasised in the interests of telling a good tale in the paper). Lloyds Banking Group's paper on 'pure brand' is a brilliant read on this topic and caused much enjoyable debate among the judges. Conversely, the five papers I focus on here all describe histories which successfully weave the short and long term together, for commercial gain and in the service of the brand over time.

WaterAid talks explicitly about the need in its first six years to generate income fast. For any charity, especially in international development, trading off short-term income for pure brand building is a risky strategy and WaterAid proves that these two aims do not need to be in competition with each other:

'The highest ROMIs for a new fast-growing client come from creating and harvesting short-term demand. We maximised 1+ reach in a month, minimised frequency and optimised for immediate response.'
WaterAid IPA Effectiveness Awards paper, 2020

It was this aggressive drive for new supporters that ultimately allowed WaterAid to model where its real value came from and to iterate its strategy over the coming year. It would simply not have had enough data on which to base a strong brand strategy without playing a great short game first.

Grocery retail is notoriously competitive and over the period covered in the Aldi paper, value was the battle ground. Whilst the focus of the paper is about building a brand over time, the data tells of incredible success in the short term too. Almost from the outset, Aldi started to outperform the category in terms of sales growth and its customer spend per trip overtook its nearest competitor, Lidl, from year one. This is not to detract from the incredible investment and belief that the team had in the strategy, but it clearly got the balance right without compromising either aim.

Building relationships for the long term

These brands are all about relationships: with their staff, their customers, and their agencies. WaterAid puts this well:

'We no longer simply measure our supporters' value to us, but also our value to them. This new, integrated approach truly connects people with the cause, making them partners in our mission.'
WaterAid IPA Effectiveness Awards paper, 2020

Value-exchange is language common in charity and not-for-profit and is a concept which commercial brands have started to adopt too.

Guinness has long embraced the societal role it plays and the execution of 'Made of more' is highly participatory. This is perhaps best exemplified in the brand's 2019 rugby sponsorship activation where, in its executions for the Six Nations, Guinness Clear and Liberty Fields were irresistible to customers and commentators alike.

In our industry, agency/client relationships have shortened: clients looking for specialist skills in newer disciplines are spreading tasks over more shops; others are consolidating into networks, prioritising budgetary efficiencies; and everyone is under pressure to deliver results in the short term. Finding, committing to and working with one lead agency, believing they are responsible and ambitious custodians of a brand is a big call for any marketer. The past 18 months have seen some apparently rock-solid client/agency relationships come to an end. But these five papers, through their results, their authorship and their confidence, are all testament to the strength of tight collaboration between client and agency teams.

Far from growing stale, these papers show that those enduring relationships have produced work which grows in ambition and effectiveness, year after year. In an industry where CMOs often have short tenures, there is a lot to be said for protecting the corporate memory for a brand within an agency.

Don't stop thinking about tomorrow

2020 has been a year for the tacticians. Businesses have had to make fundamental changes in how they get to market, how they serve customers, and in many cases, changes to what they actually make. For many brands, those without a clear sense of what they stand for, this has meant a shelving of long-term strategies in favour of short-term fixes. For others, their response to the COVID crisis has been helped by a sense of certainty about their brand and how it should behave and communicate even in such strange times. It will be fascinating to see how those brands manage to weigh the immediate needs of today against strategies made in what feels like a different time entirely.

The IPA Effectiveness Awards Databank has a wealth of papers that demonstrate the value of long-term thinking and this year will see some brilliant new additions. There is no shortage of inspiration and information there for marketers who see their role as temporary curators of a brand, responsible for preserving it for generations to come.

As we rebuild our communities, our culture and our industry against the backdrop of an economic and public health crisis, thinking about the role that brands play is essential. Trust in brands has remained high throughout a tricky 2020 and it is undoubtedly the brands that have benefitted from long-term investment that, at this stage at least, look set to survive the tests they face.

Closing the board–brand rift

How company culture and leadership drive effectiveness

By Heather Alderson
Global Planning Partner, adam&eveDDB

> *'If this business were split up, I would give you the land and bricks and mortar, and I would take the brands and the trademarks, and I would fare better than you.'*

John Stuart, Chairman, Quaker, 1900

Porridge is an excellent food. Eating porridge for breakfast immediately satisfies your hunger, yet due to its low glycaemic index, it releases nutrition over a longer period to also help keep your hunger at bay throughout the morning. Perhaps it is no surprise then that John Stuart, who made his fortune from porridge oats, was an early advocate for brands. After all, strong brands work to nourish businesses in both the short and the long term. He knew that in 1900, but now it is 2020.

Over the last few decades, the IPA Effectiveness Awards Databank has been populated by more and more evidence that advertising to make brands stronger makes businesses more prosperous. Yet, according to a June 2019 study conducted by the FT and the IPA, over half of business leaders, including 30% of senior-level marketers, rate their knowledge of brand building as average to very poor, in spite of being responsible for setting marketing objectives across both the short and long term.[1] This knowledge gap was referred to as the 'board–brand rift'.

Compared with the end of the twentieth century, let alone the start, today's marketing world is a very fast one. The latest US data shows that the average tenure of a CMO in the largest companies continued to slip to just 3.5 years in 2019.[2] CMOs are shorter in post than CEOs (6.9 years) and finance leaders (4.7 years). Many brand marketers have become addicted to the sugar rush of short-term, results-on-my-watch, communication. In recent years, short-term campaigns have drawn the prizes in creative award programmes such as Cannes. Looking across all IPA Effectiveness Awards case studies by year, we see brand building is down from 85% of entries in 2002 to 62% in 2018. A change in focus has meant an increasing perceived need for short-term sales bursts and communications that carry immediate calls to action.

Similarly, the board–brand rift study shows that the channels that tend to be most associated with fast culture, such as social media, are believed to be strong brand builders when, empirically, other channels perform better.

However, even against this backdrop, there are some encouraging signs in 2020 IPA Effectiveness Awards entries that the rift between the brand and the boardroom is beginning to close in two important ways:

1. The emergence of an effectiveness commitment culture, as exemplified by Diageo and Cotswold Co.
2. The return to customer culture, as exemplified by Tesco.

Whilst these ways are different, they have two things in common. First, the impetus for them starts in the boardroom and, second, they involve commitments that are company-wide and expertly led, not just by people, but by concepts and creative ideas.

Creating commitment culture

The IPA Effectiveness Awards Databank contains many strong multi-market case studies, including those for brands originating in the big global corporations such as Axe, Dove, Johnnie Walker, and Heineken.

However, as anyone who has tried to develop an international campaign or write an international effectiveness case knows, being able to build in the effective outcome everywhere from the outset is challenging. And that is before you attempt to put the right measures in place and gather the data, which can be even more challenging. Proving marketing effectiveness is especially difficult in big multinational companies. They are frequently structured in a way that separates the often global brand builders from the often local sales builders. Media is frequently separated from creative production and brand-building activity can be distanced from activation and day-to-day social.

Diageo is, of course, a major multinational and one of a small group of companies that puts its intangible assets on the consolidated balance sheet (£11,300m in 2020).[3] Because of the proportion of the company's intangible assets they account for, brands have had a seat at Diageo's financial top table for many years. However, in 2016, Diageo made a commitment to deliver £500m of increased productivity. As part of that, £100m of incremental gross margin was to be delivered by marketing and the brands. The commitment started and was accepted in the boardroom. It is easy to hear the words 'increase productivity' and translate that to 'cut costs' or 'improve efficiency'. To date, more than double that £100m target has been delivered back to the Diageo boardroom, but it was delivered by improved effectiveness rather than cuts. It is unlikely that such a target could have been met by individual effort or a statement of intent. Rather, Diageo embarked on a company-wide effectiveness programme touching all levels of people, all continents and all brands.

Not every company or every brand will be able to match Diageo's resources in terms of the time, finance and infrastructural investment required to build a Marketing Catalyst platform for making more effective spending decisions on marketing. However, there are three simple commitments at the heart of Diageo's programme that can be widely adopted. The first is to use robust data to facilitate decision making and reduce the impact of cognitive bias. In Diageo's case, this is where the comprehensive Marketing Catalyst platform came into its own. The second is to make a sound commitment to creativity as the proven accelerant of effectiveness. The third is a cultural commitment to ensure that everyone – in all roles, from investors to marketers, and all levels, from the boardroom to new joiners – knows what effective brand marketing is, the benefits it brings and what they personally need to do to bring it about.

A similar cultural commitment, albeit in just one country and without access to a data-driven platform like Marketing Catalyst, was made by Cotswold Co. to lift collective heads away from, in its words, 'the fetishisation of optimisation' towards being able to make a leap towards creativity and hence towards the longer-term brand building that leads to greater effectiveness. Just like in the Diageo case, the step change began in the boardroom when Cotswold Co.'s private equity investors demanded a doubling of revenue from £50m to £100m in five years. In this instance, Cotswold Co.'s target was to be achieved with no increase in marketing spend. Faced with simultaneous demand and constraint, the only way forward was to break the cultural reliance on short-term micro-management and replace it with a commitment to brand creativity. Furthermore, the data was examined and presented in a way that clearly argued the case for creativity. Therefore, the three tenets of rift-reduction of data, creativity, and culture were put to good effect.

Diageo writes:

'We've combined creativity and coordination, risk and rigour, drama and data, magic and measurement. We've made every pound, dollar, and rupee count, "every day everywhere".'

The Cotswold Co. case study describes its strategy as:

'A leap that might not seem natural in the pressurised world of private equity ownership. An approach that stands at odds to the online retail category that values the "last mile" performance above all else ... A shift to a brand-driven approach which not only paid back for itself admirably, but boosted the performance of everything around it ... the kind of creative leap that creates the kind of step change in performance that simply cannot be achieved through a culture of steady optimisation of lower-funnel activities alone.'

As methods to close the rift between the brand and the boardroom, whether a brand is big or small, we can learn from those that have successfully used the three-pronged approach of deploying data, commitment to creativity and addressing the culture of effectiveness in their organisations.

Creating customer culture

The Chartered Institute of Marketing defines marketing as:

> 'The management process responsible for identifying, anticipating and satisfying customer requirements profitably.'

There are other definitions, of course, such as the investor-friendly:

> 'The management process that seeks to maximise returns to shareholders by developing relationships with valued customers and creating a competitive advantage.'[4]

Despite these definitions, the core mission of putting the customer, let alone marketing, at the heart of an organisation has eroded over time.

As long ago as 2004, Gail McGovern, David Court, John Quelch and Blaire Crawford wrote an article in the *Harvard Business Review*,[5] arguing the case to bring the customer back into the boardroom. Central to their argument is the assertion that misguided marketing strategies have done more to destroy shareholder value than misguided fiscal practices or poor accountancy. However, they go on to explain, if marketing was just advertising and promotions, then this assertion wouldn't be true. After all, advertising works.

The problems occur when the rest of the marketing job is set aside. It is probable that in the 16 years since their article was written, the day job of the marketer has become even more removed from the 3Ps. Facebook was only launched in 2004, there was no YouTube or Twitter, and if you wanted to lip-sync to anything you probably did so with a hairbrush and a mirror rather than TikTok. These days, just managing communication is a job and a half.

The second strategy to close the rift between the board and the brand, is exemplified by this year's Tesco case study, which describes a back-to-basics programme to put the customer at the heart of the business. The strategy and initiatives that touched the entire marketing mix, not just advertising and promotions, were described as moving 'from running shops to serving customers'.

Just as in the Diageo effectiveness culture example, the shift required at Tesco was both cultural and company-wide. Also, as in the Diageo example, the impetus began in the boardroom: Tesco had an ex-marketer as its CEO. Tesco's problems were deep. They were both reputational and commercial problems. These were symptoms of more than increased competition, they were symptoms of customer neglect.

The 2000 IPA Advertising Effectiveness Grand Prix winning paper for Tesco details how 'Every little helps', as an advertising idea that was born in the early 1990s, sprung from customers' desire for a better shopping experience. The agency and Tesco then co-created totemic examples or proof points of that ethos in action, such as introducing baby-changing facilities in store. Thus, the expression made the transition from an advertising line to a brand idea. At the time, the flagship 'Dotty' campaign generated £2.25 incremental profit for every pound spent.[6]

The 2020 IPA paper details how 'Every little helps' evolved to become a company-wide mantra to rebuild customer trust from the inside out. Therefore, 'Every little helps' is no longer just an advertising line, or a brand idea, it is a way of doing business. Throughout the period from September 2015 to August 2019, the campaign generated an average of £2.75 incremental profit for every pound spent. Given that pressures on profit margins over the intervening period have been downward rather than upward pressures, it is not unreasonable to compare the profit ROI figures and conclude that the elevation of the brand idea to a way of doing business has delivered more to the business.

Visit any airport bookshelf and you will see a vast choice of 'great man' leadership books. However, when you read cases contained within *Advertising Works,* you will read stories about the leadership of concepts like an effectiveness culture or creative leaps. You will read about the leadership of ideas such as 'Every little helps'. You will learn how the board–brand rift is closed by such ideas.

These cases show that when you start with a boardroom problem and go from there, you increase your chances of coming back to that boardroom with the objectives met and more. Culture, creativity, data and customer-centricity are proven to be valuable levers to pull on that journey from the boardroom and back.

Today Tesco.com stocks 60 varieties and 12 brands of porridge. Twenty-eight of the 60 SKUs are Quaker, by far the biggest single source. So, when John Stuart spoke of the boardroom benefit of his brand back in 1900, it goes to prove that his words are still as important today as they were back then. I wonder what he would have thought about the microwavable golden syrup flavour?

Notes

1 FT in partnership with the IPA, *The Board–Brand Rift: How Business Leaders Have Stopped Building Brands*. London: IPA, 2019.
2 'Age and Tenure in the C-Suite: Korn Ferry Study Reveals Trends by Title and Industry' 21 January 2020, available from the BusinessWire website: businesswire.com/news/home/20200121005146/en/
3 Diageo Annual Report 2020.
4 Stanley J. Paliwoda and John K. Ryans, 'Back to first principles' in *International Marketing: Modern and Classic Papers*. Cheltenham: Edward Elgar, 2008.
5 Gail McGovern, David Court, John Quelch and Blair Crawford, 'Bringing the customer into the boardroom' *Harvard Business Review* 82:11 (2004) 70–80.
6 IPA Effectiveness Awards Grand Prix 2000.

Measurement and magic

The contribution of technology to creative effectiveness

By Kate Waters
Director of Client Strategy and Planning, ITV

It is a truism that the combination of data and technology has transformed our world. Almost no aspect of life is untouched by one or, more usually, both of these twin forces. We can routinely generate, gather, store and analyse trillions upon trillions of data points, revealing new insight about human intentions and behaviours, the movement of financial markets, the patterns of history, and of course, the spread of ideas.

Advertising has undergone its own transformation: the tech platforms have revolutionised and democratised the distribution of communications ideas over the last 20 years, creating an explosion in channel choice. This enables marketers to learn more about their customers than they once would have dreamed possible, to target them with an extraordinary amount of precision, and to provide almost instant and continuous feedback on performance.

So, in theory, the IPA Effectiveness Awards should be a rich source of insight and inspiration for how technology has transformed advertising effectiveness, and more specifically, *creative* effectiveness.

Except, somewhat surprisingly, they're not. This year, 64 papers were entered into the Awards and 25 were shortlisted. Yet, of these, only four were singled out by the judges as having valuable lessons for the industry on this topic, despite the IPA President's Prize being up for grabs for the paper demonstrating the Best Contribution to Effectiveness through Technology.

The four case studies that do have something to say on the subject – Central Coast, Diageo, Formula 1 and SickKids – provide valuable examples of the roles that technology, and more broadly, data can play in driving effectiveness. They also, perhaps, provide some clues as to why there aren't more case studies for us to learn from.

Each paper is very different in its scope and approach: Formula 1 explores the value of one channel – an email-based CRM programme – to enable a brand to engage fans and turn them into customers. In contrast, the Diageo paper, epic in its scope, explores the way in which aggregating insight can be harnessed to improve effectiveness across 180 brands and 200 markets. The SickKids case study demonstrates the use of technology to create more engaging and urgent creative execution, while for Central Coast, technology played a central role in shaping the overarching communications idea.

So how can technology help? There are four overarching themes that are evident across these case studies.

Size and scale of inputs and outcomes

Data has always been used by strategists and planners as the underpinning and inspiration for transformative creative strategies, but until relatively recently it's often been a comparatively simple data point or piece of analysis that has provided those foundations.

So, perhaps the most obvious theme to emerge from the four case studies examined here relates to 'size and scale'. The Central Coast and Formula 1 papers are clear demonstrations of how technology now enables parsing and interpretation of millions of data points as inputs to a creative strategy, while Diageo's Marketing Catalyst platform shows the scale of impact that's possible when technology enables insight to be easily applied across markets, channels, and brands.

Reducing the perceived risk of investing in creativity

While most marketers know the potential for creativity to transform the effectiveness of their marketing, it's still regarded by many as a 'hit-or-miss' affair and decisions relating to creative investment are frequently deemed 'risky'. For client organisations that expect evidence-based decision making across all areas of their business, an argument for a particular strategic or creative idea that is overly reliant on the assertion of experts and/or qualitative evidence, however elegantly expressed, may fall short in the eyes of non-marketing corporate stakeholders.

The Central Coast team's investment in an experimental phase to its campaign, testing four different strategic territories across six geographical segments and six further age-based demographics (generating 144 test cells and a mind-boggling 20m data points), provided the 'hard' evidence that was required to persuade many hundreds of SMEs to fund the roll-out of a two-year campaign. The clear implication is that without this level of rigour, the campaign simply wouldn't have got off the ground.

For Diageo, its Catalyst platform enables more efficient, insight-led decision making by using econometric data to predict the brands within its portfolio with the most profit potential, and the channels/approaches on individual brands which create the most positive ROI. This enables Diageo to invest ahead of sales growth, secure in the knowledge of future profitable returns. The accuracy of its modelled prediction is now so good that it's given the business the confidence to increase Diageo's marketing budgets by 31% over three years. In addition, the operational efficiency created by systematising and scaling marketing effectiveness insight has liberated the brand teams to focus on creativity. Aggregated learnings across brands, markets and touchpoints are used to sharpen understanding of the drivers of creative effectiveness, and fuel more engaging brand communications.

A further example of managing creative risk is evident in the Central Coast paper. In this case, the creative approach risked a backlash from individuals with particularly negative attitudes towards the Central Coast area. Using an algorithm which layered interest criteria against the micro-geographical areas in Sydney that indexed highly for advocacy, enabled the client to build up a mass of likes and online positive commentary for the campaign before rolling it out further, thereby reducing the risk that a polarised response to the creative could undermine its impact.

End-to-end relevance: value throughout the creative process

Viewed collectively, these four case studies demonstrate the potential of technology to drive effectiveness at all stages of the creative development process: creative idea, execution, and optimisation.

Central Coast used technology to run a real-world experiment to assess the most powerful creative territory for its campaign. The value of this was not just in creating a large and statistically robust pool of evidence to get funders on board, but also in identifying the territory that would be most effective *in the real world*. As they discovered, when trying to shift deeply entrenched negative attitudes, there is an inherent danger in relying on claimed behaviour to guide message development, as people are very bad judges of how they are likely to behave in the real world. The large-scale experiment – which formed the first phase of the campaign – not only tested different creative approaches across multiple touchpoints, it deliberately and cleverly built friction into the customer journey in order to ensure they identified the most motivating territory, which was capable of overcoming those deeply entrenched attitudes.

At the other end of the process, in an approach now routine within digital and performance channels, the Formula 1 case is a powerful reminder of the potential for technology to help optimise in-market creative performance, using weekly updates of what fans are clicking, responding to and sharing to refine the creative approach and enhance effectiveness.

SickKids, however, is the paper that best demonstrates how technology can fuel highly engaging and effective creative work at an executional level (and, as such, is the worthy winner of the 2020 President's Prize). While the idea behind the 'VS' campaign came through an insight from qualitative research, much of the executional engagement and its fundraising power was driven by technology. Recognising the power of a time-bound target, SickKids created daily targets for signing up new donors, dramatising these ambitions and progress towards them, across digital out-of-home sites in high-footfall locations and social media. The campaign captured the local community's competitive spirit, pitting one neighbourhood against each other, using technology to surface and fuel local rivalries. Smart use of technology was embedded across the customer journey, enabling donors who were motivated by the advertising to personalise their experience, choosing the cause they wanted to support or the 'crew' they wanted to join.

A fine balance: the worm's-eye view and the bird's-eye view

Muhammad Yunus, microfinance expert and Nobel Laureate, draws a distinction between two concepts that can, perhaps, help us understand why there aren't more examples of case studies that can tell us about the application of technology to creative effectiveness. He calls them the 'worm's-eye view' and the 'bird's-eye view' – contrasting the richness of personal experience that comes from a small but very detailed data set (the worm's-eye view), and the broader but less detailed view that we get by looking at the general patterns which emerge from larger data sets (the bird's-eye view).

What's evident from the four case studies that use technology to drive creative effectiveness is the importance of finding the right balance between these two viewpoints – recognising the most powerful approach to creative effectiveness can be found in a fusion of the two, rather than an over-reliance on one.

Two papers allude to this philosophy: the Diageo approach to effectiveness combines the power of applying tech-enabled insight to drive operational efficiency 'enabling brand teams to focus effort on creativity' – an explicit marriage of the bird's-eye view provided by technology and the worm's-eye view provided by the skill and craft of the brand teams. Similarly, the Formula 1 paper contrasts the purely algorithm- and rule-based approach used in more straightforward triggered service journeys, with the approach described for the fan engagement programme (the subject of the IPA entry), which is 'informed by data but also curated and crafted' – the implication being that human insight is a fundamental requirement in addition to technology for a brand-led programme of this sort.

The two other papers demonstrate the combined power of bird's-eye and worm's-eye view. The power of the 'VS' idea for SickKids comes from the fusion of a highly emotive creative idea that reimagines a fundraising brand as a performance one, with a tech-driven execution to create urgency and act as a powerful trigger for action. Whilst not explicit, the marriage of these two approaches is also evident in the Central Coast paper – in this case, the core positioning of 'adventure' was identified using a tech-driven approach, but the traditional craft of creative strategy is evident in taking this territory and refining it as a series of '*Little* adventures', which made for a far more compelling, credible and, ultimately, more effective campaign.

Polarisation of culture and capability

However, finding that elusive optimum balance between birds'-eye view and worm's-eye view presents a significant challenge for the industry.

The persistently siloed nature of communications disciplines across much of the industry reinforces a polarisation of culture and capability. While there are notable exceptions, expertise in data and technology tend to inform media choices rather than fuel big strategic or creative ideas (tellingly, the Diageo paper speaks of the integration of the Catalyst platform into media agencies, not creative agencies). In contrast, the skill most highly prized by creatives and creative strategists is the ability to create brilliant, lateral shifts in how we look at a brand or an issue, enabling us to communicate an idea in an original, relevant and memorable way. It is prized as a distinctively *human* skill – the product of creative thinking talent coupled with years of experience – and it is a skill that we are reluctant to believe can be matched by a computer.

There are critical differences too, in the process of strategy and idea generation: creative strategies and ideas tend to be approached in a 'top-down' way – the aim being to find a single, unifying insight that can inform the development of an idea, which is then expressed across multiple channels. In contrast, the aim in many digital media channels is to split populations into smaller and smaller segments, reflecting the nuances between them and creating increasingly tailored and personalised journeys, rather than championing the traits shared across segments.

So, is the fact that there are only a handful of big advertising ideas written by AI, evidence of our reluctance to let computers play at creativity? Or is it about AI's inability to write effective advertising ideas?

The best of the case studies described here suggest that there is the potential for true alchemy when we let technology in. But we will never have a robust answer unless more of us are happy to put aside our cultural differences, to learn each other's language, and to embrace the 'messy middle' where technology and creativity collide. As Diageo's Syl Saller says, it's time to get 'comfortable with the integration of measurement and magic'.

'Eureka!' moments

How uncovering true insights drives effectiveness

By Melpo Gkofa
Strategic Consultant

I am writing this chapter while I am trying to resettle my family in Greece. After 15 years living in London, we decided to go back to our homeland. The last few weeks were unimaginably busy; it turns out that moving a family to a different country (albeit your 'own') in the middle of a pandemic is not such an easy business. So I can't help asking myself, why have I committed to writing this chapter? How can I find the mental capacity while surrounded by 237 boxes and two kids screaming for attention?

But then again, I have a rich bibliography on insight at my disposal. The matter of 'insight' has been explored, discussed, debated on so many levels by so many advertising professionals. And we know that a true insight always works. Moreover, being a judge at the IPA Effectiveness Awards this summer gave me the opportunity to be exposed to some of the best-in-class advertising campaigns from recent years. So I have no excuse – I had a rich pool of examples to write about.

My mind kept going back and forth like a table-tennis ball, between this IPA chapter and our family's decision to move countries. And then I had my truly Greek eureka moment! Like our decision to leave cosmopolitan, modern, organised, open-minded London and go back to the chaotic, mad, often unwelcoming Athens, an insight is not defined by rational boundaries; it doesn't always derive from a well-calculated analysis between pros and cons. An insight speaks to the audience's heart in a unique way: it evokes memories, feelings and senses. A true insight speaks to someone's psyche and it makes you think 'this totally gets me'. The same way as the breeze on my skin after a hard day's unpacking (and arguing with the national insurance people in Athens) makes me feel 'home'.

The cases I had the pleasure of judging, all include an insight that truly gets the audience. Sometimes the insight comes from an audience segmentation (i.e. Volvo).

At other times it comes from understanding how people interact with a medium like cinema (wagamama), from social listening or semiotics (Baileys) or qualitative research (Tango). No matter what source of data and research methodology they use, all these cases simply get the audience. But how do they do this? And what are the learnings for the rest of us?

- **Learning number one from Baileys, Gordon's and Tango: Try to look outside the pre-defined boundaries of your category.** There is no need to get obsessed about how people navigate the category. Instead, look into the emotional needs and values of your audience. See them as people, not customers. Don't assume that something is obvious or too simple. Use your imagination about how to act on this insight.
- **Learning number two from Tesco: Don't focus so much on the competition.** Instead, focus on how to serve your customers better. W. Chan Kim and Renée Mauborgne talked about this principle in their best-selling book, *Blue Ocean Strategy*, which described how 'companies' time and attention is often focused on benchmarking rivals and responding to their strategic moves, rather than on understanding how to deliver a leap in value to buyers'. Tesco's case proves how focusing on customers in a consistent and holistic way can deliver phenomenal business results.
- **Learning number three from wagamama and Volvo: Don't underestimate the power of media to connect with your audience.** Insight can, of course, come from understanding the power of media touchpoints. The way people interact with a specific channel and the occasion of media consumption can be a simple but powerful solution for competitive advantage and growth.

But enough about the theory, join me in a deep dive into all these cases.

Look outside the pre-defined boundaries of your category

Baileys – from forgotten icon to global treat

Baileys, an iconic drink in the 1980s and 1990s, had become culturally irrelevant. As a result, it was suffering from a long-term sales decline.

The team from Mother and Carat had to do something radical to reverse this trend. Instead of trying to find an insight and an inspiration from within the liqueur category, they got their inspiration from a parallel one: the food category.

Food imagery was being photographed and displayed on social media provoking endless comments and reactions of admiration. More importantly, indulging in a food treat didn't need permission anymore. It didn't need a specific occasion. People felt free to indulge in treats and embrace pleasure in their own way.

This insight led to a new positioning for Baileys as the champion of free-spirited treating. This meant that Baileys could move away from the restricted and highly competitive adult liqueur occasion to a more exciting and endlessly relevant treating occasion. The 'Don't mind if I Baileys' campaign reframed Baileys from a women's drink to a real adult drink treat. I believe that the target audience clearly saw itself in the creative and felt it could relate to it. The creative was fresh, emotive and relevant.

Looking into people's real needs and liberating themselves from the boundaries of the category, the team from Mother and Carat were able to design an effective global campaign that led to a gross profit ROI of 1.7:1 over four years.

Gordon's – legacy brand turned challenger

The Gordon's Gin campaign, '… Shall we?', also looked into people's inner needs and motivations. Gordon's had the biggest market share of its category. But while the category was growing in value, Gordon's growth was falling behind. The obvious solution was for Gordon's to play to its strengths and reclaim its leadership by outshouting the competition about its botanical superiority. Instead, the Gordon's team decided to look outwardly into consumers' needs when drinking gin and unearthed a simple but powerful insight that led to phenomenal growth. A gin moment is not necessarily an appreciation of gin botanicals; people share a gin to enjoy each other's company, to share stories, to relax. It is deeply emotional, and it is true even for the most sophisticated gin drinker. The creative idea '… Shall we?' was born out of this universal insight and it was so different from the rest of the category. It was fun, cheeky, playful, and colourful in a category that celebrated sophistication, smartness, and botanicals. It basically understood the members of its audience and talked straight to their hearts. The results were phenomenal: Gordon's value doubled and the profit ROI was estimated at 2.11:1.

Tango – rescuing Tango from a sticky situation

Tango's case is another extraordinary example of how a fresh human insight led the brand to an unexpected growth and re-positioning.

The Tango team from VCCP and Britvic discovered an insight beyond the category; an insight that is true to the core target audience (16–24-year-olds), regardless of the reasons why someone would drink a carbonated orange drink. Looking truthfully into the core of the target audience, the Tango team discovered that what 16–24-year-olds worried about most was making a show of themselves. Tango decided to help its audience gain control over awkwardness. The 'sticky situations' campaign stood out with its humour about awkward situations and unexpected resolutions. The campaign smashed advertising research group Kantar's norms for advertising distinctiveness, being well-remembered and well-talked-about. Most importantly, it helped with the product's distribution and resulted in an increase in penetration of five percentage points.

Focus on customers not your competition

Tesco – from running shops to serving customers

Tesco's case is one of the most holistic and comprehensive cases of true dedication to customer understanding and service, which led to impressive business results. The turnaround at Tesco wasn't due to the implementation of one campaign insight, but a consistent and well-coordinated effort over several years. New players in the category and new buying habits were challenging Tesco, once the dominant player in UK supermarkets. Crucially, its trust and perception scores were plummeting. Instead of trying to react to the new competition and enter another price war, Tesco decided to do what it did best: serve customers. 'Serving Britain's shoppers, a little better every day' became Tesco's purpose and it was translated across all touchpoints (paid, owned and earned). New creative was developed, a new media approach, which better reflected contemporary media consumption, was put in place, and a clearer promotion strategy was executed. What happened as a result? Market reputation and quality perception scores bounced back and profit was restored. And to those who are sceptical about marketing and communications, a sophisticated econometrics analysis proved marketing's impact on profit with an estimated average ROI of £2.73 for every £1 invested in marketing between September 2015 and August 2019.

Don't underestimate the power of media

Volvo – a defiantly human success story

Volvo is an innovative and safe car manufacturer, but prior to this campaign, the brand suffered from 'boring' image perceptions. It was described as 'old' and 'boring' while its German competitors were 'young', 'fun' and 'trendy'. Volvo (similar to the other brands in this chapter) focused on discovering an insight that 'got' its audience instead of trying to deliver a trendier image and imitate the competition. The brand understood that its audience cared much more about how to make the world a better place than about status and economic success. This insight distinguished it from the prevailing advertising strategies of the premium car sector, which focused on success in relation to power, status, and cars. So far, so good. But I believe that what makes this case really interesting is the media execution of this insight. Volvo partnered with the Sky Atlantic TV channel and created seven docudramas about pioneers who have tried to improve the world. If this campaign had been executed as standard spot advertising without the element of storytelling, Volvo would have been unable to cut through. Instead, Volvo's brand shone, and it clearly aligned with people's expectations and aspirations.

wagamama – stirring souls and selling bowls the wagamama way, through the secret power of cinema

wagamama faced extremely challenging market conditions. A lot of food restaurant chains were closing, margins were being squeezed, and competition was fierce. The team from MullenLowe and the7stars knew that, despite these conditions, the only right strategy was a brand-building one. Focusing solely on promotional activity would only make things worse. The beauty of this case lies in the fact that wagamama used cinema as a brand-building vehicle that cleverly drove sales too. The brand knew its audience well. It knew that in the cinema, it would find its audience not interrupted (by texts or social media), and, in a sense, 'captive'. wagamama cherry-picked cinemas close to one of its restaurants to show its advertising – a playful, energetic ad which suggested the chain's food nourished the soul as well as the stomach.

In this way, it simultaneously primed the audience emotionally and enabled an action (visit a nearby wagamama). The choice of cinema was well crafted and it is no surprise that the campaign delivered brand and business results.

Epilogue

These six cases from the 2020 IPA Effectiveness Awards all used the power of insight to overcome brand and business problems. They went beyond their category boundaries, they focused on their customers rather than reacting to the competition, and they used the power of media to come closer to their customers and prompt them for action.

For me, it is not surprising that these cases were effective, smashing brand-building scores while delivering business results for their shareholders. They are valuable to the industry because they provide evidence that insights work and give ammunition to all strategists and planners to deliver campaigns based on insight and imagination rather than simply react to the market.

When I opened this chapter, I shared with you my worries about my family's move to Greece. Closing this chapter, I just hope that my family's insight and decision to come back to our homeland will in future prove to have been as effective as these cases were. Time will tell …

Diversifying the discourse on advertising effectiveness

Proving the effectiveness of not-for-profit communications

By Harjot Singh
CSO EMEA & UK, McCann Worldgroup

At its heart, effectiveness has always been about impact. The measurement and evaluation of effectiveness is the only credible way of discerning the *impact of the impact,* contextualising it across three key factors, evidenced by:

- the audacity of the objectives,
- the bravery of the approach,
- the causality of the work.

Did I make this up? Yes.

I call it 'the ABC of effectiveness'. It's my way of landing the plane.

If this sounds simplistic, I'd rather we dwell on the existing discourse on effectiveness instead. I find that it is oversimplistic and inadequate in how it relates to representing the diversity of marketing challenges, particularly those faced by non-profits.

The current discourse on effectiveness is dominated by stories in which the tools, norms, resources and collective wisdom as it applies to evaluating, proving and contextualising effectiveness across 'the ABC of effectiveness' are disproportionately abundant, for marketing effectiveness cases across categories that have clear commercial motives and challenges.

Tried, tested, proven, accepted, cited, and held as a definitive standard; as if to imply that these methods, assumptions and considerations apply to every marketing effectiveness case and category in principle.

Simply put, the discourse on effectiveness as it relates to our industry is not diverse enough.

One way of understanding the issue of under-representation of successful not-for-profit effectiveness cases and the subsequent paucity of learning that exists around the unique nuances of proving effectiveness for not-for-profit cases across the world is to reflect on how our industry works: inadvertently placing certain kinds of stories in a position of strength to be seen, glorified and valorised more than others.

In 2020, less than 20% of all submissions to the IPA Effectiveness Awards were for not-for-profit. Since 2004, not-for-profit cases have always hovered between 10% to 15% of total entries. Winners are even fewer. International winners are even more scarce.

In the last 22 years, there have only been four not-for-profit cases that have been awarded a Grand Prix. Only one of those was an international, multi-market case.

They were the Health Education Authority (1998), Barnardos (2002), The Metropolitan Police Service (2007) and FARC (2011 – the only international Grand Prix winner to date).

In culture, dominant identities establish their superiority from constant representation, repetitive affirmation and recognition of their ideal. As a result, they are seen, heard, shared and socialised more. They become and inform the dominant, desired and idealised narrative and standard.

What's happened in the IPA Effectiveness Awards to date is quite similar. Not-for-profit stories just don't have the same exposure, or recognition, and it's time we fixed that.

Maya Angelou said, 'when you know better, you do better'.

That is the point of this chapter.

There is such little learning on methodologies, principles, techniques and approaches focused on proving effectiveness for not-for-profit cases vs. the rest – in the IPA and across the board. As a result, the industry remains disproportionately more educated, familiar and informed on marketing and proving marketing effectiveness in its classical sense.

It is time to start creating a narrative that is focused and sensitised to the unique nuances that exist in marketing challenges faced by an organisation that's trying to stop child abuse (Truth Project), raise awareness of the stigma associated with mental health and suicide (CALM), save a nation's healthcare system (NHS England), raise funds for research and medical science to save terminally ill children (SickKids) or prevent half a million children from dying because they don't have access to drinking water (WaterAid).

I am by no means suggesting that it's not challenging to sell more mayonnaise, cars, alcohol, fast food or groceries in a highly competitive, connected and fast-paced attention economy. I am by no means suggesting that it's a competition, even though, in this case, this is one.

But what I am saying is that we need to consider and create a set of principles that can inspire and educate not-for-profit organisations to experience and share in the success of proving the effectiveness of their communications just like the existing majority of for-profit stories.

Since there isn't enough of a repository of successful not-for-profit cases this year or in the past 20 years to base these principles on, I want to refrain from the expected approach of glorifying or vilifying any particular case.

We need a forward-looking conversation. Because we cannot base it on past performance alone. We just don't have enough of a sample size to afford the kind of strident views one might expect to read in a chapter like this. That's why I want to base this point of view on the potential of what can and should make it against what actually made it through to the IPA Awards in 2020.

Unless more not-for-profit cases make it to the top, gain visibility and exposure in effectiveness award shows, we will not have enough learning to determine the range of ways in which not-for-profit cases can and should measure and prove effectiveness.

When I started researching what was available and what was in development, I was filled with optimism, and that is the sentiment I want to share with you from here on. I say this because there is something very progressive that non-profits create.

A different playbook, if you will, to respond to the ABC effectiveness framework of proving the audacity of the objectives, the bravery of the solution and the causality of the work to the impact.

I recently learned that the most compelling starting point in proving effectiveness for non-profits in particular is a clearly identified and articulated theory of change.

It is the most irrefutable foundation to build your effectiveness argument on.

Simply put, a theory of change maps out the organisation's *path to impact*.

In doing so, it specifies the causal relationships between the activities and the eventual outcomes. It specifies which of these outcomes are short-, medium- or long-term, at the outset.

Ultimately, this argument is the basis to communicate the rationale behind why it is believed that the campaign will deliver the *impact* that the organisation's programme or intervention seeks to create.

Speaking of impact, it is particularly important that not-for-profit cases differentiate outputs from outcomes. Often this is not as complex or nuanced as for other, dare I say, more straightforward, commercial cases.

When proving effectiveness for not-for-profits, it is important to clearly establish that the outcome is the change that occurred because of the work.

Outputs usually only demonstrate that, for example, a certain amount of activities have occurred – whether it's number of hours of training, calls, products delivered, etc.

In proving effectiveness for non-profits, it becomes critical to demonstrate how those outputs then lead to the change, i.e. the outcome(s).

It is not enough to conduct activities, there needs to be a clear rationale that links the execution of those activities with expected changes in the lives of beneficiaries – much like the SickKids submission endeavours to do.

One can't really have a conversation about outcomes, impact or effectiveness without metrics. In the case of non-profits these metrics have to be very precisely and thoughtfully linked to the mission or purpose.

Yes, mission or purpose is important, and we've talked about it incessantly as an industry. In the case of non-profits, the importance of linking the metrics to the mission is critical, more so than it may be in other categories where the key metrics can be credibly linked, argued and proven purely in relation to a marketing objective.

Further, for non-profits, proving effectiveness means measuring the success of the campaign or intervention in achieving their purpose.

This means that non-profits have to consider some very distinctive conditions and options in identifying and articulating their mission or purpose and linking their metrics to it.

Given the diversity of organisations in the non-profit sector, no single measure of effectiveness and no generic set of indicators will work for all of them, to the extent they do for cars and condiments.

This means we have to explore a different set of strategies.

Intuitively, the simplest strategy would be for a non-profit to narrowly and precisely define its purpose so that progress can be measured and attributed directly. While this approach works for non-profits that have a very straightforward and quantifiable mission, as seen in the NHS England submission, it doesn't work for all and it doesn't take into consideration the diversity that exists within the non-profit sector.

The other issue with this approach is that defining a purpose very narrowly can trivialise or oversimplify the narrative in such a way that it undermines the impact, treating the symptoms rather than the cause of a particular social problem, much like non-profits like CALM and the Truth Project seek to impact with their work.

For them, proving effectiveness relies on being judged not just on key statistics as they relate to fewer deaths etc., but also on changes in public attitudes as expressed in popular culture and opinion surveys.

The second strategy for measuring and proving effectiveness by linking the metrics to purpose is to invest in and cite research to determine the extent to which the activities of the not-for-profit actually help to mitigate the problem(s) or promote the benefits that the mission involves. The Truth Project submission would have been even stronger and more compelling with this kind of context.

The CALM submission is a good example to cite here. CALM's urgent and important mission is to compel the nation to recognise male suicide and its increase as a matter of national outrage. Its submission this year was evidenced by research that illuminated and contextualised the challenge, which wasn't raising awareness of the issue – as this had been increasing – but rather getting the UK to truly engage with it.

Its research placed the charity's purpose in a position of strength because it was focused on the cultural inability to talk about death, especially in our society, the degree to which suicide was still a taboo in communications across many if not most mental health charities, and the existing attitudes among British men. These made them five times more likely to believe that depression is 'not a real illness', much more inclined to treat mental health issues disdainfully, twice as likely as women to call suicide an embarrassment, three times more likely to call it pathetic and four times more likely to call it immoral.

Whilst CALM had a quantifiable element in its approach and in its mission, which made linking metrics to the mission possible, this approach doesn't work nearly as well for others.

Investing in research to substantiate why we believe the activities of the non-profit in question are genuinely meaningful and worthy of creating the social impact they're after is even more important for them.

However, for some not-for-profits, narrowing the scope of the mission to a quantifiable goal isn't an option and investing in research outcomes isn't as feasible.

In my experience, I find that this is especially true for non-profits that operate in the environment/conservation area. There was a paper that made it into the entries this year, but it did not advance.

And it made me think about why proving effectiveness might have been more difficult or perhaps less straightforward for them. In my research, I came upon an example that helped me understand this better.

A charity like the Nature Conservancy, for example, can potentially calculate changes in the Earth's total biodiversity to substantiate their mission and link metrics to it in order to prove effectiveness, but the benefits of engaging in an approach as sophisticated and expensive as calculating our planet's biodiversity wouldn't justify the cost.

Come to think about it, the work of any conservation charity arguably has at best only a modest, if not imperceptible, effect on global biodiversity, which is affected on a far greater scale by other factors such as deforestation, climate change, conversion of habitats, etc.

So how can non-profits such as these prove effectiveness? In researching this, I found that they have another option. They can develop micro-level goals that, if achieved, would imply success on a grander scale.

An effectiveness paper from such a non-profit should focus on determining success in proving effectiveness by using a baseline set of data established by existing scientific surveys to measure the success of its efforts across a series of microgoals that will ultimately count towards creating a lasting, positive impact.

Every milestone matters: charting a path to success and impact. It's about brand direction thinking vs. brand position thinking.

It should also be added that not-for-profits are in service of impacting positive social change. It is not as easy to clearly and squarely discount the impact of communications efforts and the value they add from that of other social change strategies and policies being implemented at the same time.

Truth is, it takes creativity and perseverance to prove effectiveness irrespective of the category you operate in.

Not-for-profits have to apply creativity and perseverance differently – in the way they apply precision in defining their purpose to make it quantifiable, in the way they apply discretion in investing in research to show how their purpose and the specific pursuits that follow from it work, and in the way they apply foresight in identifying and developing concrete micro-goals that imply success on a larger scale.

As of today, we don't have enough learning around measuring and proving effectiveness for non-profits to the extent that we could claim that there is a clear and defined right and wrong way to evaluate non-profit communication campaigns, which are often if not always unique and diverse, making the creation and adoption of standard evaluating guidelines difficult.

Different evaluation designs will have different interpretive boundaries. Designing and investing in evaluation approaches that take into consideration the unique realities of the non-profit sector and the diversity that exists within that sector must become a clear priority for us as an industry, so that we can maximise the opportunities for both learning and assessing impact in future.

Despite the unique challenges that non-profits are faced with, they can, and must, measure and prove their effectiveness, tracking their progress towards making their purpose real in a way that helps them play and earn a meaningful role in people's lives.

And we need to see more of them be recognised in the effectiveness competitions.

Juries have a responsibility to discern and elevate the best for us all to learn from.

But we need to create the learning first. Juries will only be as experienced and advanced as the learning that exists.

Ultimately, the discourse on effectiveness will only be as contemporary and representative as the diversity of learning and the diversity in the learning that exists.

We know better. Let's do better.

(Re)discovering the challenger spirit

By Susan Poole
Strategic Consultant

Writing this in the summer of 2020, the notion of challenge doesn't seem abstract. With protests worldwide supporting causes including Black Lives Matter and trans rights, challenge seems commonplace. Over time, whilst some brands take up causes to fight for them overtly, there are other brands that you wouldn't think of as challenging. This applies in the arena of marketing as much as it does around causes. There is always a steady stream of new brands that seem exciting and are often badged as 'challengers', for rewriting the rules of their category, like Purplebricks,[1] or forging their own category, like Oatly. It's not often we think of large or established brands as challengers, yet that is what this chapter is about.

When 'challenger brand' thinking was first popularised over 20 years ago in Adam Morgan's book, *Eating The Big Fish*,[2] it was an era of new upstart brands snapping at the heels of the establishment. Challenger brands took on the leaders, often making this competitiveness overt as Virgin Atlantic did with its jibes at British Airways.[3] Challengers often framed their position as 'David versus Goliath' narratives. In addition, big brands often also launched their own challenger brands to compete with rivals, rather than get involved directly, as the Co-op Bank did with its online venture, Smile, and British Airways did with its discount airline, Go.

But since its heyday, the notion of a challenger brand appears to have fallen out of favour. Yet amongst this year's IPA Effectiveness Award winners we have seen a new cohort of challenger brands. These challengers weren't the new upstart brands on the street and they weren't forging a new category. Nor were they challenger brands started by big brands to fight in a way their parent brands couldn't. These were large or legacy brands that discovered (or rediscovered) challenger mindsets. These brands adopted challenger mentalities to change their own fortunes – proving that being a challenger truly is a reflection of outlook, not size.

This new breed of challenger brand often isn't waging a 'David versus Goliath' battle, and they aren't calling out a competitor like the challenger brands of yesteryear.

They are large or legacy brands – the establishment, if you will. Yet they have adopted challenger mindsets to change their fortunes, often in the face of adversity or decline. They have been eschewing conventional approaches to managing a large or legacy brand and have been unwilling to accept their fates without a fight. They have been smart in finding ways to fund new activity to prove its value, and smart in how they changed their marketing approaches to improve their fortunes. Some have also taken advantage of the benefits of being a bigger brand.

The new breed of challenger brands

Brands in this year's IPA Effectiveness Awards that have (re)discovered a challenger spirit include Gordon's, Aldi, Heineken, Tango, and Heinz. These are well-known brands that could never be described as young whippersnappers. In fact, they have all been around for 20–250 years! They each faced different challenges but what unites them is a refusal to accept limitations or the fate of share decline or delisting. They looked to their categories and sought to change consumer perceptions by doing things differently, using a challenger mindset. In doing so, they avoided conventional marketing approaches typical of brands of their age or stature. They often had to think quite smartly to secure bigger budgets to enable them to make a step change. To quote Adam Morgan, they all shared 'ambitions bigger than conventional resources'.[4]

Eschewing typical marketing conventions

These established brands were all facing challenges that typical marketing wisdom would have suggested they should accept as their fate, including managed decline, divesting the brand, remaining niche or accepting the risk of another failed launch. But each of these brands spurned these futures in favour of a challenger approach that proved effective.

Gordon's was facing the conventional path of 'managed decline' for a brand experiencing dramatically increasing competition. The gin market was seeing literally hundreds of new launches, and Gordon's was a legacy brand in the standard segment of a market that was turning premium. Gordon's was growing slower than the market and losing share. Rather than adopt a strategy of managed decline, Gordon's rejected the category's dominant narrative of provenance, recipes or ingredients, and put its focus on the consumer and the social occasions associated with drinking gin. It launched a new variant, Gordon's Pink, and playful advertising with the line, 'Gordon's … Shall we?'

It didn't just do this with a hope to turn around market share and report steady growth. Instead, Gordon's aimed for dramatic growth and achieved it. Despite 700 new brands entering the category, Gordon's doubled in size in three years, grew faster than the market and increased profits from communications tenfold.

Tango, a famous UK brand and a celebrated name in UK advertising history, had fallen a long way since its advertising heyday 20 years ago. The brand was threatened with delisting due to falling sales and share loss versus major competitors. Rather than the conventional approach of divesting or just milking the brand, Tango's owner, Britvic, chose to give it one last chance. Tango opted to go against the category codes set by its big competitor (Fanta) and reignited dominant brand codes from its advertising history for a whole new audience that wasn't even born when 'you've been Tango-ed' ran. Tango outgrew the market with 38% growth year on year. It drove switching from Fanta and drew new people into the category, accounting for 19% of category growth in the process.

Aldi had been part of the UK supermarket landscape for 20 years, yet its share wasn't above 2%. Rather than accept a future as a niche player, Aldi changed approach to grow into fifth place in the market. It focused on the role it played in people's lives, utilising distinctly British humour. Its 10-year case showed how Aldi knew that change takes time to happen and therefore played a long game and ultimately turned shame into pride, delivering a ROMI of 21.6:1 over 10 years.

Heineken was looking to launch into the growing non-alcoholic beer segment globally. But it rejected the lower-price approach typical in the category and instead launched a premium 0.0% product that fitted with the upscale nature of the parent brand. It changed the discourse around non-alcoholic beer to reframe it as a positive choice and 0.0 became the biggest global non-alcoholic beer brand.

Lastly, Heinz [Seriously] Good Mayonnaise chose to actively avoid failure in the tricky second stage of launch – a common fate of the vast majority of FMCG launches. After its successful launch two years earlier, growth had started to falter, and so the brand chose to act like a challenger and not be afraid to do things differently. Its strategy led to 67% growth versus category growth of just 7%.

Disruptive category thinking

As well as eschewing typical marketing conventions for how to manage brands in their circumstances, some of these challenger brands also disrupted the dominant discourse in the category. In the words of Adam Morgan, they were 'enlightened zaggers': 'The enlightened zagger deliberately swims against a prevailing cultural or category tide'.[5] They deliberately chose to talk and behave differently from others or the norm in their categories.

For example, Aldi reframed a category negative into a positive. After 20 years in the UK, Aldi was still pigeonholed as a 'supermarket for poor people'. Rather than trying to fit in with the 'regular' supermarkets, Aldi chose to double down on its distinctive features to bring to life its founding principles. The retailer chose to 'act like the pirates rather than the navy'. It focused on what made it different, even when those differences were currently contributing to the 'shame' of shopping at Aldi. It used British humour to engage with people and presented its difference in a way that showed how it could fit with people's lives, and in doing so, generated 'pride' in the brand. It kept up this challenger mindset over a prolonged period. If Aldi had ended up as a wannabe regular supermarket, it would have left itself exposed to attack from the next tranche of challengers.

Gordon's chose to go against the dominant gin category narrative of ingredients and provenance, and instead focused on an insight-led way of talking about the gin occasion and the emotion associated with it. A whole new generation of gin drinkers were being trained to seek out provenance stories and had little reason to associate Gordon's with this world. To quote the qualitative strategy research, Gordon's felt 'stuck in time, lacking in energy or movement'. Not only did Gordon's have little hope of being distinctive against small distillers' craft stories, it wasn't even being considered in the same competitive set. So, despite being No.1 in the category, the brand risked a managed decline as the market moved on. Instead of an inward-focused approach like its competitors (focus on own ingredients or provenance), Gordon's focused outwardly (on people and their motivations). Its '… Shall we?' campaign invited people to stop and enjoy a Gordon's and a catch up. The approach used smart and understated wit to stand out in a serious category.

Heineken launched into the non-alcoholic sector with its 0.0% product. Its analysis showed that non-alcoholic beers were presented in three ways: one, for when you can't have beer; two, 'as good as beer'; and three, as a 'healthier beer'. In all these scenarios, non-alcoholic beer was seen as a compromise. Heineken wanted to act differently and present non-alcoholic beer as a beer with added value. Making it something that can be drunk anytime, a positive choice and one that gives people permission to drink it on more occasions. Heineken reframed the category with its 'Now you can' campaign and extended the category into new occasions.

Smart thinking to find budgets

New ways of approaching a category require budgets to support them which, in the face of adversity, aren't always easy to find. But Gordon's took a smart approach to carve out a budget to prove its new concept. It redesigned the bottle and used the cost-of-goods saving to carve out a test budget. If the test worked then more budget would be released. And it was.

Utilising ESOV

Evidence shows that you need to punch above your weight to grow – i.e. share of spend needs to be greater than your share of voice (excess share of voice).[6] This new breed of challenger brands all understood this and factored excess share of voice (ESOV) into their budget setting. Aldi overtly used ESOV to guide its media planning. Heineken required all its markets to make a three-year commitment to devote at least 25% of their total spend to the new launch. The authors of the Heineken paper note that the brand 'heavily and unapologetically' outspent competitors. Tango also showed ESOV in action: it had a SOV of 12% to help it grow from 4% to 6.5%.

Many of this new breed of challenger brands had one other advantage over smaller, newer challengers: they were often already large brands. The downside of this is that the brands often needed large spend to have a positive ESOV to drive growth. But it has also been shown that the relationship between spend and share isn't completely linear: larger brands have an advantage as they don't need such a large positive ESOV to grow.[7] Nielsen research shows that larger brands benefit most from a positive ESOV – per 10% of ESOV the leading brands in a category can benefit on average from 1.4% market share growth vs. 0.4% growth for smaller brands with the equivalent ESOV.[8]

Being a large or legacy brand doesn't hold you back from being a challenger

What this selection of cases from the 2020 IPA Effectiveness Awards has shown is that size isn't a barrier to challenger thinking. These large or legacy brands have employed challenger thinking whilst being far from spring chickens. Gordon's is a 250-year-old brand, Heineken has been around since 1873, Tango and Aldi had been around over 20 years and Heinz is a 150-year-old favourite. This didn't hold them back. This shows that challenger thinking has grown up. It is no longer the confine of startups or small brands (if it ever really was). It is a powerful way of driving growth and giving new life to brands whilst making them fit for the future.

Finding the challenger at the heart of the brand

One thing that was clear from reading the papers is that they weren't all brands you would automatically think of as challengers. But many papers showed how they looked to brand history to rediscover the challenger thinking that was inherent in the brand. For example, challenge was inherent in Aldi's business model, but hadn't been dramatised in its first 20 years in the UK. Challenge was inherent in the Tango brand history, but had been dulled since the brand's prime. Challenge was part of the Heineken story with its distinctive singular-product approach in a category filled with multi-product ranges, but this actually made its non-alcoholic launch trickier.

Brands weren't just jumping around sporadically, but were rediscovering the element of challenge that fitted their brand and using it to build an emotionally powerful brand and drive the growth that comes with it.

Challenger brand thinking has grown up

In the words of Peter Field:

> *'20 years ago, challenger thinking was a seductive theory based on some observations on particular players who had done it. But there was always the temptation to say that these were special cases, maybe distinctive founders or unique cases. But this is not weird; this is smart. This is how to drive growth. It might have been something only a few had spotted, but it actually makes huge business sense and has grown and spread. The mantra of powerful emotional brand identities is now well understood.'*[9]

Notes

1 2018 IPA Effectiveness Awards, 'How Purplebricks brought Commisery to the UK's estate agents'.
2 Adam Morgan, *Eating the Big Fish: How Challenger Brands Can Compete Against Brand Leaders.* Hoboken, NJ: Wiley, 2009.
3 Graham Ruddick, 'Virgin v British Airways: was the Corbyn saga part of the old rivalry?' *The Guardian*, 26 August 2016. https://www.theguardian.com/business/2016/aug/26/virgin-v-british-airways-jeremy-corbyn-rivalry-richard-branson.
4 Morgan, *Eating the Big Fish*.
5 'Enlightened Zagger' available from the Overthrow II website: https://www.overthrow2.com/challenger-type/enlightened-zagger/.
6 Les Binet and Peter Field, *The Long and Short of It*. London: IPA, 2013.
7 Data2Decisions.

8 Nikki Clark, 'Budgeting for the upturn – Does share of voice matter?' available from the Neilsen website: https://www.nielsen.com/us/en/insights/article/2009/budgeting-for-the-upturn-does-share-of-voice-matter/.

9 Peter Field, '"Challenger thinking is how brands drive growth": Peter Field on 20 years of challenger brands' available from the Challenger Project website: https://thechallengerproject.com/blog/2019/peter-field-on-challenger-brands.

Time to take a fresh look at PR

By Helen Weavers
Strategic Consultant, Real World Planning

It appears that there has never been a focus on PR in the observations made by judges in the new learning chapters of the *Advertising Works* books.

This is surprising. Since 2002, the IPA Effectiveness Awards have actively encouraged entries about communications in all channels, not just advertising, with the intention of demonstrating the commercial impact of communication ideas per se, regardless of where they appeared. Moreover, we have been aware since the 2013 IPA publication, *The Long and the Short of It,* that campaigns designed to create brand fame are extremely effective, and many IPA winners have ably demonstrated that. Agencies now use 'fame' principles such as 'how do we get the idea talked about?' or 'how do we get the brand into culture?' as part of their planning process … so we might expect PR to feature prominently in effectiveness cases.

However, in other ways, the lack of focus on PR is not all that surprising. IPA cases are rarely purely, or even mostly, driven by PR. Of the 1500+ entries since 1980 in the IPA's EASE database, only 28 are listed as having PR as a lead channel (less than 0.02%). Only three of these won Gold awards, and all of those were for non-commercial campaigns (Stoptober, 2016; Art Fund, 2016; Organ Donation, 2007) where limited funding precluded the use of advertising. With its typically small budgets, it's not easy for PR-led activity to be extensive or long-lasting enough to generate the behaviour changes and payback that the IPA Effectiveness Awards require.

Of the larger number of cases that mention PR as a support channel or show earned media coverage as a communication outcome, the specific impact is rarely, if ever, quantified – understandably, since it's usually difficult to do so.

Another challenge is the difficulty of even defining PR. Is it a channel, a marketing discipline, any earned media, work originated by PR agencies …? PR has evolved considerably over the years. It's no longer simply 'press relations' that aim to indirectly influence consumers and stakeholders via achieving favourable newspaper coverage.

It's now a much broader range of activity that can also go direct to consumers and often involves the creation of impactful communication ideas in their own right. PR agencies are often now a key part of multi-agency working, involved early on in strategic planning as well as a vital component in the execution and dissemination of ideas.

Have we perhaps failed to keep up with this evolution in the Awards cases and related insights that the IPA publishes, or even in the way we judge the Awards? PR can trigger heated debate in the judging sessions: accusations that 'it was just a stunt', 'it's only buzz', or that successful instances are accidental and opportunistic rather than strategic or planned (hence hard to replicate or scale). There is no doubt that the effectiveness of PR is hard to evaluate and demonstrate, but does the marketing community suffer from a lingering subconscious prejudice about PR?

Therefore, it was very interesting to see among this year's winners four cases that featured PR prominently, only one of which was for a charitable cause. These cases deployed PR in quite different ways, illustrating the range of 'use cases' and approaches now possible.

PR to drive perception change

The KFC Australia 'Michelin Impossible' campaign was striking for being powered almost exclusively by PR and earned media, making its impact relatively easy to isolate and quantify. It was also notable for using PR to tackle a tricky perception challenge for a long-established brand (not to create buzz for something new or to shock on behalf of a charity).

KFC has been operating in Australia for over 50 years, but faces stiff competition from the much larger McDonald's and from newer fast-food brands perceived to offer better quality food. It suffers from the nickname 'the dirty bird' and various communication approaches in previous years had failed to convince sceptical Aussies that KFC food was good quality. The brand needed to find another way; a PR-led, 'aim for fame' strategy proved to be a very effective answer.

The agency observed that no Michelin star had ever been awarded to an Australian restaurant but that, given the criteria were that a restaurant be considered 'very good in its category' and 'worth a special journey', KFC could theoretically qualify – especially the KFC restaurant in Alice Springs, one of the most isolated places in the Australian outback. The owner of that restaurant, Sam, was enlisted to champion the mission and travel to Paris to meet with the director of Michelin. A carefully orchestrated local and national PR campaign ensued.

The media loved the story, achieving a staggering 564 pieces of coverage, delivering 29 impressions for every person in Australia. The public also loved the idea and talked about it, with KFC achieving a category-record YouGov Brand Buzz score. Food quality perceptions improved while transactions and revenue grew significantly, paying back the modest investment many times over.

While the submitted case covers a short period, it will be interesting to see if the idea will prove memorable enough amongst a broad audience to influence brand perceptions and sales for years to come.

PR to dramatise a cause

The entry from CALM was perhaps a more 'conventional' PR-led case in that CALM, the Campaign Against Living Miserably, is a suicide-prevention charity lacking the budget to promote its cause through advertising. However, it was unconventional for the scale and variety of outcomes achieved against a difficult brief.

The campaign's aim was to get lots of people talking about something that no one wants to talk about: death and more specifically male suicide, the biggest killer of men in the UK under 45. The agency identified a vicious circle or 'doom loop' that it wanted to disrupt with its campaign: the less we talk about male suicide, the more we stigmatise male suicide, with fatal consequences.

With a donated budget of £100k, the charity was forced to look beyond advertising channels and instead examined the dynamics of 'cultural transmission', identifying the role of powerful images in getting ideas shared and talked about on a mass scale. This thinking resulted in Project 84, where 84 statues of men were placed on the top of a huge building in central London, as if they were about to jump, creating a disturbing image that highlighted the shocking statistic that 84 men a week in England and Wales had taken their own lives in the previous year.

The clever PR thinking went beyond the creation of this image. Each statue represented a real life lost, with families of men who had taken their lives involved in production, providing additional moving content with which to engage the media. The building used belonged to ITV, adding gravitas and ensuring wide coverage, and the ITV programme, 'This Morning', became an active partner in the campaign, interviewing celebrities and families affected by male suicide and highlighting CALM's helpline, ensuring that people didn't just talk about the statues but also the services that could prevent further tragedies occurring. The campaign also asked people to sign a petition that called on the government to appoint a minister for suicide prevention and provide bereavement support.

This striking idea generated a huge amount of media coverage and social media conversation, plus an unprecedented amount of donations and fundraising, making it possible to increase staffing of the helpline. Moreover, 400k signatures to the petition resulted in CALM being invited to Number 10 by Theresa May, who announced a new Minister for Suicide Prevention on World Mental Health Day: demonstrating how a short-term 'PR stunt' can have a very significant long-term impact.

PR to amplify advertising

Another notable entry this year featured PR in an effective support role to talked-about advertising. We've seen evidence in many IPA cases of the earned media generated by popular ads such as those run at Christmas by retailers. But this was different: it was a topic that bored and irritated the country, yet required urgent personal action: PPI mis-selling.

Compensation for mis-sold payment protection insurance (PPI) had been available since 2007. Complaints peaked in 2012 when claims management companies (CMCs) started to advertise services complaining to financial providers on consumers' behalf. However, claims had been declining since then and inertia had set in; there was no deadline for making a claim and aggressive CMC marketing deterred many who distrusted the process, dismissing it as a scam.

Millions of people who were legitimately owed compensation had not received it, so the Financial Conduct Authority decided that a deadline and supporting communications campaign would encourage people to make a decision to claim if they felt they had a case.

The deadline itself was a PR-able entity, supported by a press release, and the announcement did cause a small uplift in complaints amongst those already interested in claiming. However, without anything memorable or emotive to maintain salience and catalyse action amongst the less engaged, levels dropped back.

Therefore, in planning the communications campaign, the agency perceived a need for an idea that was unforgettable enough to cut through very strongly, get talked about and then stay in the mind. An animatronic head of Arnold Schwarzenegger became the key campaign asset, used in a variety of media channels to support a range of strategic tasks over a two-year campaign.

A key element of effectiveness was the earned media impact: the bizarre use of Arnie transformed the coverage of PPI in the media, taking the topic from the financial sections of newspapers to the front, and onto TV news and consumer affairs programmes. This independent media coverage will not only have increased reach and frequency but also helped to make the deadline and free claims process seem official. The campaign very successfully reversed the decline in PPI interest and helped to generate over 11m complaints and £10bn in compensation payouts.

PR to refresh salience

The final example demonstrates the way PR can ably support a challenger brand strategy within FMCG, not at launch stage but during the 'difficult second stage' of years three to four, a period which many new brands do not survive. Heinz had always struggled in mayonnaise against the dominant Hellmann's, and launched a new premium product, Heinz [Seriously] Good Mayonnaise, in early 2016. TV advertising helped the new product achieve a promising 11% value share by the end of the year. However, the same advertising and spend levels deployed again in 2017 did not drive any growth; the product's share and penetration plateaued.

The team felt that a critical issue was lack of salience in the 'sea of blue and white' that is the mayonnaise fixture. It cleverly chose to think and act not like one of the biggest brands in the world but rather as the little guy in this category, the upstart. Heinz [Seriously] Good Mayonnaise adjusted its advertising approach, including using bold, high-impact outdoor formats, but also turned to specific PR-led ideas as a different way to demand attention in the sector.

Heinz's PR agency used a Twitter poll to incite interest in a hybrid product combining Heinz [Seriously] Good Mayonnaise with the much-loved Heinz Tomato Ketchup. The poll got 100k votes in 48 hours and a lot of media coverage, so that by the time the product was launched, demand drove Heinz's mayonnaise share to its highest-ever level.

To drive salience and get the brand embedded in popular culture, the PR agency introduced Heinz [Seriously] Good Cadbury Creme Egg Mayo, in partnership with

Cadbury, on 1 April. This apparent April Fool's joke garnered a lot of media attention, and then even more when the product was revealed as genuine and sampled at a pop-up event.

Over two years, the combination of PR-led activity and advertising helped generate incremental sales of £12m–£16m for Heinz [Seriously] Good Mayonnaise from a total communications budget of under £5m.

These four cases used PR quite differently and to different ends, but some common themes are evident, giving us some principles for when PR could be an effective choice and how to deploy it well.

1. None of these cases were for new entities or causes, but all were looking for a new way to communicate, in order to tackle inertia, hard-to-shift perceptions or a disinclination to engage with their message.

    PR and earned media offered the advantage of communications that didn't look like classic paid marketing: it can be more impactful or persuasive to find out about something via people you know or your media sources than via advertising, when there is an instinctive awareness that one is being sold to. The use of PR helped to create a new shared reality or public experience of these topics that disposed people to start behaving differently.

    Others passing on your idea can, of course, amplify its reach and frequency many times beyond what the budget affords. The use of PR seems to have allowed these campaigns to get noticed by a large number and a broad range of people, including those not currently 'in market'. This is the role of brand-building communications, indicating PR's potential (when executed really well) to create demand and grow penetration, rather than just to mop up existing demand, as activation does.

2. All these campaigns understood how to make their ideas easily transmissible and 'sticky'. They reminded me of the advice given in *Made to Stick* by Chip and Dan Heath and *Hit Makers* by Derek Thompson: aim for a combination of the simple *and* the unexpected, the familiar *and* the surprising ... so that the concepts are instantly easy to understand yet also rewarding in their originality, encouraging sharing and media coverage.

    All these ideas borrow interest from other well-known entities so our brains find it easy to notice and process them quickly, but then they go on to do something new, interesting and emotive, which sustains and rewards our attention and inclines us to pass them onto others.

    These cases remind us not to forget the power of bold, singular ideas amidst all our complex messaging matrices and integrated campaign plans. And they remind us of the power of surprise (one of the core emotions universal across all human cultures – hard-wired because it's so useful for survival) to make people pay attention afresh.

3. All these cases appreciated the PR power of an unfolding story, and then carefully orchestrated one that repeatedly drew people in. These weren't just brief one-off stunts; these stories built over time to maximise engagement encouraging longer-term memories to develop. And you couldn't cover those stories without appreciating their messages; they were built into the ideas.

These campaigns also all had something to push against: some kind of cause to champion or 'enemy' to compete with that helped create a newsworthy story. A challenger brand mindset seems useful when developing PR-able ideas.

What these cases have made me appreciate is that PR, in many ways, is an acid test of strategic and creative thinking: it takes real skill to develop ideas that are sufficiently unignorable that they get covered, shared and talked about, and that also deliver on hard objectives of behaviour change and increased sales despite usually small budgets. It's not easy to pull this off, but these campaigns demonstrate that it's possible to do it in a variety of sectors.

But here's a plea to those developing future PR-led activity and effectiveness papers: it would be really helpful to both judges and the wider community to see more isolation of the impact of PR/earned media and more discussion of how it worked, in order to continue to drive the continued reappraisal of the discipline that these cases indicate that PR deserves.

SECTION 2

Gold winners

Tesco

From running shops to serving customers: The Tesco turnaround story

By Simon Gregory, BBH; James Parnum, MediaCom
Contributing authors: Kevin Fitzgibbon, MediaCom – Business Science; Nick Ashley, Tesco
Credited company: MediaCom – Business Science

Summary

This paper details the Tesco turnaround from 2015 when it reported a historic loss and declining brand trust. Consumer perceptions of the supermarket's value for money and quality had fallen sharply, along with willingness to recommend it. Tesco adopted a new purpose, 'Serving Britain's shoppers a little better every day', and other changes to make it more customer-led. Media was re-balanced and given new investment. Creative, often featuring Tesco colleagues, focused on communicating helpfulness and stories about quality food. Innovations included Tesco Clubcard Plus, a subscription service. It is estimated the marketing contributed £4.3bn in incremental revenue in 2015–2019.

Editor's comment

In showing how marketing can be a catalyst for change across a huge and struggling business, this case makes an ambitious and important contribution to the IPA's Effectiveness Awards Databank. The judges thought the authors did a great job of linking effects across Tesco's fast-moving and complicated operations back to the impact of marketing across several years. It is a brilliantly written paper about a true transformation journey.

Client comment

Nick Ashley, Head of Media and Campaign Planning, Tesco

This IPA paper has both confirmed and enhanced our understanding of the role of marketing and communications in building both business and brand. More explicitly, as we develop the plan for the next five years, there are three fundamental pieces of learning that we will take forward:

- Serving customers. This is the overall focus of the paper and the thinking that has helped us put the customer at the heart of marketing in terms of messaging, targeting, media selections and product development.
- Getting the fundamentals right. Bringing clarity to the drivers of the business, installing both long- and short-term objectives, bringing media and creative together, and understanding the importance of both short- and medium-term results are all well understood building blocks. However, it's easy to lose sight of them when caught up in the frantic day-to-day. Building this solid foundation gives us the time, head space and guidance with decision making.
- Differentiating. This paper has shown how much can change in both the market and fortune in a short space of time. By shining a light on our strengths and weaknesses with customers, and amongst our competitor set, we have more insight to guide how we differentiate. And, in doing so, ensure that we actively differentiate rather than waiting for the market to move around us.

Marketing has always had a clear and strong role within the Tesco business. Now, with the 2020 IPA paper, we have even more evidence to ensure that it remains a vital tool in serving our customers a little better every day.

Tesco has been at the heart of British retail for 100 years, growing from one stall in London in 1919 to a shop in almost every town in 2020. Then, after decades of growth spurred on by the promise of 'Every little helps', shoppers began deserting. In 2015, Tesco reported a painful combination of the biggest loss of a retailer in UK history and the lowest-ever scores in customer trust experienced by the brand. Shoppers were turning away in droves.

However, through the oft-said but rarely delivered strategy of putting the customer back at the centre of the business, Tesco initiated a turnaround on a scale rarely seen. By the end of 2019, the brand posted its highest trust, quality and value scores in more than nine years whilst the business posted a profit of £2.21bn.

This paper covers these turnaround years (2015–2019), describing the strategies, actions and communications that initiated and contributed to this change. Much of the success comes from a few key ingredients that we often forget in planning for today's world, and all is borne from a simple ambition of shifting back 'from running shops to serving customers'.

Introduction

Background

For many years, Tesco and Sainsbury's competed head-to-head for the top spot in UK retail. By 1995, Tesco had claimed number one, where it remains today (Figure 1). Marketing, with brand and business working hand in glove, delivered Tesco's well-known promise of 'Every little helps' which guided much of Tesco's success.[1]

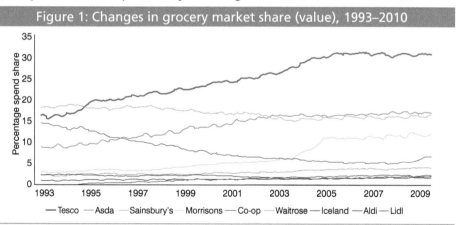

Figure 1: Changes in grocery market share (value), 1993–2010

Source: Kantar World Panel, 1993–2009.

During this period the brand built a winning proposition through a mix of service initiatives (e.g. parent-and-child parking, Tesco Clubcard, wider aisles), innovations (e.g. online shopping, Computers for Schools), and best-in-class communications, all centred on the customer (Figure 2).

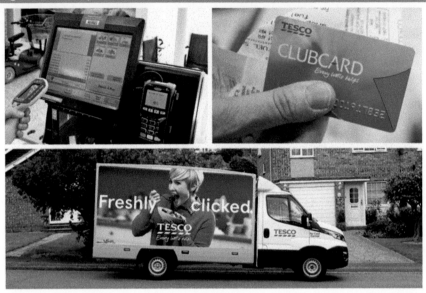

Figure 2: Examples of historical initiatives and 'firsts' launched by Tesco

However, come the early 'teenies', whilst the business continued to post healthy profits, the brand was beginning to show signs of decline. In 2014, exacerbated by a series of external and internal forces, share price fell too.

New competitors

The grocery market was experiencing one of its biggest periods of change. The introduction and aggressive expansion of the German retailers (Aldi and Lidl) brought a new value offering, stealing share across the category (Table 1).

Table 1: Changes in discounter market share (value), 2009–2019

Year	Lidl market share value (%)	Increase in market share	Aldi market share value (%)	Increase in market share
2009	2.4		2.0	
2011	2.5	4%	2.3	15%
2013	3.0	20%	3.6	57%
2015	4.0	33%	5.4	50%
2017	5.0	25%	6.8	26%
2019	6.1	22%	8.0	18%

Source: Kantar World Panel (52-week till roll), 2009–2019.

At the other end of the spectrum, the premium players such as Waitrose, Marks & Spencer and Sainsbury's positioned themselves around higher-quality food.

New behaviours

Shopping behaviour had also changed. By 2014, over 50% of shoppers chose to complete their main shop across two to four grocers, shifting away from the traditional out-of-town one-stop big shop that had served Tesco so well through the 1990s.

Home delivery made an impact too, with small but growing brands like Just Eat (takeaway), Hello Fresh (delivered ingredients) and Amazon (online shopping) offering customers new choices.

Tesco's middle ground was being squeezed (Figure 3).

Figure 3: Trapped in the middle and pressured from all sides

Internal head-winds

A series of internal failings brought more strain to the business.

Stories emerged of supplier payments being knowingly delayed and customers being misled, whilst the category-wide 'horse meat contamination' crisis raised questions about supply chains. Then, in 2014, Tesco's share price plunged after it emerged that the business had been overstating profits.

Net result

And so, Tesco experienced the double-punch of a steep decline in both brand health and share price.

Figure 4: The decline of Tesco's brand index and share price over time, 2009–2014

Source: YouGov (12-week moving average), 2009–2014; Tesco PLC, 2009–2014. Brand index is an aggregate measure of brand health.

... and customers turned away from the stores in droves (Figure 5).

Figure 5: Shoppers increasingly turned away from Tesco, coming less often and buying fewer things

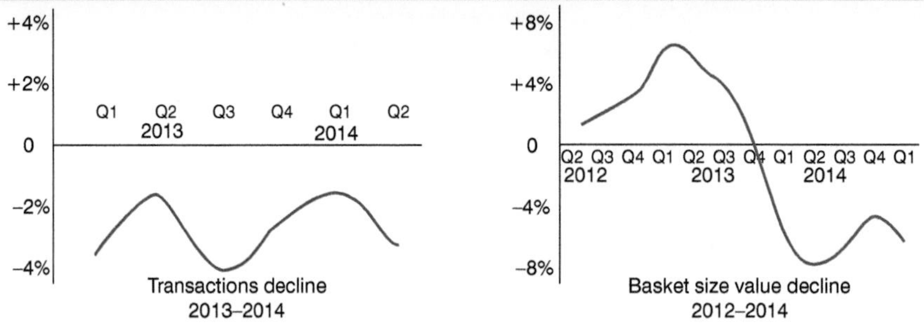

Source: Tesco PLC, (12-week rolling) 2012–2014.

Isolating the problem

Perceptions of 'quality' and 'value for money' – the two critical drivers of choice – had fallen heavily since 2009 (Figure 6).

In fact, Tesco was underperforming on 'quality' and 'value' perceptions to such an extent that these key drivers represented points of *negative* differentiation (Figure 7).

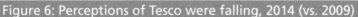

Figure 6: Perceptions of Tesco were falling, 2014 (vs. 2009)

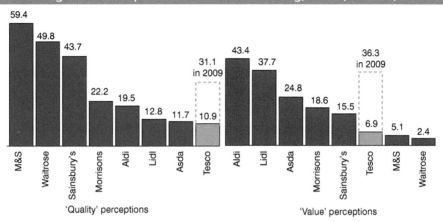

'Quality' perceptions   'Value' perceptions

Source: YouGov (12-week rolling), 2014

Figure 7: Tesco's brand image profile analysis against drivers of store choice ranked in terms of performance

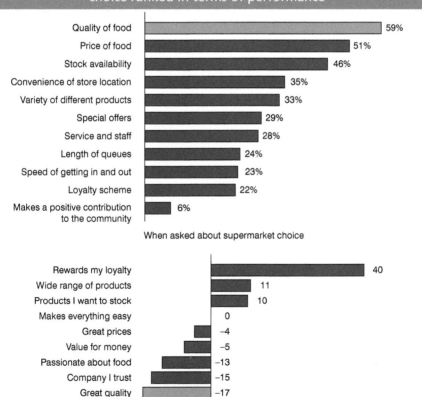

Source: Millward Brown Brand Tracker, 2015. Q: 'When deciding which supermarket to use, how important are the following factors to you and your household?'

Tesco was facing a crisis of broader brand perception. Sentiment about the corporate brand and the store offering was weakening. The result was 'reputation' and 'recommendation' scores were in sharp decline.

Tesco's NPS became negative in late 2014 (Figure 8).

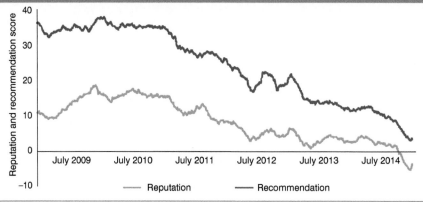

Figure 8: Decline in customer perception of 'reputation' (as a proxy for 'trust') and whether they would recommend Tesco, 2009–2014

Source: YouGov (12-week rolling), 2009–2014.

Symptomatic of this decline was the use of 'Every little helps', a line that had become name-checked by millions, against the brand (Figure 9).

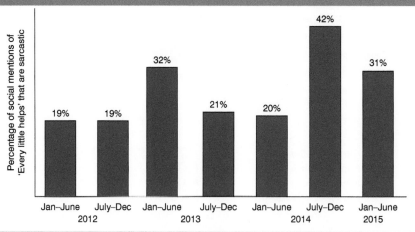

Figure 9: Increasing sarcastic use of 'Every little helps' in social conversation, 2012–2015

Source: BBH Social Listening, Brandwatch: Tesco conversation.

Bringing shoppers back to Tesco and repairing its reputation would require more than a quick-fix solution. Tesco would have to reset and rebuild the relationship between the brand and its customers.

What we did

A plan for recovery

As part of a total business turnaround, rebuilding the Tesco brand became a priority, with marketing recognised as the key lever that could re-engage customers.

Marketing had three clear tasks (Figure 10):

- rebuild trust
- repair quality perception (focusing on food)
- restore value perceptions

Figure 10: The marketing strategy for Tesco's recovery

1. Rebuild trust...

... by putting 'serving customers' back at the heart of the Tesco business.

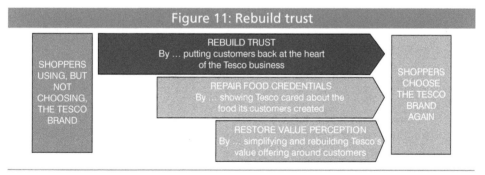

Figure 11: Rebuild trust

The first act was setting the customer agenda from the top down. The arrival of Dave Lewis as Tesco's first CEO from outside the business reset the ethos of the company by emphasising transparency, acts over words, and serving customers.

> *'Having been a marketer, I come with very much a customer lens to any business as that's what I care about most ... I will say let's do what's right for the customer and then let's deal with the consequences from that on finance and the cost, because it's ultimately worth it.'*
>
> Dave Lewis, Tesco CEO, Tesco Annual Report 2015

A series of speeches[2] established a new narrative of moving 'From running shops to serving customers' to both the City and the sector.

This became the cornerstone of Tesco's new purpose – 'Serving Britain's shoppers a little better every day' – connecting to the great Tesco of the past and putting customers back at the heart of the business.

The purpose was installed, quite literally, across the entire estate (Figure 12).

Figure 12: A new brand purpose focused on serving customers

Driven by its new purpose, the Customer Team developed a new approach to communicating change to colleagues and customers alike.

A new media strategy

The new five-year strategy required a new approach to media designed to deliver long-term growth.

1. **Rebalance investment** to campaigns with long-term objectives that better served customers to create a balance of 'brand over time, trade over-night.' Previous campaigns had focused solely on short term (Figure 13).

Figure 13: Pre-2015 examples of Tesco's focus on short-term trade advertising

2. **Regain market-leading share of voice.** Tesco's share of voice correlated to share of market, and spend was in long-term decline. Share of voice (SOV) needed to be restored to the stature of Tesco's scale and ambition to serve (Figures 14 and 15).[3]

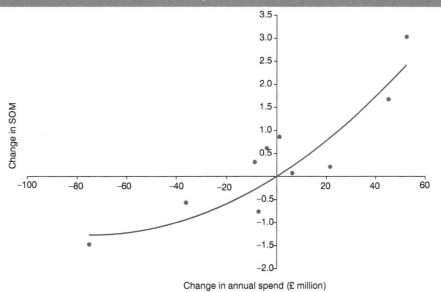

Figure 14: The relationship between Tesco's share of voice and share of market, 2010–2016[4]

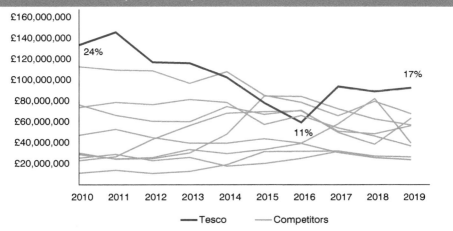

Figure 15: Since 2011, Tesco's spend in market and share of voice (annotated) had been in decline

Source: Nielsen Ad Dynamix – estimated supermarket spend 2010–2019 (SOV figures annotated).

3. **Reweight our media mix** to better reflect people's changing media consumption. By 2014, Tesco's media spend was out of kilter with where consumers were spending time. Going forward we would down-weight print and up-weight digital spend to reflect this (Figure 16).

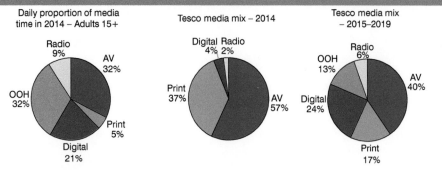

Figure 16: Overhauling Tesco's media investment to align with media consumption (2014–2019)

Source: TGI Touchpoints (2014 survey); Tesco internal (marketing spend data, 2014–2019). Note: 'AV' includes TV, VOD and cinema, while 'digital' includes display, video and social media.

4. **Working 'inside-out'** to rebuild relationships both in and out of the business. Communications were planned from an owned channel perspective of serving colleagues and customers, maximising Tesco's unique owned channel advantage: over 2,300 stores, 330,000 employees, 2,500 trucks, 17 million Tesco Clubcard members, the most-read magazine, and a host of other websites. This would reach over half of the nation before even paying for any media and was estimated to be worth £147m[5] in annual media value. Communications were then extended to serving 'communities' – both geographic and shared communities of interests and needs (e.g. vegans, new dads, foodies) – and then the national public (Figure 17). Size became Tesco's strength; integrating owned, earned and then paid would help develop stronger through-the-line plans (Figure 18).

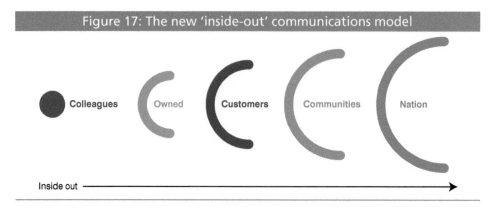

Figure 17: The new 'inside-out' communications model

Figure 18: Tesco's owned media estate is valued at £147m and is a clear competitive advantage

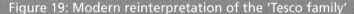

A new creative approach: a return to helpfulness

Customers and Tesco colleagues were placed front and centre in our campaigns to demonstrate our shift to serving customers through messages of 'helpfulness'.

A modern reinterpretation of the classic and much-loved 'Tesco family' carried a series of new, customer-focused, in-store initiatives from reducing queues and matching prices on branded goods, to same-day click and collect and 'no quibble' returns. Branding, cut-through and likeability instantly improved with the new focus on helpfulness.[6]

Figure 19: Modern reinterpretation of the 'Tesco family'

Colleagues were actively engaged to bring a more emotional side of helpfulness to life. They consistently featured in communications showing how we served shoppers, helping them find love on Valentine's Day, giving dads recognition on Father's Day, and finding the perfect school uniform for kids (Figure 20).

Figure 20: A return to helpfulness

A 'Little helps plan' borne from customer and colleague research instigated a range of helpful acts to better serve *all* of our shoppers, such as removal of the 'Tampon Tax', Free Fruit for Kids, Junior Nappies, and Bags of Help.

These and other helpful campaigns – such as Food Waste, the Fair for Farmers Guarantee, Pride, and Dance Beats – became a drumbeat of activity throughout the year (Figure 21).

Figure 21: Tesco's 'Little helps' plan

2. Repair food credentials …

… by showing Tesco cared about the food its customers created.

Figure 22: Repair food credentials

In 2015, the business set about a full food product range review and reset.

The desired output was a simpler, easier to navigate, and improved quality range. However, if this was to be successful, Tesco had to convince customers that the brand represented quality.

Research showed that the biggest barrier was one of perception. Blind taste tests of Tesco food vs. branded showed that the brand was having a negative impact on quality perceptions (Figure 23).

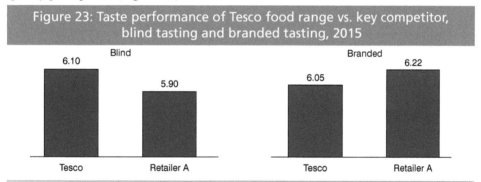
Figure 23: Taste performance of Tesco food range vs. key competitor, blind tasting and branded tasting, 2015

Source: Tesco Insights, Marketing Sciences, 450+ consumer interviews, 10 product categories.

The lack of trust and food scandals mentioned earlier had been exacerbated by a lack of food-quality communications between 2010–2014 (focusing on pricing instead) compared with our competitors and a lack of product development (Tesco's 'Everyday value' range had become perceived as cheap and dated).

To combat this, Tesco began having conversations with the public about real supplier stories and food provenance, but was met with scepticism and disbelief; the 'too big to care' image dominated.

To better serve customers, we had to re-engage with them.

Food plays an integral role in our lives: evoking memories, anniversaries, holidays, special occasions and good times shared. We may, on average, only know five recipes, but both the toast-burners and amateur-chefs have a dish that helps us connect to or create these moments. A dish made with passion and care.

Tesco made a shift in focus: from the food it sells, to the food you love to make for the people you love.

A holy trinity of *people*, *stories* and *food* was created (Figure 24).

Figure 24: 'Food love stories', brought to you by Tesco

The most famous expression of this new approach became 'Food love stories, brought to you by Tesco' – tales that use food to deliver love.

We saw Birdie's 'Everybody welcome' jerk chicken bring love to a foster home, Nana's 'Magic soup' cheer up a child, and Carl's 'All-change' casserole use a sausage that divided the nation (Figure 25).

Figure 25: 'Food love stories'

This redefined how Tesco treated food both internally and externally, from new dialogue with suppliers and colleagues, to new recipes, food inspiration and meal deals (Figure 26).

Beyond 'Food love stories', Tesco further demonstrated its care with health initiatives through a long-standing partnership with Jamie Oliver.

It upped the ante even further for Tesco Finest*, with an immersive event focused on the range and a media-first sponsorship of Friday and Saturday night Sky VOD on the big screen for further *treat night* indulgence (Figure 27).

Figure 26: 'Food love stories'

Figure 27: Tesco Finest* sponsorship of Friday and Saturday SKY VOD and Devour Finest* experiential event (2018)

Media: a long-term storytelling platform

'Food love stories' was Tesco's first food campaign in many years and the media strategy had to reflect that changing people's perceptions of Tesco's food quality would take time, while also providing multiple layers across the 'inside out' model for the stories to be told (Figure 28).

Four ingredients guided the media approach:

1. **Amplify the tastiest stories.** AV and OOH drove national reach and built brand. Radio was added as a natural storytelling medium.
2. **Make stories personal.** Using media owners, sales and insight-led stories were segmented by meal type, occasion, family make-up and convenience to add further relevance.
3. **Deep and meaningful.** The idea was brought to life in helpful ways in stores and owned media including POS, recipe cards, emails, Tesco Magazine and Tesco.com.

4.   **Stories unfold, evolve, and are retold.** Tracking provided constant optimisation and resulted in shifts from display to video, upweighting OOH in poor-quality regions, testing short- and long-form content strategies on social, and monitoring creative wear-out to extend TV stories' lifespans.

Figure 28: The 'Food love stories' storytelling platform as exemplified by Birdie's 'Everyone's welcome' jerk chicken story, which has been run four times (2017–ongoing)

The Tesco food story shifted from 'pile it high and sell it cheap', to serving customers through the food they love to make.

3. Restore value perception ...

... by simplifying and rebuilding Tesco's value offering around serving customers.

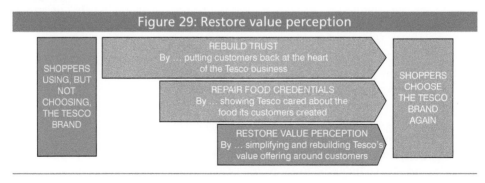

Figure 29: Restore value perception

By 2014, Tesco had 32 in-store and value-promotion mechanics (i.e. buy-one-get-one-free) and focused the vast majority of its in-store media budget on price communications.[7]

Clubcard, whilst still a strength for Tesco, had become complex and cluttered with myriad equations for using points and the once innovative 'Value range' had aged poorly, creeping into 'cheap and nasty' (Figure 30).

Figure 30: A Tesco store c. 2014

Next to the German retailers' simplicity of low prices, Tesco looked complicated, confusing and out of touch.

Customers were walking away with extra items in their basket that they felt they didn't need and contradictory price-per-pack discounts meant uncertainty on whether they were getting value or not.[8]

Again, Tesco looked to how best to serve its customers and reorganised around the needs of shoppers (Table 2).

Table 2: The switch to a customer-first approach in Tesco's value offering, 2014–2019

From Tesco led	To customer led
Multiple and confusing value mechanics	Seven simple and consistent value mechanics (including a simplified Clubcard) based on easy maths
What and when Tesco could sell at a good price	A trading plan and value products (e.g. 'Exclusively at Tesco' brands) based on customer needs
Transactional and basic retail mechanics	Innovative products and services that brought value to customers in new ways. (e.g. Clubcard Plus – a subscription service that brought Tesco, Tesco Mobile and Tesco Bank closer together)

Communicating these changes effectively required an equally important shift.

To date, most research had focused on transactional impacts of value such as the rational equation of getting more for less. However, talking further to customers revealed the importance of the *feeling* of value.

The emotion-driven pride of being able to provide more for the family, the reassurance that you knew where you stood, or the excitement of buying something you wouldn't normally be able to afford. Tesco's role was to help make this achievable.

Trading with emotion

Daily communications brought 'Weekly little helps' that flexed with time of the month (e.g. bulk items near payday and meal solutions near the start of the week) and became themes during seasonal events (e.g. Easter and Halloween).

Bigger acts reassured on the essentials such as the new value range of Exclusively at Tesco brands. In each case, communications were framed around shopper needs (Figure 31).

Figure 31: Exclusively at Tesco

These messages were delivered through a 'virtual shop window', created by bringing together both front pages and first impressions of the nation's 'red tops' (a first), and combining it with a long-term media partnership with *The Sun*, *Daily Mirror* and 27 regional titles (Figure 32).

Figure 32: Tesco's exclusive news brand partnership with *The Sun* and Reach blocking out the competition with 'Weekly little helps' in paper and online (2017–ongoing)

This was complemented by a greater emphasis on targeting shoppers using first-party data from Tesco's first-ever data-management platform (DMP) to deliver greater relevancy in social, display, video, digital audio, and addressable TV (Figure 33).

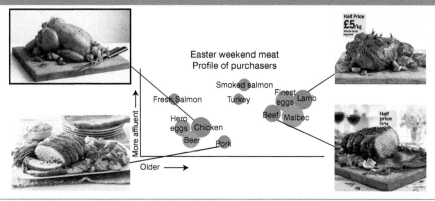

Figure 33: Easter example of Tesco's data-led approach to targeting, which delivered different roast ads depending on a person's age and affluence (2018)

Source: Global Data (Easter Report)

Winning hearts and minds with value

Tesco's 100th birthday in 2019 marked a significant shift in value. Rather than focus on Tesco's history and back story, the brand conducted a series of innovative acts to better serve its customers in a celebration of '100 years of great value'.

Four hero-price events, special prices for Clubcard members, a new Christmas campaign and an innovative new Clubcard Plus subscription service were all launched under the banner of 'Prices that take you back'.

This platform brought together Tesco and a host of nostalgic cultural moments and characters from 'Bullseye' to Mr Blobby to highlight the relationship between the brand and the nation. And, in doing so, positioned the prices as so good they felt like they were from a time gone by (Figure 34).

Figure 34: 'Prices that take you back'

Such was the conversation around the campaign that Freddos returned to their original 10p price following a Twitter petition (resulting in 20 weeks' worth of sales within a week!), and the nation taking part in a Tweet-off between Frazzles and Skips for a similar deal (Figure 35).

Figure 35: Freddos, Cadbury Dairy Milk, Skips and Frazzles

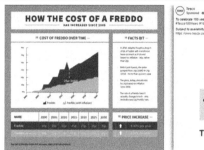

Customer-first value thinking drove activations that got the nation *talking* about Tesco's great value – a combination of quality and price. Creativity and context, both proven to enhance recall, would be key to these activations.[9]

For Christmas 2018, nine spots were created with ITV's 'I'm a Celebrity ... Get Me Out of Here!', and in 2019 all of the main broadcasters co-created ten spots running across ITV, Channel 4 and Sky (an industry first). In both cases, IP, talent and branding were brought together contextually around the programmes (Figure 36).

Figure 36: ITV 'I'm a Celebrity ... Get Me Out of Here!' partnership (2018) – ITV, Channel 4 and Sky partnership including first-ever cross-channel introductory ident (2019)

The launch of Clubcard Plus resulted in a news hijack through an activation matching key headlines to the ads (and some late nights working with *Metro*'s editorial team the day before printing!), while the nostalgia of the Centenary campaign was further enhanced through an ad-funded programming partnership that brought back the classic game show 'Supermarket Sweep'. The latter brought Tesco sponsorship, product placement and amplification rights to build into the 100-year anniversary campaign (Figure 37).

Price confusion had been replaced with simple, good value to serve customer need.

Figure 37: *Metro* editorial partnership for the launch of Clubcard Plus (2019); Tesco, Freemantle and ITV recommissioned 'Supermarket Sweep' (2019)

What happened

Over the five years of Tesco's recovery plan, 'reputation' (as a proxy for 'trust'), 'quality' and 'value' all experienced improvements on a scale previously unseen in the category.

'Trust' was rebuilt and restored, with 'reputation' rebounding from –6% to +14% and reducing the competitor gap to only 2.5 points (Figure 38).

Figure 38: Significant improvement in Tesco's 'reputation' score from 2015

Source: YouGov (12-week rolling), 2009–2019. The competitor set includes: Tesco, Sainsbury's, Asda, Morrisons, Aldi, Lidl, Waitrose, Marks & Spencer, Ocado, The Co-operative.

As trust and reputation improved, so did Tesco's relationship with its own colleagues and suppliers (Figure 39).

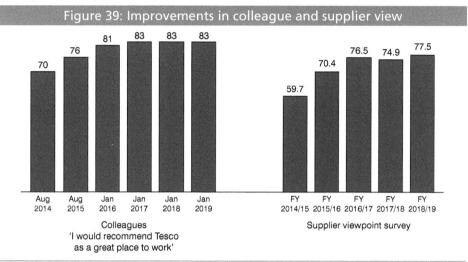

Figure 39: Improvements in colleague and supplier view

Source: Tesco Annual Reports, 2014–2019.

Quality perceptions rose from 9% to 28% and again closed to within four points of market average (Figure 40).

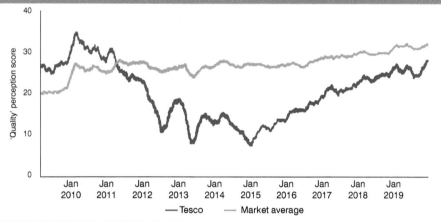

Figure 40: Significant improvement in Tesco's 'quality' perception score from 2015

Source: YouGov (12-week rolling), 2009–2019. The competitor set includes: Tesco, Sainsbury's, Asda, Morrisons, Aldi, Lidl, Waitrose, Marks & Spencer, Ocado, The Co-operative.

Value perceptions increased from 4% to 22%, and, in mid–2016, Tesco overtook the competitor average. Tesco now holds a 5-point lead (Figure 41).

GOLD
GRAND
PRIX

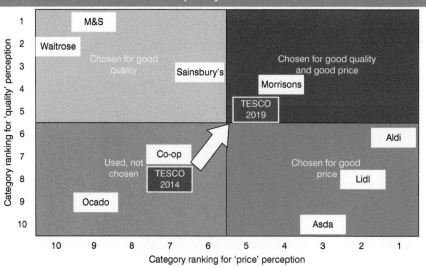

Figure 41: Significant improvement in Tesco's 'value' perception score from 2015

Source: YouGov (12-week rolling), 2009–2019. The competitor set includes: Tesco, Sainsbury's, Asda, Morrisons, Aldi, Lidl, Waitrose, Marks & Spencer, Ocado, The Co-operative.

As testament to this, sales of 'Exclusively at Tesco' grew to 6% of Tesco's total offering and the Centenary activity generated, on average, 50% incremental revenue per event (compared to a normal Tesco week of trading).

Customers were given a clear reason to choose Tesco again, offering better quality than Aldi, Lidl and Asda, and a better price than M&S, Waitrose and Sainsbury's. Tesco had reclaimed its position as a mid-market leader (Figure 42).

Figure 42: Change in Tesco's ranking vs. competitors for key drivers of store choice – 'quality' and 'value', 2019

Source: YouGov, 2011–2019.

Customers returned to Tesco

Customers spoke with their wallet, with more of them choosing Tesco more often and with like-for-like sales increasing by 28% between 2014 and 2019 (Figure 43).

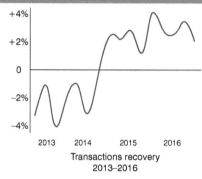

Figure 43: Shoppers came back to Tesco, making more trips to the store and buying more with each visit

Transactions recovery 2013–2016

Basket size value recovery 2012–2019

Source: Tesco PLC (12-week rolling), 2012–2019.

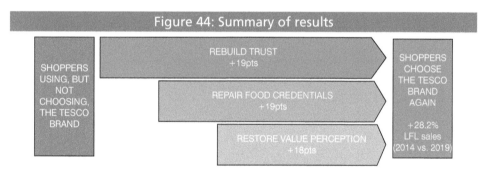

Figure 44: Summary of results

Then, in April 2019, the business posted its highest profits in five years, reflecting 16 consecutive quarters of growth since a pre-tax loss of £6.4bn in February 2015. Profit (before tax and exceptional costs), driven by increases in like-for-like sales growth, had surpassed pre-2014 levels at +£2.21bn (Figure 45).

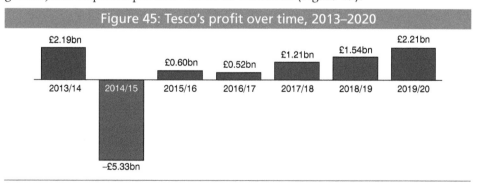

Figure 45: Tesco's profit over time, 2013–2020

Source: Tesco Annual Reports.

By putting the customer back at the heart of Tesco, brand and business had recovered as one.

Share price and brand health rose by 36% and 630% respectively between 2015 and 2019 (Figure 46).

Figure 46: The recovery of Tesco's brand index and share price over time, 2009–2019

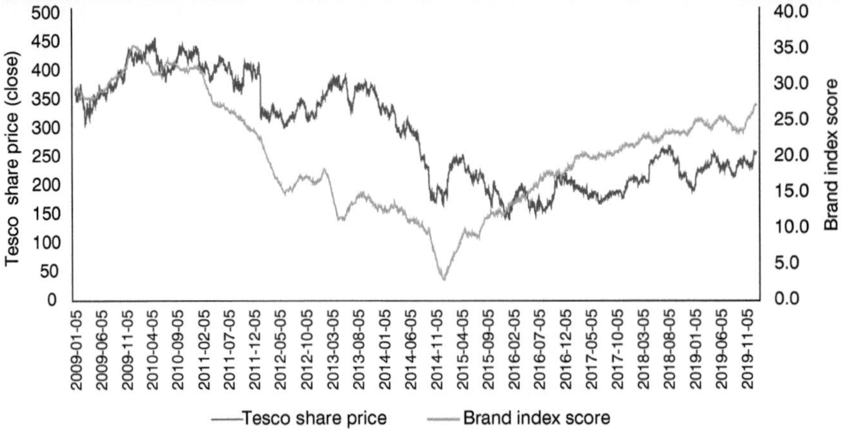

Source: YouGov (12-week moving average), 2009–2019; Tesco PLC, 2009–2019.

The impact of marketing

We have shown that Tesco's revitalised brand was driven by a customer-first approach that transformed the brand's fortunes.

However, grocery is a complex and fast-moving business, and the long-term focus of this paper means that there were numerous factors beyond marketing that could have played a part in driving results.

The following section will prove the impact across three dimensions:

- How marketing alone drove customer perceptions of 'quality', 'value for money', and overall brand strength
- The revenue and profit returns from our media spend, building long-term brand value and short-term sales
- The longer-term improvements and efficiencies delivered by media spend over time

Isolating the impact

There are a number of broad factors that can be discounted from the offset.

Distribution

Over the last five years, Tesco's store footprint has only nominally grown by 1.3% square feet versus a market that has expanded significantly by 11.3%. In fact,

Tesco's share of space has dropped 2.4 points from 26.5% to 24.1%, which means distribution is unlikely to have been a core lever of its growth (Table 3).

Table 3: Total Tesco store space versus market (2015 vs. 2019)

	2015	2019	Change
Tesco space	38,108,273	38,619,701	1.3%
Total market space – including Tesco	143,665,700	159,953,194	11.3%
Tesco share of total market space	26.5%	24.1%	-2.4%

Source: Tesco internal data, w/c 05.01.2015 versus 30.12.2019. Competitor square footage collected by Glenigan.

Consumer confidence

Confidence levels have not helped Tesco. Since 2015, they have plunged from positive to four years of negative with an average score of –6 across the five years of the turnaround (Figure 47).

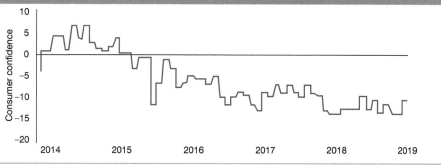

Figure 47: Over the last five years, consumer confidence has experienced a significant decline (2015–2019)

Source: GFK (weekly scores), 2015–2019.

Inflation

Between 2015 and 2019, inflation in the grocery market has oscillated between –1.6% and 2.7%; in most of these years Tesco has lagged behind the market, benefitting less than its rivals (Table 4).

Table 4: Tesco and grocery market inflation (2015–2019)

	2015	2016	2017	2018	2019
Total grocery market	−1.60%	−1.20%	2.70%	2.10%	1.10%
Tesco	−1.80%	−1.50%	2.60%	2.50%	0.70%

Source: Kantar, annual inflation figures, 2015–2019.

Promotions

Tesco operates a high-low business model with promotions crucial to stimulating sales. However, the number of products on promotion has remained flat since 2015 (Table 5).

Table 5: Tesco and total grocery market inflation (2016–2019)					
	2015	**2016**	**2017**	**2018**	**2019**
Products on promotion	n/a	3,895,184	3,810,714	3,876,270	3,789,517

Source: Tesco internal. In 2016, how promotions were accounted for changed, hence no comparable data for 2015 (2016–2019).

Using an econometric model, we can quantify a number of factors,[10] including those above, allowing us to forecast what would have happened to our key brand metrics if the new marketing approach had not happened.

Firstly, quality perceptions would have risen more slowly and largely plateaued by the end of 2017, with a 5% gap versus our actual result (Figure 48).

Figure 48: Tesco 'quality' perception – actual versus forecast score assuming marketing effectiveness had not improved since 2015

—— Tesco 'quality' – actual score   —— Tesco 'quality' – forecast score without marketing improvement

Sources: MediaCom Business Science, YouGov (12-week rolling) – actual vs. forecast assuming marketing effectiveness remained the same as 2015.

Similarly, 'value' perceptions would have largely plateaued by November 2016 with a gap of 4.8% versus what we actually achieved (Figure 49).

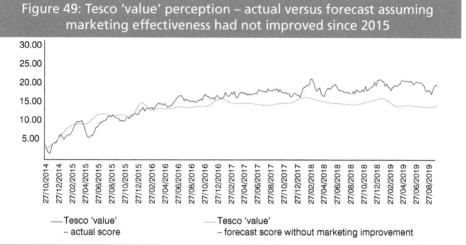

Figure 49: Tesco 'value' perception – actual versus forecast assuming marketing effectiveness had not improved since 2015

—— Tesco 'value' – actual score —— Tesco 'value' – forecast score without marketing improvement

Source: MediaCom Business Science, YouGov (12-week rolling) – actual vs. forecast assuming marketing effectiveness remained the same as 2015.

In summary, we see an average drop of 5% for 'quality' and 4.8% for 'value' if the marketing had not improved since 2015.

Whilst we are not able to model 'trust' within the model, the overall contribution of marketing to 'quality', 'value' and brand index scores more than demonstrates the broader impact of spend (Table 6).

Table 6: Marketing's contribution to YouGov 'quality', 'value' and brand index scores are all over 30% (2015–2019)

	Quality	Value	Brand index
2015 score	18.5	13.7	15.0
2019 score	26.8	17.7	24.1
Increase	8.4	4.0	9.1
Media contribution	2.7	1.2	3.2
Media contribution %	32.5%	30.9%	35.3%

Source: MediaCom Business Science, contribution to YouGov 'quality', 'value' and brand index scores – absolutes taken in line with first and last available model dates (04.01.16 and 30.09.19).

Return on investment

Econometric modelling suggests that marketing spend represents between 2.8% and 3.4% of total revenue for Tesco. Whilst this is a small percentage, the impact on a business the size of Tesco is substantial (Table 7).

Table 7: Marketing investment impact on revenue as a percentage of total Tesco revenue (2015–2019)	
Contribution to revenue – media by year	
September 2015–August 2016	2.8%
September 2016–August 2017	3.4%
September 2017–August 2018	3.2%
September 2018–August 2019	3.1%

Source: Tesco Econometrics, MediaCom Business Science – published until 2017 and now updated to September 2019.

Marketing spend drives revenue through two effects:

1. its impact on brand health
2. its effect on sales.

The econometric analysis developed by MediaCom Business Science allows us to quantify both.[11]

Impact on brand health

Since 2015, an improved brand has grown revenue and marketing has driven 45% of this revenue growth, equating to £1.8bn (Figure 50).

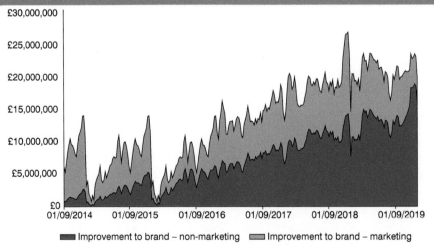

Figure 50: Revenue delivered by brand performance (long term) with and without marketing investment, 2014–2019

Source: Tesco Econometrics, MediaCom Business Science – published until 2017 and now updated to September 2019.

Impact on sales

Modelling allows us to quantify two sales effects:

1. a long-term effect on base sales (impact 3–24 months after the activity has run)
2. a short-term impact on sales (impact within the first three months)

While the main focus of Tesco's marketing efforts has been brand revitalisation, marketing has achieved both.

On average, two-thirds of the media-driven profit has been delivered in the short term, proving our marketing effect worked to deliver short-term commercial return as well as long-term growth (Table 8).

Table 8: Profit delivered in the short and long term (2015–2019)

Year	Short term	Long term
September 2015–August 2016	66%	34%
September 2016–August 2017	61%	39%
September 2017–August 2018	66%	34%
September 2018–August 2019	73%	27%
Total	**66%**	**34%**

Source: Tesco Econometrics, MediaCom Business Science.

When isolated versus other factors, we can see the combined impact of short-term and long-term improvements on revenue over time (Figure 51 and Table 9).

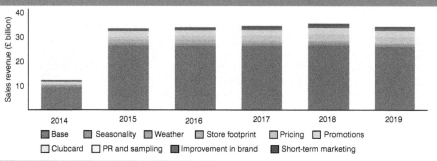

Figure 51: Isolation of revenue driven by long-term improvements of the brand and short-term sales impact associated with marketing investment

Source: Tesco Econometrics, MediaCom Business Science.

Table 9: Revenue driven from brand improvement and short-term sales impact

	Revenue driven from brand improvement	Revenue driven from short-term sales impact
2014	£175,391,273	£349,957,753
2015	£371,945,348	£776,272,564
2016	£371,251,227	£701,844,022
2017	£741,676,313	£910,496,312
2018	£1,014,880,108	£972,348,625
2019	£1,100,194,837	£607,808,082

Source: Tesco Econometrics, MediaCom Business Science.

Between 2015 and 2019, this equates to £4.3bn incremental revenue, with every £1 invested in marketing returning £13.65 (Table 10).

Table 10: Revenue return on investment from marketing spend over time

	Incremental revenue	Revenue ROI	Total modelled media spend
Sep 2015–Aug 2016	£919,008,029	£13.94	£65,904,575
Sep 2016–Aug 2017	£1,177,069,246	£13.30	£88,484,201
Sep 2017–Aug 2018	£1,109,468,118	£14.14	£78,437,019
Sep 2018–Aug 2019	£1,111,722,871	£13.34	£83,361,159
Total	**£4,317,268,264**	**£13.65**	**£316,186,954**

Source: Tesco Econometrics, MediaCom Business Science.

Converting revenue to profit is no easy task in a business as complex as the nation's biggest grocer, so we have applied a category-specific margin based on learnings from the IPA Effectiveness Awards Databank.[12]

Applying this margin shows we delivered £863m incremental profit between 2015 and 2019 with a profit ROMI of £2.73.[13] To put this profit ROI into perspective, the Grand Prix winning Tesco paper from 2000 delivered a profit ROI of £2.25, which is 18% less than the paper calculates we have achieved (Tables 11 and 12).

Table 11: Profit return on investment from marketing spend over time

	Incremental profit	Profit ROI	Total modelled media spend
Sep 2015–Aug 2016	£183,801,606	£2.79	£65,904,575
Sep 2016–Aug 2017	£235,413,849	£2.66	£88,484,201
Sep 2017–Aug 2018	£221,893,624	£2.83	£78,437,019
Sep 2018–Aug 2019	£222,344,574	£2.67	£83,361,159
Total	**£863,453,653**	**£2.73**	**£316,186,954**

Source: Tesco Econometrics, MediaCom Business Science.

Table 12: Summary of revenue and profit ROIs over time		
	Revenue ROI	Profit ROI
Sep 2015–Aug 2016	£13.94	£2.79
Sep 2016–Aug 2017	£13.30	£2.66
Sep 2017–Aug 2018	£14.14	£2.83
Sep 2018–Aug 2019	£13.34	£2.67
Total	**£13.65**	**£2.73**

Source: Tesco Econometrics, MediaCom Business Science.

Since marketing also creates a halo effect for the future, these short-term sales are 6% higher for each £1 spent on media in 2019 versus 2015 (an extra £60m), creating a long-term improvement in both effectiveness and efficiency over time (Figure 52).

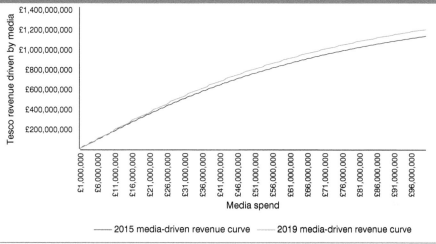

Figure 52: Revenue delivered in the short term per £m spent on media, (2015 vs. 2019)

Source: MediaCom Business Science.

Broader impact

'It is right to be investing in advertising. Over the three years you see a strong strengthening in the brand. More people are choosing to shop at Tesco and our brand is stronger, as customers recognise improvements in both quality and value.'

Dave Lewis, 2018

Communications became a vital part of the recovery narrative to the City and Tesco's stakeholders. As customers returned, Tesco's rebound made the headlines (Figures 53 and 54).

Figure 53: Media coverage marking Tesco's recovery

Tesco chief hails 'progress' as profits pass £1bn

Dave Lewis says more people shopping at chain as 'brand is stronger'

Tesco advertising push pays off as profits rebound almost 800%

Tesco beats forecast with 28% rise in annual profits

Retailer makes profit of £1.64bn on sales of £57.5bn in ninth consecutive quarter of growth

Tesco to issue annual dividend after profits eclipse £1bn

Earnings rise almost 800% as grocer dodges high street gloom

Tesco profits rebound as turnaround continues

By Daniel Thomas
Business reporter, BBC News

News > Business > Business News

Tesco share price surges after it unveils 800% profit rise and resumes dividend

The supermarket said its turnaround strategy is 'firmly' on track

Figure 54: Tesco Annual Reports 2017 and 2018

If you look over the last three years, you'll see a very deliberate strategy in how we spend our marketing money. The combination of 'Food love stories' and 'Weekly little helps' meant it was the right time to be investing in [advertising]. If I look at the quality perception of the brand – it's continued to improve strongly – over the three years you see a strong strengthening in the brand.

Dave Lewis,
Tesco Annual Report 2018

Source: Tesco Annual Reports.

Though Tesco may not yet be the darling of the nation it once was, its transformation has not gone unnoticed.

Throughout the five years of recovery, Tesco won a host of awards including Britain's Favourite Supermarket (five times),[14] Grocer of the Year (three times)[15] and YouGov's most improved brand of the year three times in a row.

Learning

1. The brand fundamentals

Central to this recovery was the reparation of the relationship between customer and brand. For a brand to succeed, customers must trust that the seemingly simple colours, logos and language stand for a consistent delivery of what's promised. For Tesco, whilst communications had previously tried to show the basic quality-versus-price value equation and Tesco's helpfulness, customers had simply stopped believing them. Restoring 'Every little helps' to a promise rather than an endline required a fundamental reparation of customer trust.

2. The marketing catalyst

In the Tesco turnaround, marketing stood tall and played two crucial roles beyond communications: (a) aligning the business and colleagues around shopper needs and barriers (led from the top with ex-marketer Dave Lewis and Chief *Customer* – not Marketing – Officer Alessandra Bellini); and (b) acting as an agile and immediate lever to communicate business intent and 'buy' the time needed to make more substantial changes in operations.

3. Think long – act fast

The establishment of long-term objectives and strategies around 'trust', 'quality' and 'value' brought a new alignment in the business across all 'P's of Tesco's customer mix (price, product, promotion, place, people, packaging). This not only ensured that we were all 'singing from the same hymn sheet', but also freed the business to move quickly when it needed to.

Though not covered in the timeframe of this paper, these pillars and associated communications allowed Tesco to lead the way during the recent COVID–19 pandemic. By reassuring shoppers through simple colleague comms and flexing 'Food love stories' to connect the nation with emotion, the brand has seen market-leading shifts in 'reputation', 'quality' and 'value'.[16]

4. Return to the craft of media planning

Whilst a lot changed in the media landscape during these five years, Tesco's approach proves that you can simultaneously embrace the new (e.g. digital, data, DMP) with the old principles of media planning and buying.

Reweighting the plan to support campaigns with long-term objectives, a single-minded focus on winning SOV, and a media mix that reflected shopper consumption, gave Tesco a strong foundation from which to grow. It enabled meticulous systems to flourish and allowed long-term platforms to thrive on all available paid, owned and earned touchpoints.

The success here encouraged further bravery through exclusive activations, media creativity and partnerships – all underpinned by context – proving again that marketing is at its best when medium and creative are planned in harmony.

Conclusion

In 2014, Tesco represented a somewhat poisoned chalice: a great British brand, steeped in marketing history and embedded in culture. However, with this came one of the biggest-ever losses in UK retail history and a broken relationship with shoppers.

This paper explores the five-year turnaround undertaken by the grocer, linking the brand recovery (+640% increase in brand index score), the increase in sales (+28.2% like-for-like sales) and the huge shift in profit (from –£6.4bn to +£2.21bn), to a fundamental shift from 'running shops to serving customers'.

It is a tough story to simplify; it has many authors, multiple variables, no end of mistakes, slices of luck and lessons. Yet, at heart, it is driven by a simple belief in using marketing to connect business and brand to work in union.

Five years ago, this may have been an uncomfortable conclusion, but now it is said with great pride: 'Every little helps'.

Notes

1 IPA Effectiveness Awards Databank, 'How Every Little Helps was a Great Help to Tesco'. IPA Grand Prix Paper, 2000.
2 For example, Marketing Society, 2015.
3 A market leader's SOV does not necessarily need to equal its SOM due to its scale advantage – Harvard Business School, 'Ad Spending: Growing Market Share' (January–February 1990).
4 In total, five methodologies were utilised – all over the same six-year period, 2010–2016 – to prove the relationship of SOV and SOM and forecast the approximate media spend required for SOM growth: 1. Using IPA benchmark – expected share growth of 0.5% for each 10% excess SOV (£123m); 2. Bespoke MediaCom Business Science Model I: modelled SOV as the dependent variable (£115m); 3. Bespoke MediaCom Business Science Model II: modelled change in SOM as the dependent variable (£73m); 4. Bespoke MediaCom Business Science Model III: modelled change in spend as the dependent variable (£83m); 5. MediaCom Business Science Econometric Model: calculated by the short-term and long-term curves (£86m).
5 MediaCom. Tesco's owned-media value calculated by finding a suitable paid-for media equivalent and costing up at market rates and averages.
6 Millward Brown, 2014.
7 Nielsen, 2014.
8 'Drivers of Shopper Value', Tesco, 2015.
9 GroupM and Newsworks 'Value of Quality' (2018); Integral Ad Science, 'The Halo Effect' (2019).
10 The 25 variables accounted for in the econometric modelling process include: share of grocery retail space, versus competitors; availability of products within each category; space allocated to each category in-store; average selling price by category; base price by category; price inflation by category; promotion participation by category – including sales driven by promoted products, and the proportion of products that are on a promotion; Tesco Clubcard coupons and vouchers; new product/range launches; brand health metrics; weather impacts; economic indicators; payday; bank holidays; school holidays; seasonal and cultural events; sporting events; general market trends (e.g. the rise of veganism); Tesco paid-media activity; DM and emails sent; PR data; Tesco-owned assets (Tesco magazine and other owned media assets); experiential and sampling activity; competitors, communications activity; competitor pricing.
11 The long-term impact is determined by modelling YouGov brand metrics to calculate the uplift driven by marketing. This is combined with calculating the uplift in sales driven by movements in brand metrics, to capture the future demand created by marketing. While the short-term impact is determined through traditional market-mix modelling. Quantifying and combining each of these effects give us the total return from Tesco's media investment.
12 IPA Effectiveness Awards Databank– since 2000, there have been 32 supermarket IPA entries; of those which have specified a category norm to calculate marginal profit, the figure used ranges from 20% to 32%. As the biggest supermarket, we have used the conservative end of this range – a margin of 20% – to calculate our profit figures.
13 Tesco Econometrics, MediaCom Business Science.
14 *The Grocer.*
15 *The Grocer.*
16 YouGov / Kantar.

Audi

The value of 'Vorsprung durch Technik' over four decades

By Will Lion and Thomas Gwin, BBH
Credited company: The Effectiveness Partnership

Summary

This paper identifies consistent themes behind effective Audi UK advertising from 1982 to 2019. Building on the brand purpose of 'Vorsprung durch Technik' ('progress through technology'), communications succeeded in elevating the auto brand from the mass market to the prestige sector and defended its position as most desired prestige brand. Unvarying principles included the use of 'hero' car models 'with personality' in creative and the choice of film to convey premium values. Audi UK grew its sales faster than other European Audi markets and the UK car sector as a whole. It is estimated that since 1982 communications returned £2.33 per £1 invested.

Editor's comment

The judges thought this case was an important demonstration of how a strong brand idea can power impressive business results over almost 40 years. This case convincingly shows how a long-term client–agency partnership reinterpreted this idea for changes in the market and media-consumption habits to make the Audi brand consistently more desirable and more commercially valuable.

Client comment

Anna Russell, National Brand & Retail Marketing Lead, Audi UK

As 'Vorsprung durch Technik' soon turns 40, we reflect on an incredible journey. Most of us were still children or twinkles in our parents' eyes when this story began.

While Audi has always had the engineering prowess, in the early 1980s it lagged the premium image to go with the price tag for all the finely-tuned kit. Over four decades that all changed. In the UK, Audi is now considered more desirable than BMW and Mercedes, and our price point is now up there with our competitors.

How did we get there? Through incredible cars, first and foremost. But also through that other thing engineered into all Audi cars, three words that mean the belief in progress through technology. Through our brand and the communications, this made the cars more famous and moved people emotionally, all the way to the showrooms. There are millions of Audi cars on the road now as a result.

What have we learned? Company values and beliefs matter. They help steer us in a changing world. 'Vorsprung durch Technik' is often the guide through any decision. Going long matters. We must keep looking up and out, especially as a premium brand. Data and people matter. Science and art matter. When these two are put together in the right mix, you can really 'Vorsprung'.

Thank you to all the guardians over the years for everything that made Audi UK what it is today. As you can see, it worked a treat.

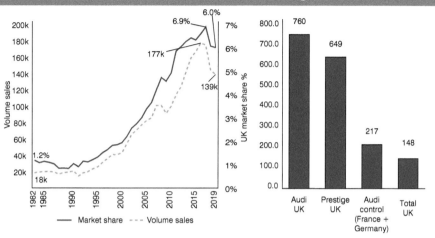

Figure 1: Audi UK volume sales and share 1982–2019 (left) and 2019 volume sales indexed to 1982 (right)

Sources: SMMT data 1982–2019 (Audi UK, UK car market, prestige UK car market); JATO data 1982–2019 (Audi control: France + Germany).

What is the long-term value of creativity for communications effectiveness? The graphs above offer a clue. In this paper we will show the large role communications played in fuelling Audi's exceptional growth, by helping to turn an ordinary brand into an extraordinary one.

It's the story of how a mid-market brand with sales of 18k and 1.2% share became the most desirable mass-prestige car brand, selling nearly 10 times that amount each year,[1] increasing market share by a factor of 5, and supercharging its pricing power – growing 7.6 times faster than the UK car market and 2.2 times faster than similar European Audi markets.[2]

It's about how communications engineered one last invisible component into every car – 'Vorsprung durch Technik'[3] – and how these words helped steer a brand over the decades of change, kept us thinking long in an increasingly short-term world, energised an agency and an industry, became part of British culture and created some of the UK's best advertising along the way.

And, for the first time, we have put a value to what these three words have created since 1982: **£31.8bn**. Today, Audi UK enjoys an additional £0.7bn year in sales (and that's excluding fleet and used) because of this communications engine. For context, that's almost identical to the sale value of Instagram being created every single year.

Overall, for every £1 spent since 1982, **£2.33 of profit** has been returned.

This is the complete story of 'Vorsprung durch Technik' – and the value it has created.

Introduction

Find a child. Give her a marshmallow. Tell her if she can resist eating it for 15 minutes she'll get a second one.

This is the 'marshmallow test' and children who are patient enough to wait for that second marshmallow have been found to do better at school, at work and in life.[4] Delaying immediate gratification and thinking long seems to have magical effects.[5]

Brands appear to be the same.[6]

With the knives of effectiveness being blunted by short-termism[7] and a 'crisis in creative effectiveness',[8] this Audi case study is perhaps the definitive story of long-term creative thinking and effectiveness in UK advertising.

But it goes one step further.

Everyone knows 'going long' works. The question for the industry is now a practical one: how? How, in a world that is changing fast and 'going short', do you resist eating that marshmallow?

While the commercial effectiveness of Audi's communications creativity has been consistently demonstrated across four decades with the IPA (Table 1), this is the first time we have taken a step back to look at the long-term value that 'Vorsprung durch Technik' has created since it was invented. And it is the first time we share the culture and techniques that ensured it kept 'going long'.

Table 1: Audi IPA Effectiveness Awards over the last four decades

Period	Paper	Key results
1982–1987	'Vorsprung durch Technik: The Change of Audi Marque Image'	Improved sales mix within range (higher profit margin) and reduced price elasticity, driven by jumps in awareness, image consideration, as well as improved advertising efficiency.
1995–1997	'Members only: How Advertising Helped Audi Join the Prestige Car Club' (Bronze)	33% increase in demand, improved dealer margins, and dramatic improvements in residual value of cars, driven by jumps in awareness, driver imagery, brand favourability and consideration.
2000–2005	'From Private to Public Prestige'	65,505 incremental sales, driven by increases in awareness, brand prestige measures, desirability, enquiries and conversion.
1999–2007	'Firing Up the Quattro: how Audi Accelerated into the 21st Century' (Silver)	£1.29bn incremental sales, driven by further improvements in brand image, consideration, enquiries, as well as efficiency gains.
2008–2009	'The New More Fuel-Efficient Audi Communications Model' (Silver)	£51.3m of profit and greater prestige market share, driven through increased efficiency image and desire metrics at the time of a recession.
2012	'Audi A1: A Big Idea, Condensed' (Bronze)	£21.2m of incremental profit, impressive share growth of new category in compact premium and attracted new customers from mass market during a recession.
2015–2018	'Beauty and Brains: How We Supercharged the Audi Premium' (Grand Prix)	£1.8bn of incremental sales, growth 3 times faster than the UK market and 2.5 times faster than Audi globally, closed the price gap to competitors, increased lifetime customer value, sold more cars at higher specification, through image and desire improvements.

We will show that Audi's guardians[9] over the years would pass the 'marshmallow test', dreaming of a greater brand down the line, and in doing so pulled off marketing's greatest magic trick: more sales, at a higher price, with lower marketing costs.

But to appreciate this trick properly, we will need to go back four decades.

One brief, three chapters

Imagine this brief arriving on your desk in 1982:[10]

> *'Take a brand of solid engineering but vague provenance and personality out of the middle market, give it a fresh vision and hurl it credibly into the prestige club of marketing aristocrats. We're more expensive than our mass market competitors[11] but lack the credibility to enter the prestige club. We have been called "for the man who can't afford a Merc" and "for the failed BMW man".'*

Essentially, take on 'The Ultimate Driving Machine' and the brand Janis Joplin asked God to buy her.[12]

Figure 2: BBH pitch response characterising the state of Audi in 1982[13]

```
AUDI - PRESENT IMAGE


 -   We believe Audi's image is presently very low
     profile, very bland, amongst non-owners.
     When considered, it is seen as functional,
     serious and sensible.  A good all round purchase,
```

Audi and the car market have certainly moved on since 1982 – but the fundamental brief remained much the same over four decades.

In a sentence, the brief has been: build a marketing machine to sell more cars, at a higher price, and do it more efficiently.

In a word: premiumise.

Looking back, it's clear there were three distinct chapters that powered that transformation.

Table 2: The three chapters of Audi's transformation, with key issues at each stage

Chapter 1: Elevate Lift out of the mass market	Chapter 2: Join Become part of 'the club'	Chapter 3: Lead Supercharge the premium
Key issue Not considered in the prestige club at all. Tethered Ford/Saab in associations. Prestige price without prestige image.	**Key issue** Only 17% said Audi was a prestige brand vs. 80% Mercedes, yet prestige volume sales needed.	**Key issue** Defend and grow premium to take a bigger value share of the slowing prestige market.

These created the following objectives

Figure 3: Overall objectives 1982 to present and specific objectives of the three chapters

Overall

Business
- Increase share of the UK car market, selling 'more cars'
- Increase average price point and increase car specification, selling 'more cars'
- Make marketing more efficient

Behaviour
- Get more drivers into the Audi brand having bought higher-specification models
- Drive more enquiries and test drives with the brand

Brand
- Increase awareness of the Audi brand
- Make Audi a credible, desirable and distinct brand among the prestige car audience
- Drive consideration of the brand and its models

Chapter 1: Elevate	Chapter 2: Join	Chapter 3: Lead
Business	**Business**	**Business**
• Reduce price elasticity	• Drive volume sales without	• Drive volume sales, higher
• Drive more profitable sales mix	discounting	customer value and
		profitability
Behaviour	**Behaviour**	
• Drive higher-specification	• Drive higher-specification	**Behaviour**
model choice	model choice	• Drive higher-specification
		model choice and conversion
Brand	**Brand**	to aftersales
• Drive image gains and close	• Drive image gains and become	
gap to prestige competitors	firmly part of the prestige club	**Brand**
		• Defend and grow image lead

What we did

The strategy in a nutshell

Chapter 1. Elevate.

Lift out of the mass market. To drive image and sales mix, a progressive, technical, German identity with a sophisticated, warm, and understated tone was created. On a German factory tour in 1982, Sir John Hegarty spotted three words on an old Audi poster that would embody all that meaning – 'Vorsprung durch Technik'. When John enquired what the phrase meant he was told: 'It's an Audi belief about progress or advancement through technology'. The phrase had been around internally from 1971, but a decade later it was re-ignited and made relevant for a different time and country.[14] Communications then brought this spirit to life with stylish people doing stylish things in stylish places.

Chapter 2. Join.

Become part of 'the club'. That meant defining what the brand wasn't – stuffy or brash – by seducing new drivers with its more modern, witty approach to success. Communications characterised the driver and the designs in this light.

Chapter 3. Lead.

Supercharge the premium. To get drivers to buy 'more car', communications focused on the brand's shiniest jewels – its best models and technologies – and the brand started behaving like a progressive luxury brand.

Fundamentally, the values of the brand were the strategy. They just flexed to the varying product launches, marketing tasks and media changes dealt out over the decade (Figure 4).

Figure 4: The Audi brand and communications model 1982–2020

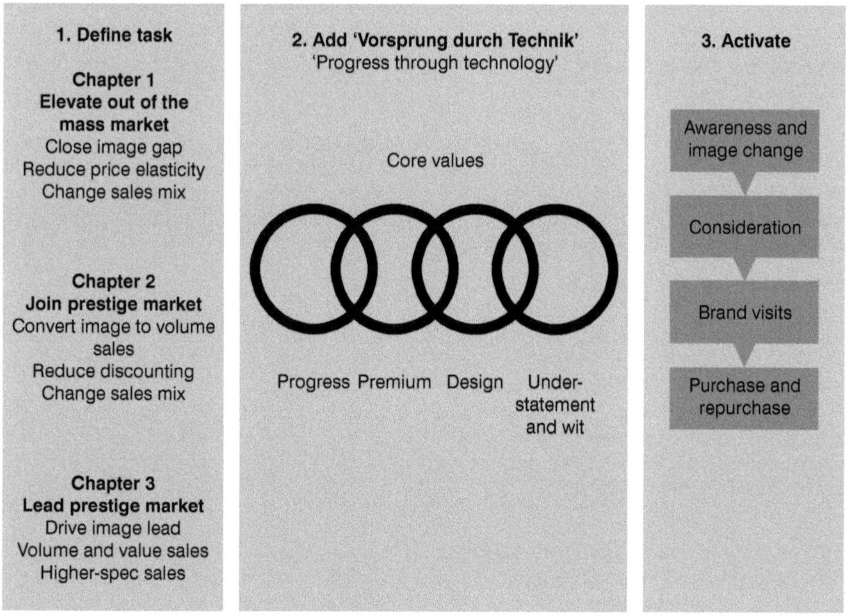

Communications and media principles

Over four decades, there have been some immutable principles (Table 3).

Table 3: Communications and media principles 1982–2020

Communications principles	Media principles
Screw down the invisible components Progress, premium, design, understatement and wit created a brand body language that allowed a warmer, more whimsical way of talking about engineering. This was put into an aspirational context, such as Geoffrey Palmer's lugubrious voice, 'twinkle in the eye' endlines and the brand's more recent musical handwriting.	**The medium is also the message** Choices were made to put image returns ahead of immediate financial returns and make sure the media signalled those values too. From dominating breaks in new TV franchises (e.g. TV-am), gold spots in cinema, placing in high-tension moments like sports finales, launching a TV channel, ringtones embedded in print ads, GQ takeovers and Shazam partnerships, progress and premium have been communicated through the medium, not just the message.
Some of the metal is more magic Distinctive hero cars, like the TT, R8, Q8, e-tron, and features have allowed the brand's best stories to be used disproportionately for their sales to halo across all its models. Indeed until the mid-2000s, the rule was nothing below A6 gets on air.	**Film for feeling, other media for ammo** Since 1982, film was used to build image at speed and to stand out from the print-heavy automotive world. Later, econometrics would prove film to be the most effective medium for both long- and short-term sales as well as image building. But it was important that the head had reasons to follow the heart, so emotionally wrapped facts in print, outdoor and later digital created ammo for bragging rights and justified the premium.
Don't hand the pen to the car Early advertising for Audi was technical and unremarkable. The client said to Nigel Bogle: 'You've handed the pen to the car. I don't want that, I want you to give them personality'. Since then, we have written their characters like screenwriters might. Their personality features have mattered more than their technical features.	**Outmanoeuvre instead of outspending** Audi's share of voice (SOV) rank since 1982 has often been behind competitors, yet its media visibility and awareness has often been ahead. Powering this was a belief that 'share of creativity' would supercharge pure media spend, by commanding attention through more compelling advertising.
People decide, not the research 'Vorsprung durch Technik' did not do well in research. It was considered arrogant, annoying and raised 'the whole issue of Germanness'. But clients Brian Bowler and John Meszaros felt it was right for a German company. Since then, the Audi account has used research heavily, but we have not been used by it. As with the cars, engineering and art worked together.	
Zag The tropes of the automotive category have been actively avoided, since the pitch called for 'a more salient, single-minded image that does justice to the character of the cars in a compelling fashion'.	

Strategy in action

Chapter 1. Elevate from mass market with image   1980s

Task: Elevate out of mass market with image.

Creative strategy: Establish provenance with distinct technical, Germanic, progressive identity combined with witty, understated tone. Sum this up in a line: *Vorsprung durch Technik*, or 'progress through technology'.

Media strategy: Weighed against volume and towards image shifts. Television used, as most cars used press advertising and it could drive emotional image change fastest. Press used to create "saloon bar ammo" - facts that supported the emotion.

TV advertising: 'Glider', 'Odd Couple', 'Villas'.

A thousand miles on one tankful.

The new Audi 100 TDI recently travelled 1338 miles on a single tank of diesel, averaging 76 mile per gallon, and taking the world record into the bargain. Which makes it the perfect car for those who can't choose between luxury and economy. For a free brochure call 0800 585685.

Cornering has never been so sweet.

Do you react like a dummy in an accident?

Figure 6: Chapter 2. Join

Chapter 2. Join

1990—2010

Task: Join the prestige ranks and sell volume.

Creative strategy: Cement the Audi values through celebrating the driver, the design and hero models.

Media strategy: Broadened media strategy for volume: 80% to mass market, 20% to prestige audience. Full integrated media mix balancing image and volume goals, joined by 'cultural strategy' - content, editorial, TV station launch and PR strategy to flex more into popular imagination and cater to 'always on' audience.

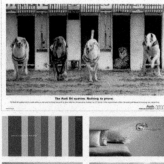

Figure 7: Chapter 3. Lead

Chapter 3. Lead   2010—2020

Task: Supercharge the premium and sell at scale.

Creative strategy: Draw on the codes of progressive luxury and focus on 'beautiful cars with amazing brains' - the sports cars and the intelligent tech.

Media strategy: Fully connected user journeys. 50:50 brand stories/product launches in media mix. "Best seat in the house" prestige media choices, innovative use of programmatic and progressive partners, e.g. Shazam.

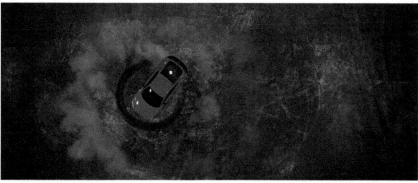

The Audi website 2018

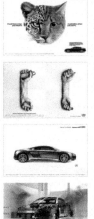

The results

Figure 8: Audi UK volume sales and share 1982–2019 (left) and 2019 volume sales indexed to 1982 (right)

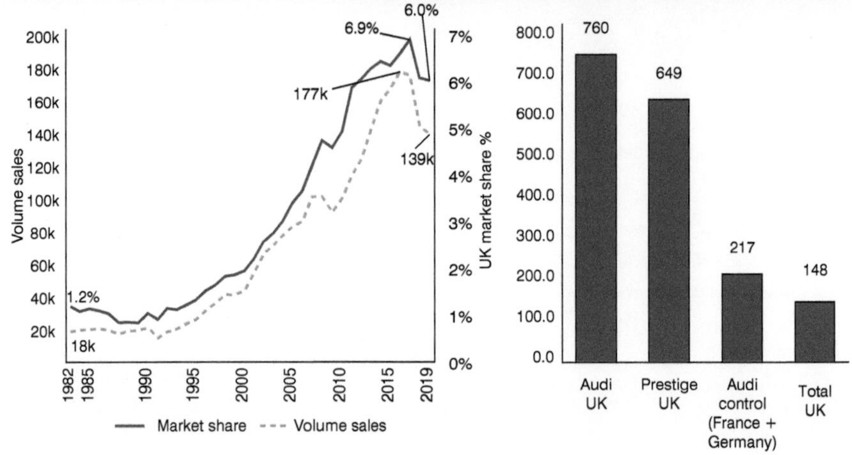

Sources: SMMT data 1982–2019 (Audi UK, UK car market, prestige UK car market); JATO data 1982–2019 (Audi control: France + Germany).

The case for effectiveness begins and ends with extraordinary sales and share growth. Between 1982–2019, Audi UK hugely outperformed the UK market and an Audi Europe Control Group, where the only significant difference was the communications.

We will show that a large part of this growth is driven by the Audi brand, powered by its communications, and this has had an undeniable effect on Audi UK's trajectory, advertising creativity and British culture over four decades.

We will also discount the impact of:

- **Product** – similar Audi markets with the same products grew at a slower rate
- **Price** – Audi's premium has in fact grown
- **Promotion** – Audi's discounting is below competitors
- **Prestige market growth** – Audi has grown faster
- **Reduced competition in the prestige sector** – competition has in fact expanded and intensified
- **Distribution** – we can model out impacts and when distribution shrunk Audi sales still grew
- **Increased marketing spend** – Audi has not spent more than competitors, often it spent less

We will then isolate effects and estimate ROMI.

But first we look at how Audi communications have delivered versus the objectives set in terms of:

- **Brand** impact – changing how favourably people think about Audi
- **Behavioural** impact – getting more people into Audi, spending more
- **Business** impact – increasing revenue and profit

A note on four decades of data

Data collection is highly complex even for short campaigns, but across four decades it has proven uniquely challenging. Where we have longitudinal data from 1982, we have shared it. Where results gaps exist, we have shown how the strategy and shifts are connected across the three chapters. In the Appendix, we clearly outline our assumptions and calculations.

Brand

We changed how people thought about Audi

More people knew Audi for the attributes the strategy wanted to shift, putting the brand firmly in the prestige car club and embedding 'Vorsprung durch Technik' into British culture.

Communications stood out and were well branded (Figure 9).

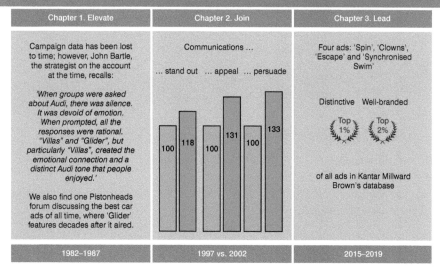

Figure 9: Communications standout, appeal, persuasion, distinctiveness and well-branded score

Sources: John Bartle interview 2020; Pistonheads forum; Harris Brand Tracking as seen in Audi IPA 1998 paper; Kantar Millward Brown 2015–2019.

Spontaneous awareness of the brand increased, even in 2010 when media visibility declined (Figure 10).

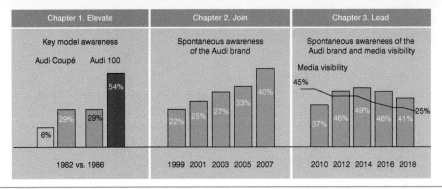

Figure 10: Key model and brand spontaneous awareness, set against media visibility

Sources: RAM average quarterly figures as seen in Audi IPA 1988 paper; Hall & Partners Brand Tracking Study; Stampon Carpenter Brand Tracking Study (base new car buyers) as seen in Audi 2001 IPA paper; Kantar Millward Brown 2010–2018.

Spontaneous awareness of the brand exceeded competitors, despite lower share of voice, since 2010 (Figure 11).

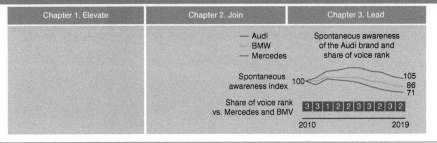

Figure 11: Spontaneous brand awareness and share of voice rank versus competitors

Sources: Kantar Millward Brown 2010–2019; Nielsen Media Expenditure Data 2010–2019.

The brand was discussed more in the press, tripling its share of prestige news between 1994–2019.

Puns in headlines (e.g. 'Vorsprung durch Becknik') have only served to give the brand extra free publicity.

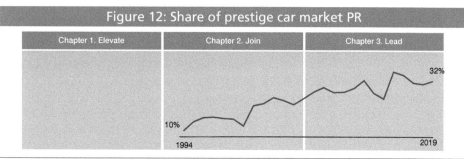

Figure 12: Share of prestige car market PR

| Chapter 1. Elevate | Chapter 2. Join | Chapter 3. Lead |

Source: Factiva data (1994–2019).

'Vorsprung durch Technik' was mentioned in the press 30 times more between Chapter 1 and 3, suggesting it was the brand being discussed, not just the cars (Figure 13).

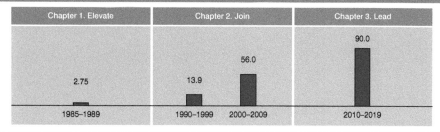

Figure 13: Average annual press mentions of 'Vorsprung durch Technik'

Source: Factiva data (1985–2019).

For each chapter, the strategy's specific image metrics increased (Figure 14).

Figure 14: Key brand image metrics

Chapter 1. Elevate	Chapter 2. Join	Chapter 3. Lead
Task: Move away from the mass market	Task: Define a distinct Audi driver image	Task: Become more desirable and famous for sporty, intelligent cars
Overall image score / Competitive set	1995 indexed perceptions of Audi is for the …	2015 indexed perceptions of Audi as …
vs. positive gap to Mercedes / most associated with	… successful … intelligent … different	… intelligent …desirable … sporty
–18 –8	100 200 100 158 100 145	100 104 100 104 100 106
1982–1987 1982 1987	1995 vs. 1998	2015 vs. 2018
(NB Audi and Vauxhall are the only brands during the period to shift image metrics, suggesting this is not a category effect)		

Sources: Louis Harris Analysis 1987, as seen in Audi IPA 1988 paper; Harris Tracking 1998, as seen in Audi IPA 1998 paper; Kantar Millward Brown 2015–2018.

We also see similar shifts with staff and dealers. In 2000, 70% thought the brand was an asset and were proud to work at Audi. By 2019, this had jumped to 90%.[15]

In Chapter 3, Audi became the most desirable mass prestige brand. It continues to hold that lead.

As discussed in Audi's 2018 IPA paper, 'desire' is Audi's most important 'soft' metric as it strongly predicts future sales growth. Specifically, econometrics has shown from 2015 that a 10% lift in 'desire' had a 3.7% sales impact (Figure 15).

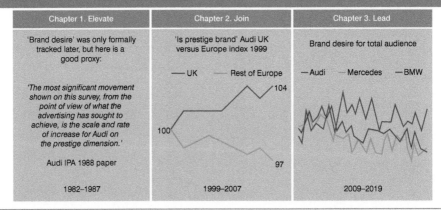

Figure 15: Brand desire or proxies for the total audience of car buyers 1982–2019

Sources: Audi IPA Paper 1988; Audi AG Brand Tracking Study 2007; Kantar Millward Brown 2009–2019.

In late Chapter 3, Audi became the most desirable brand among the prestige audience (those who already owned a prestige car) (Figure 16).

Figure 16: Brand desire for the prestige audience 2019

Chapter 1. Elevate	Chapter 2. Join	Chapter 3. Lead			
		Audi 1st	BMW 2nd	Mercedes 3rd	Jaguar 4th
		38%	37%	30%	24%
			2019		

Source: Kantar Millward Brown 2019.

Consideration for the brand and its models increased (Figure 17).

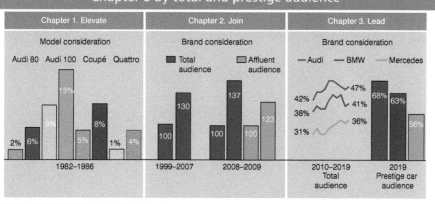

Figure 17: Consideration for key models, the Audi brand and in Chapter 3 by total and prestige audience

Sources: RAM quarterly average data, as seen in Audi IPA paper 1988; VAG data 1999–2007, as seen in Audi IPA 2008 paper; Kantar Millward Brown data 2008–2009, as seen in the Audi IPA 2010 paper; Kantar Millward Brown data 2010–2019.

Behaviour

Communications attracted more affluent people and got them spending more with the brand

More people with more disposable income engaged with the brand and its higher-specification products, and ordered its higher-priced models. This increased overall customer value.

Buying signals such as enquiries, visits to centers and test drives increased (Figure 18).

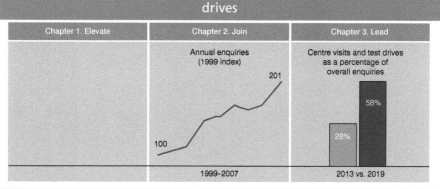

Figure 18: Buying signals including enquiries, centre visits and test drives

Sources: Audi UK data 1999–2007; Audi UK data 2013–2019.

Those exposed to communications had a higher chance of converting to order and future services (Figure 19).

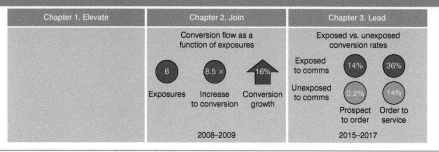

Figure 19: Conversion rates as a function of exposure to communications

Sources: Audi UK 2008 data, as seen in Audi 2010 IPA paper; Audi UK data 2017 fallow cell versus non-fallow cell study.

A wealthier group of people bought higher-specification, higher-priced, higher-margin models (Figure 20).

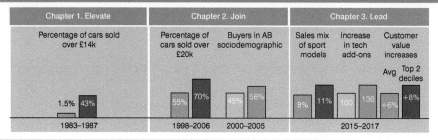

Figure 20: Sales mix, buyer mix and specification mix

Sources: SMMT, What Car? 1983, as seen in Audi 1988 IPA paper; SMMT data, as seen in Audi 2006 paper; GB Target Group Index data 2005–2008; Audi UK data 2015–2017; VWG customer value segmentation data 2015–2017.

Loyalty grew steadily and net migration into the brand stayed positive (Figure 21).

Figure 21: Loyalty and net migration into the Audi brand

Sources: Audi UK data 1988; Audi UK data 1998–2008; Audi UK data 2016–2019; Audi UK data 2015–2018.

Commercial

Communications created more sales, more revenue, and more profit – all at increasing efficiency

Audi UK grew faster than other similar Audi markets and the UK prestige market. It was able to improve the sales mix to deliver greater profitability, all while making more efficient use of communications budgets.

Volume and share increased at a rate above that of i) the UK car market, ii) the prestige market and iii) an Audi Europe control group. Overall, Audi sales volumes grew from 18k in 1982 to 139k in 2019, and total market share grew from 1.2% to 6.0%. Volume peaked at 177k in 2016 and share peaked at 6.9% in 2017. Declines since then can be in large part explained by factors beyond marketing's control.[16] It's also worth noting that during sales dips on this chart, while short-term strategies may have been amplified, the long-term brand building never ceased (Figure 22).

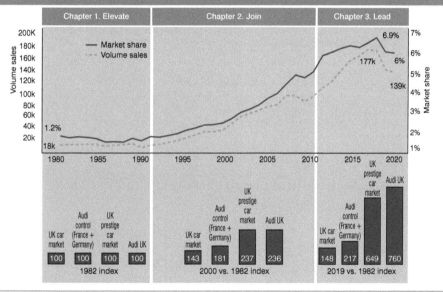

Figure 22: Audi UK sales and share growth 1982–2019 with 1982 volume indexes by chapter

Sources: SMMT data 1982–2019 (Audi UK, UK car market, prestige UK car market); JATO data 1982–2019 (Audi control: France + Germany).

These increased volume sales were of a higher value.

In Chapter 3, inflation-adjusted price increased by 7% (versus BMW and Mercedes which increased 3%).

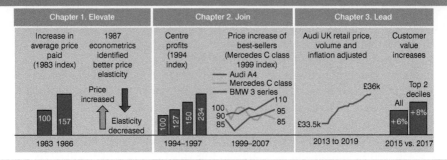

Figure 23: Proxies for profitability, including average price paid, price elasticity, and customer value (the total customer contribution, with car, finance and aftersales combined)

Sources: Audi UK 1981–1987 median price data, as seen in Audi 1988 IPA paper; econometrics by Robert Young, as seen in Audi 1988 IPA paper; Audi UK data 1994–1997, as seen in Audi 1998 IPA paper; VAG data 1999–2007, as seen in the Audi 2008 IPA paper; JATO data 2013–2019; VWG customer value segmentation data 2015–2017.

There was greater adoption of profitable aftersales (Figure 24).

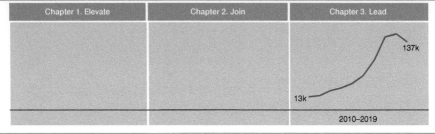

Figure 24: Customers who have completed an aftersales event at an Audi centre

Source: Audi UK data 2010–2019.

Flagship halo models sold across the range and made communications more efficient (Figure 25).

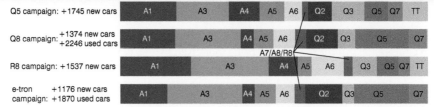

Figure 25: Sales halos across the marque created by flagship model campaigns

Source: Neustar MarketShare Econometrics Data 2015–2019.

Marketing efficiency improved, and was among the most efficient in the market. (Figure 26).

Figure 26: Marketing efficiency metrics

Sources: MEAL/RAM data 1988, as seen in Audi 1988 IPA paper; Hall & Partners data 1997/9–2000/3; Audi IPA paper 2006; Kantar Millward Brown media visibility data 2015–2019; Nielsen media expenditure data 2015–2019.

More sales were delivered with less and less media spend per car (Figure 27).

Figure 27: Media spend per sale (indexed to 1982, inflation adjusted)

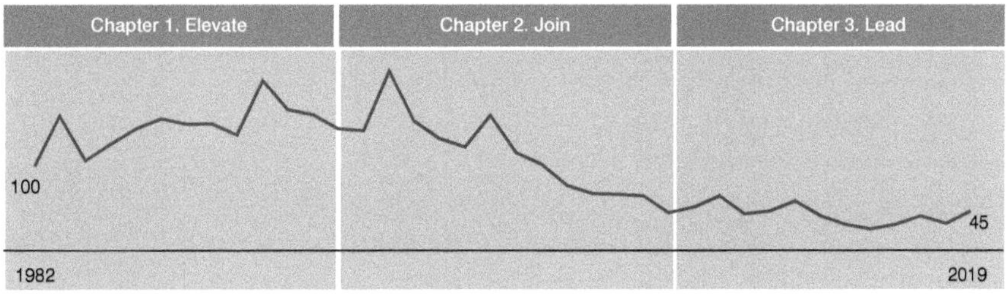

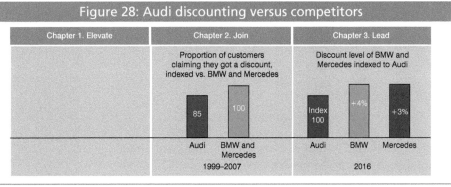

Sources: Media spend per sale index based on Nielsen media expenditure data 1982–2019 (NB 1986–1994 is modelled); SMMT data volume sales data 1982–2019.

Discounting was below that of competitors (Figure 28).

Figure 28: Audi discounting versus competitors

Sources: Audi UK data 1999–2007, as seen in the Audi 2008 IPA paper; Audi UK data from Strategic Review Report 2016.

Discounting other influences on sales growth

By discounting other factors, we can strongly suggest communications played a large role in driving these effects.

Was it the cars getting better?

Without excellent cars, we would not have been able to achieve these results. But as Audi UK has grown faster than other similar Audi markets with identical cars (Figure 22), this can be discounted as a factor.

Was it the price?

No. The Audi average price has grown (Figure 23).

Was it price promotion?

No. Discounting was below competitors (Figure 28).

Was it prestige market growth?

No. That helped, but Audi grew faster. Comparing the first and last five years, 1982–1986 and 2015–2019, Audi UK grew 8.3 times vs. 5.6 times for the prestige market.[17]

Was it reduced competition in the prestige sector?

No. Competition has nearly doubled (Figure 29).

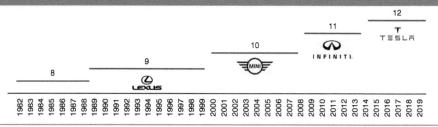

Figure 29: Number of prestige car brands in the UK car market 1982–2019

Source: SMMT data. Note the starting eight are: Audi, BMW, Jaguar, Land Rover, Maserati, Mercedes, Porsche, Volvo.

Was it increased distribution?

No. We can either econometrically model these out from 2015 or show instances of reducing distribution and increasing sales effects due to communications. For example, during 1999–2007, distribution shrunk from index 100 to index 90, but Audi's sales still surged during this period (Figure 23).

Was it increased marketing spend?

No. Audi's share of voice was often second or third versus BMW and Mercedes (Figure 30).

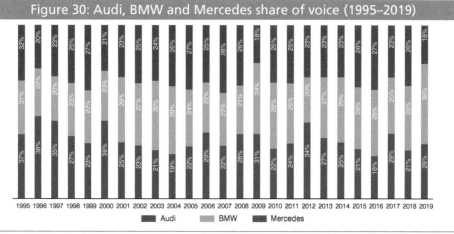

Figure 30: Audi, BMW and Mercedes share of voice (1995–2019)

Source: Nielsen media expenditure data 1995–2019.

Measuring return on investment

So what is the long-term value of creativity in communications?

We can look at this through 'triangulating' a number of methods:

- recent econometrics
- econometrics modelled backwards
- stating more intangible returns

By doing this, we estimate that communications have created between £23.9–31.8bn of value over four decades.

Let's unpack that.

Econometrics summarised

Econometrics 2015–2018 have demonstrated how 26% of Audi new car sales are media-driven, creating a return of £2.8bn. In other words, Audi realises £0.69bn per year of additional sales because of this strategy. This is likely a large underestimate as the model does not account for fleet sales, which make up 58% of sales[18] and comprise higher-priced cars, or used car sales (Table 4).

	Table 4: Incremental value from new car sales as calculated by econometrics 2015–2018				
	2015	2016	2017	2018	Total
Incremental value from new car sales	£684,161,444.56	£736,260,104.87	£730,080,430.94	£603,170,291.26	£2,753,672,271.62

Source: Neustar MarketShare Econometrics Data 2015–2018.

Econometrics modelled backwards

We can interpolate using this model to get an estimate for the value of 'Vorsprung durch Technik' communications over four decades in the UK.

We do this by modelling back in the used and fleet sales to the more recent econometrics – all the way back to 1982. We feel this assumption is solid as the dynamics by which people buy new or company cars are not significantly different to retail cars. As Tom Brennan, Audi UK's Head of Fleet puts it:

> *'It's easy to assume fleet is a different thing to retail when it comes to marketing, but ultimately it's the same people choosing a brand just by slightly different means, so the comms matters to us too.'*

Because the present may not be like the past, we then discount this figure by 25% to give a lower estimate.

Doing this, we estimate the incremental value of 'Vorsprung durch Technik' over four decades in the UK to be between £23.9– 31.8bn (Table 5).

Table 5: Incremental value from new car and used sales 1982–2019 as suggested by econometrics 2015–2018		
Estimate of sales	**Detail on calculation**	**Value**
Incremental retail car value sales	26% retail sales 1982–2019	£9.8bn
Incremental fleet value sales	26% fleet sales 1982–2019	£13.7bn
Incremental used car value sales	27% used car sales	£8.3bn[19]
Total incremental value sales	Total	£31.8bn
Total incremental value sales discounted 25% for conservative lower estimate[20]	Total x 25%	£23.9bn

Measuring ROMI

Given the amount spent on marketing over four decades, we calculate a revenue ROMI of £29.56 for every £1 spent.[21] In the absence of four decades of profit data, we use the profit figure stated in Audi's investor report to get a profit ROMI of £2.33 over the time series. Again, to be conservative, we use the reduced revenue figure to mitigate against lower marketing power and lower margins. That creates a lower estimate of £22.17 revenue ROMI and £1.50 profit ROMI (Table 6).

Table 6: ROMI calculation based on Audi profit data[22]		
Element	**Notes/Source**	**Value**
Incremental order take revenue	Econometric data (2015-2018) + Modelled data (1982-2014, 2019)	£31,822,168,620.13
Retailer gross margin (%)	IPA average for automotive (retailer margin)	5%
Retailer cash margin (£)	Calculation = Incremental order take revenue × Retailer gross margin	£1,591,108,431.01
Incremental sales revenue to manufacturer	Calculation = Incremental order take revenue – Retailer cash margin	£30,231,060,189.12
Profit margin (%)	Global margin Q1 2018 – Q3 2019	11.3%
Cost of campaign	Net media spend: Nielsen (1982–1985; 1995–2019) + Modelled data (1986–1994) + Agency fees	£1,022,701,620.65
Revenue ROMI	Calculation = Incremental sales revenue to manufacturer / Cost of campaign	£29.56
Discounted revenue ROMI	As above but based on 75% incremental order take revenue	£22.17
Net profit generated by campaign	Calculation = (Incremental sales revenue to manufacturer × Profit margin) – Cost of campaign	£2,385,475,072.05
Return on profit calculation	Calculation = Net profit generated by campaign / Cost of campaign	£2.33
Discounted return on profit calculation	As above but based on 75% incremental order take revenue	£1.50

Source: Audi Investor and Analyst Day presentation discloses a profit margin of 8.07% before special items, but after marketing costs for Q1 2018 – Q3 2019. The 11.3% referenced relates to the same, but accounts for cost of campaign listed in the table.

Measuring a ROAI (return on agency investment)

We introduce a new metric for the field: return on agency investment (ROAI). Put another way: was BBH worth it? The adoption of 'Vorsprung durch Technik' as Audi global's marketing positioning in the early 1990s allows an interesting experiment. Given Germany and France are very similar-sized countries to the UK, with nearly identical factors but different communications, we can isolate 'The BBH Effect'. To be clear, 'Vorsprung durch Technik' was still guiding their comms, but BBH was not making them.

We calculate that every £1 spent with BBH generated £34 of sales. That's an ROAI of 34 times.[23] Or put another way, the total agency costs to Audi over four decades are recouped in a year and a bit of incremental returns (Table 7).[24]

Table 7: Return on agency investment	
Audi UK sales if same as control	2.55m
Audi UK actual sales	2.63m
Difference between UK and control	83,484
Value of difference	£2.87bn
BBH fees 1982-2019	£85m[25]
Return (value/fees)	34 times (every £1 invested in BBH returned an extra £34)

Intangible returns

Beyond the numbers, there are broader effects to consider

'Vorsprung durch Technik' impacted creativity, careers, international relations, British culture and Audi globally.

To advertising

Audi UK has generated admiration, awards and knighthoods. It has helped to define an agency and a way of doing car advertising, picking up 65 major creative awards (Figure 31).

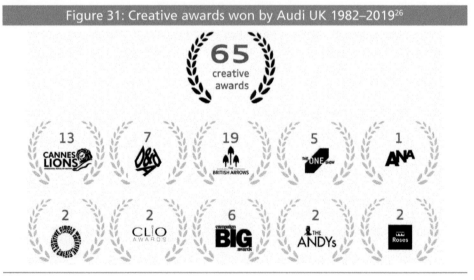

Figure 31: Creative awards won by Audi UK 1982–2019[26]

By 2004, it had been declared a 'Superbrand', and 2019 commentators reflect the original strategy in their words (Table 8).

Table 8: Audi becoming a 'Superbrand' – 15 years of commentary from Superbrands UK		
2004	**2013**	**2019**
Audi named one of the most iconic brands for the first time by Superbrands UK.	Superbrands UK celebrates Audi's creativity: 'Any motor advertising that breaks the mould of the traditional car commercial ... is to be welcomed. Clearly a supporter of this philosophy, Audi has made a point of applying creative thinking in the development, not only of its cars but also to its marketing.'	Superbrands UK comments on the brand's strategy, consistent from 1982 but updated for the times: 'Always ahead, always exciting and always with a twinkle in the eye.'

Sources: Superbrands 2004, Superbrands 2013, Superbrands 2019.

To Audi

'Vorsprung durch Technik' was so successful, Audi HQ in Germany adopted it as the brand's endline in the early 1990s (important to note the UK ran its own communications). How deeply that philosophy inspired Audi business, engineering, design and marketing decisions we cannot quantify. But actions like launching a supercar, an electric SUV, a hydrogen car, a moon buggy and even a car whose headlights detach as drones, all feel like things a company who believes in progress through technology would do. In 1982, Audi certainly had designs on becoming a different kind of company. 'Vorsprung durch Technik' almost certainly helped accelerate that new trajectory. It may have even helped to define the company.

To culture

The Guardian has argued 'Vorsprung durch Technik' changed international relations, see quote in Table 9.[27] We'll take it. But arguably the measure of getting into the British psyche is getting into its culture, especially its comedy. 'Vorsprung durch Technik' made it into two of the definitive comedies of its day – *Only Fools and Horses* and *Peep Show*. It became part of the cultural furniture. (Table 9)

Conclusion

As 'Vorsprung durch Technik' turns 40 soon, it is fitting to reflect on its remarkable journey.

From 18k sales a year to 177k sales a year at peak; from being unremarkable to becoming not just a credible choice against 'The Ultimate Driving Machine' and the brand Janis Joplin asked 'The Lord' to buy her – but the most desired choice.

It's the story of an ordinary brand evolving into an extraordinary icon.

Table 9: Audi's cultural horsepower – international relations and entering the culture		
International relations	**Films & TV**	**Songs**
Headline: 'Vorsprung durch Technik – ad slogan that changed how we saw Germany'	*Lock, Stock and Two Smoking Barrels*	U2 – 'Zooropa'
	Only Fools and Horses	Blazin' Squad – 'Easy Come Easy Go'
'[In the 1980s], popular perceptions of Germany – in Britain at least – were still wrapped up in the legacy of the past. "Don't mention the war," barked Basil Fawlty, but people still did. A three-word slogan, drawled lugubriously by Geoffrey Palmer in a series of Audi ads, changed all that. "Vorsprung durch Technik" became a motto for a nation that was putting the past behind it and restyling itself as a byword for quality, efficiency, progress and technology.'[28]	*Peep Show*, expressing the desire metrics in other words:[29] *Mark*: So, what's he like? *Gerard*: Graphic designer. *Mark*: Oh, please! 'Hello, can I redesign your logo? Yes, that'll be a £100,000 for a squiggle.' *Mark* [voiceover]: Wish I was a graphic designer. *Gerard*: And he drives an Audi. *Mark*: But of course, Vorsprung Dick Technik! *Mark* [voiceover]: Wish I had an Audi.	Blur – 'Parklife': 'Parklife (Parklife!) Parklife (Parklife!) It's got nothing to do with your Vorsprung durch Technik, you know Parklife (Parklife!)'
The Guardian (2012)		

Source: BBH Archive.

What we have shown here is how much of that success came from the meaning packed into three words and the unique way they've been brought to life through communications, changing:

1. How the brand existed in people's minds
   - From something bland to the most desirable car brand among prestige owners and the general population.
   - Becoming a part of British culture.
2. How people engaged with the brand
   - Converting indifference to interest, action and loyalty.
3. The fortunes and trajectory of the brand in the UK
   - Generating £23.9–31.8bn of estimated incremental value 1982–2019.
   - Creating an average of £0.69bn of actual modelled value per year recently – and that's just for new cars. It is likely even more including fleet and used sales. For context, Instagram sold for $1bn or approximately £0.7bn in 2013. The Audi UK communications machine creates an Instagram every year. That's something to like.
   - Growing at 7.6 times faster than the UK market and 2.2 times faster than the European Audi control group with increasing efficiency of marketing budgets.
   - Every pound that went into this machine didn't just pay for itself, an additional £1.50–2.33 of profit was delivered back.

Overall, we've pulled off that marketing magic trick: selling more cars, at a higher price, more efficiently.

Crowning it all, 'Vorsprung durch Technik' gave the now-$60bn global car brand not just its endline. It gave it its spirit.

But back to that marshmallow.

What lessons can we share for resisting a little longer?

Advice for 'going long'

Create a culture of long-termism

There was a shared client and agency belief 'going long' worked. At first it was a feeling. Then it was built on data. It has overruled testing, warded off putting prices on TV ads and kept all heads looking out to the horizon. Don't stop believin'.

Think premium

Commoditisation is hell. Successive generations shared the belief that it is not just sales that matter, but the value of those sales. We all felt marketing was best when it unlocked something in people's minds that made them feel like paying more. If you see yourself as premium, *not 'going long'* starts to look like a dangerous commercial risk.

Look within

Martial artists say if you hold your arm up and someone tries to knock it back down, it's fairly easy. If you ask the person to point and focus at something while that arm is up, it's much harder. 'Going long' is perhaps so tricky because successive guardians cannot agree where to focus. Such focus is a gift – but it is our belief it is best when it comes *from within*. Remember, 'Vorsprung durch Technik' was not invented by BBH. It was re-invented. Original greatness is a clue to further greatness. Why? Because spiritual answers from within a brand are much more likely to be embraced by the organisation and people out in the world eventually, simply because they are true. Everyone can feel it. As such, we deliberately never really defined the brand too tightly. The brand onions made our eyes water. We knew what it stood for and let the guardians make the right calls to flex to the times.

Hardwire the soft and hard metrics

Whether it was factor or regression analysis, we mathematically linked 'soft' metrics like 'desire' with 'hard' metrics like revenues. Financially minded people stopped thinking of them as soft but as necessary and proven routes to growth. Communications became investments, not costs. It even caused one CFO to ask if *'you have enough budget?'*

Put those metrics in the cockpit

In addition to the sales, those growth-driver metrics like 'desire' were central to the marketing team. Teams were reminded about them and rewarded on them.

Put short into long

Expertise in conversion has undoubtedly made those creative and effectiveness highs possible by not letting it become an outsized concern. Great 'short' makes great 'long' possible.

Find and polish your jewels

Long-termism is about telling your best stories in the best media. Everything else can be said in other places. It is focus that truly moves the needle. A few great things a year, that say the most about your brand, is all long-termism requires.

Zag

Difference. Feeling. Simplicity. These elevated the brand out of blandness, beyond engineering and into a statement on life and how it could be lived. A true zag contains an energy that inspires all the people working on that brand to protect it, embrace it and reinvent it. It has kept the engine running for four decades.

Enjoy your marshmallows. Just later if you can.

Notes

1 (2015–2019 mean sales of 160k/year) / (1982 sales of 18k) = 8.8 times and versus peak sales in 2016 (177k) it's 9.7 times.
2 Comparing Audi UK volume sales 1982 (18,277) to 2019 (138,924) vs. Audi Germany and France aggregate volume sales 1982 (149,172) to 2019 (324,719). This holds true if we compare longer time periods like 1982–1986 vs. 2015–2019. Here Audi UK volume sales (96k sales 1982–1986 to 802k sales 2015–2019) grew 5.8 times faster than the UK car market (8.8m sales 1982–1986 to 12.5m sales 2015–2019) and 4.2 times faster than similar European Audi markets (Audi Germany and France: 839k aggregate volume sales 1982–1986 to 1.7m sales 2015–2019).
3 Meaning the belief in 'progress through technology'.
4 Walter Mischel, *The Marshmallow Test: Understanding Self-Control and How to Master It*, London: Corgi Books, 2014.
5 Watts, Duncan and Quan have recently found this may be due to a child's social and economic background instead, but please allow us the metaphor for storytelling. Tyler W. Watts, Greg J. Duncan and Haonan Quan, 'Revisiting the Marshmallow Test: A Conceptual Replication Investigating Links Between Early Delay of Gratification and Later Outcomes', *Psychological Science*, 29(7): 1159–1177.
6 Les Binet and Peter Field, *Marketing in the Era of Accountability: Identifying the Marketing Practices and Metrics That Truly Increase Profitability*, London: IPA, 2007. Les Binet and Peter Field, *Selling Creativity Short: Creativity and Effectiveness under Threat*, London: IPA, 2016.
7 Binet and Field, *Selling Creativity Short*.
8 Orlando Wood, *Lemon: How the Advertising Brain Turned Sour*, London: IPA, 2019.
9 While this paper bears the names of the authors who just happen to be around at this time on the Audi account, we would like to salute all the previous 'guardians' who are too many to mention, but too great to not credit.
10 As summarised following conversations with Sir Nigel Bogle and John Bartle.
11 In 1982, the Audi 80 had a list price of £6,680, while the very similar Ford Sierra was £5,071.
12 '(Oh Lord Won't You Buy Me A) Mercedes Benz' by Janis Joplin (1970).
13 BBH Archives.
14 Nigel Bogle interview (2020).
15 Audi UK dealers and staff data questionnaire.
16 Why the dip? First, the UK car market was slowing. Second, there was lower consumer confidence after Brexit and there was a sharp fall in the pound versus the euro in mid-2016. Third, Audi had to reconfigure many of its cars following new laws on determining levels of pollutants (WLTP). This severely limited supply as Audi has to reduce production to meet these standards. Econometrics identified this as the biggest single factor in volume reduction with 44% of the attributable difference (Neustar MarketShare, 2018).
17 Audi UK unit sales increased by 8.3 between 1982–1986 (96,489) and 2015–2019 (801,658). Prestige UK unit sales increased by 5.6 between 1982–1986 (681,807) and 2015–2019 (3,801,454).
18 Neustar MarketsShare Econometric Report 2018 and SMMT data 2018.
19 New econometric modelling in 2018 has used car sales as part of the model for the very first time and demonstrated that 27% of Audi used car sales are driven by media.
20 In the event that prior to 2015 media-driven sales were less than that identified by econometrics, we have applied a 25% discount to this figure to establish a conservative estimate for the lower end of the range.
21 Revenue ROMI is calculated from the incremental sales revenue to the manufacturer after deduction of retailer cash margin.
22 In the event that prior to 2015 media-driven sales were less than that identified by econometrics, we have applied a 25% discount to this figure to establish a conservative estimate for the lower end of the range.
23 £2.87bn / £85m = 33.7.
24 £2.87bn of incremental sales / 38 years = 71.7m; £85m / 71.7m = 1.2 years.
25 BBH archive.
26 BBH archive.
27 https://www.theguardian.com/world/2012/sep/18/vorsprung-durch-technik-advertising-germany
28 theguardian.com/world/2012/sep/18/vorsprung-durch-technik-advertising-germany
29 From the episode 'Man Jam' as sourced from https://www.imdb.com/title/tt1774080/characters/nm1377114
30 1982–1985 Nielsen Data for Audi expenditure values provided by John Aylings Associates, 1995–2019 data obtained from Nielsen.

Diageo portfolio

Marketing Catalyst: Creating a culture of marketing effectiveness

By Andrew Geoghegan, Diageo
Contributing authors: Andrew Bertolaso, Gain Theory; Jack Carrington and Neasa McGuinness, Mother; Andrew Deykin, Data2Decisions; Sinan Erhan, Boston Consulting Group; Vicki Holgate, Kiel Petersen and Filina Spanodimou, Diageo; Craig Mawdsley and Lisa Stoney, AMV BBDO

Credited companies: adam&eveDDB, Anomaly, Hey Human, Kantar, Metropolitan Republic, Leo Burnett Sydney, Scanad, Nielsen

Summary

In 2016, Diageo committed to delivering an incremental £100m in profit from marketing within three years via an initiative encompassing its wide brand portfolio. The approach applied to its many brands such as Guinness, Baileys and Smirnoff, and to both mature and developing markets including the Americas, Africa, and Australia. Approaches to data were standardised. Marketing Catalyst, a bespoke tool to advise marketers on effective spending, and Creative Sparks, a programme to refocus staff on creative excellence, were used to embed marketing effectiveness into the company culture. It is estimated the initiative produced more than twice its £100m target, returned its investment 16 times over, and enabled Diageo to widen the scope of effective measurement from brands accounting for 30% of its marketing spend to 90%.

Editor's comment

The judges thought this was a brilliant example of how to embed consistent marketing effectiveness practices across a complex organisation, whilst encouraging the role of innovative creativity and insight in driving the growth of individual brands. The success of Diageo's approach can provide lessons for many businesses.

Client comment

Syl Saller, Outgoing CMO, Diageo

Our marketing effectiveness programme has changed the fabric of marketing, reinforcing our role as business leaders first and foremost, agitating for better business outcomes. We have a deeper understanding of how to create the conditions for creativity and have a learning mindset. We understand how it all works and are comfortable with the integration of measurement and magic.

In 2016, as part of a bold company-wide initiative, Diageo made a commitment to deliver an incremental £100m gross profit from its marketing.

This required an acceleration in Diageo's culture of marketing effectiveness on over 200 brands across 180 markets, ensuring every pound, dollar, and rupee would count.

We sought to reimagine the role of people and process, and introduce innovative leading-edge analytics and technology, creating a system integrating creative magic and measurement every bit as good as the brands it served.

Not only did we create this culture, we more than doubled the financial ambition.

Introduction

This case study is entirely typical of an IPA Effectiveness Awards paper in seeking to demonstrate outstanding results from communications. However, it's different from every IPA paper ever written in that it demonstrates those improvements across an entire global organisation with over 200 brands. The sheer scale of this paper is unprecedented. This is about creating a global effectiveness culture that cascades down to every brand in the portfolio.

In 2016, Diageo was one of Britain's most admired companies, with some of the greatest brands in marketing and a trophy cabinet full of IPA Effectiveness Awards.

However, if you cast your mind back, it was a time when businesses felt significant pressure from economic uncertainty and low growth. Many companies were under pressure to focus on short-term cost saving. It looked like last orders for investing in brands for the long term.

That year, Diageo announced to investors its intention to deliver £500m in productivity savings, with the aim of reinvesting two-thirds back into the business. For an organisation like Diageo, brands and advertising would play an essential role, and marketing made a commitment to contribute £100m incremental profit on top of what it already delivered from its communications. But how could we achieve this?

From the outside, it's easy to imagine that Diageo marketing was already the best in the business, recognised for its creative flair and informed by the sterling work of Binet and Field, Kahneman, and the Ehrenberg-Bass Institute. What's perhaps less appreciated is the complexity of our operating environment, the breadth of our market footprint, the sheer number of our brands, and therefore the everyday challenges in achieving such an ambition.

We'd have to design a new marketing system which combined creativity and coordination, risk and rigour, drama and data, magic and measurement. We needed to make every pound, dollar, and rupee count, 'every day, everywhere'.

A marketing culture every bit as good as the brands it served. And we found it.

This is the story of how.

The problem

Context

Diageo is the world's largest premium alcohol company, home to over 200 brands including Johnnie Walker, Guinness, Smirnoff, and Baileys.

With revenues of £12bn and 28,400 employees, including 1,200 marketers, Diageo brands are enjoyed in over 180 countries from business operations in 54 countries.

Diageo is derived from the Latin for day ('dia') and Greek for world ('geo'), and refers to our purpose in enabling people to celebrate responsibly with our brands every day, everywhere.

Figure 1: Diageo brands

The challenge

Creating a new effectiveness culture throughout the business demanded that we redesign our approach to marketing, considering people and process, data and technology. To deliver better future business outcomes and free our marketers to focus on brilliant creativity, we'd need to improve and embed a more consistent approach to measurement.

For people and process there were some big shifts to achieve:

- establishing common, transparent KPIs everywhere;
- ensuring insight was always easy to access and right at the heart of marketing decisions;
- building deep understanding about effective marketing practice, unleashing creativity and a learning mindset;
- building deeper collaboration cross-functionally and conviction in marketing investment.

Data and technology would play a big role, requiring a different approach to:

- data quality, coverage, infrastructure, and housing;
- developing best-in-class analytics for different market contexts;
- providing a frictionless user experience.

The challenge was different by geography. In some markets we needed to increase coverage and shift from rear-view evaluation to always aligning measurement to long-term business objectives. In other markets we had to overcome significant data or capability issues to establish new approaches.

Removing friction and time spent on manually assembling data would increase time available for creativity to flourish. We would have to work with our agency partners to redesign how our teams approached all aspects of the creative development process. We sought to create a whole-brained approach to marketing, integrating measurement sympathetically with strategy and creativity, and powering decisions with the right combination of fact and judgement.

To create the analytics we sought, we'd need a dramatic improvement in data availability and quality across numerous types including media data, sales data, and other causal information. We needed a common taxonomy across datasets and within datasets covering different geographies. We'd need a common approach to cleaning and housing our data which could cope with low levels of detail, frequency, and accuracy.

The scale of change was exciting and significant: we'd have to take the whole organisation with us to make the change happen, including general managers and finance partners.

Objectives

We had clear three-year objectives for F17–19, financial years which ran from July 2016 (Figure 2).

Figure 2: Objectives
Business objectives
Deliver £500m in productivity savings, reinvesting two-thirds
Deliver 100 basis points (1ppt) incremental organic operating margin growth
Marketing objectives
Deliver £100m incremental gross profit attributable to marketing (i.e. above and beyond the expected contribution)
Increase effective measurement of brands accounting for 30% of marketing spend to 80%
Communications objectives
These continued in place for each brand through our marketing business planning cycle

Delivering the financial target and quantifying active users of measurement would allow us to understand if we'd achieved the behavioural change.

The solution

The cornerstone of this programme was Marketing Catalyst, a web-based tool that helps marketers decide how to spend their money more astutely.

We complemented it with Creative Sparks, a programme designed to refocus our teams on creative excellence.

They were integrated in a change programme designed to build belief and change behaviours.

Figure 3: A culture of marketing effectiveness

Marketing Catalyst

Catalyst sits on top of a newly created marketing data platform, unifying, automating, and consistently structuring all our data. It enables us to deduce how much each brand should spend as well as how that spend can best be deployed. Catalyst slots into our marketing planning process, linking through to our media agencies.

As we designed it, we recognised two ways we could realise extra value from our brand communications.

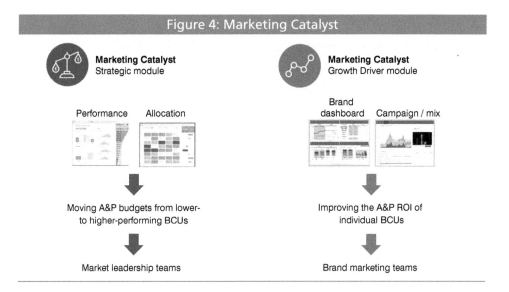

Figure 4: Marketing Catalyst

Strategic module

Most marketing effectiveness programmes focus on individual brands. As a portfolio business, we hypothesised there was value in making polarised investment choices across brands – because they don't all have the same growth potential, profitability, or brand strength. We developed a recipe for 'future profit potential'.

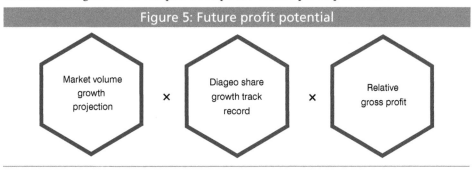

Figure 5: Future profit potential

The strategic module provokes us to consider how much to spend on each brand relative to its future profit potential. For example, in Figure 6, brand A is overspent versus its opportunity, and that money could be redeployed to brand B or C.

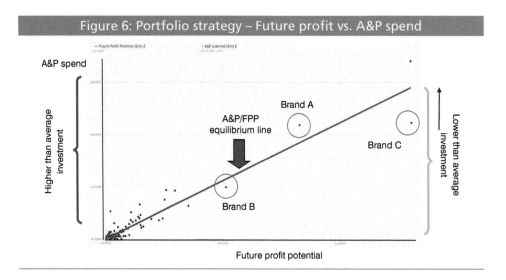

Figure 6: Portfolio strategy – Future profit vs. A&P spend

A second lens considers relative brand strength versus the short-term ROI of each brand. Based on this, brand B looks like a better choice in which to increase investment (Figure 7).

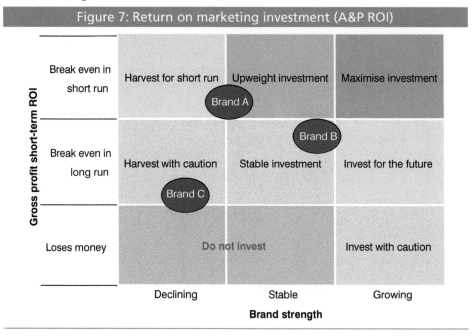

Figure 7: Return on marketing investment (A&P ROI)

With these perspectives, the model suggests how much to increase or decrease spend on each brand to generate the optimum profit outcome or achieve a specific target. A user can add constraints, such as budget limitations or caps for individual brands. Users can account for uncertainties or changes in the external environment that might affect ROI – meaning it can deliver competitive advantage in normal times, as well as adapting to a financial crisis or other unexpected events.

Figure 8: The change in budget and corresponding benefits identified by the new allocation

The change in budget and corresponding benefits identified by the new allocation.

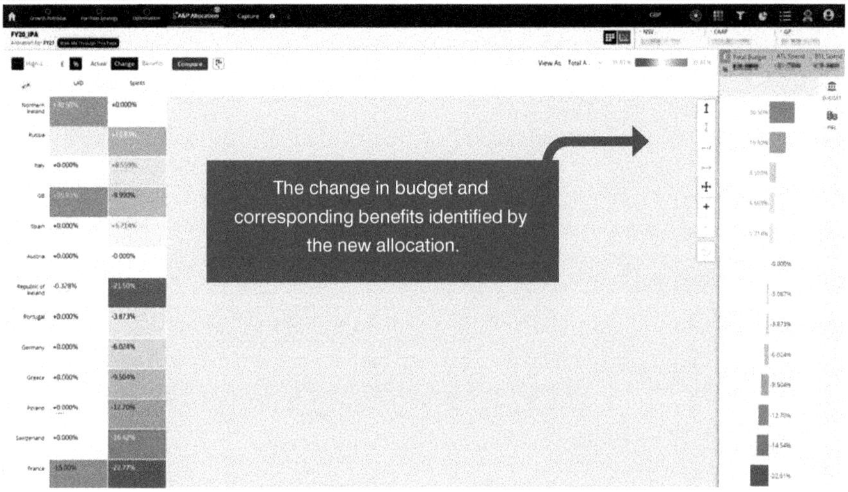

The platform was designed for marketing leadership to use with finance and general management alongside their portfolio strategy, considering investment scenarios annually with assumptions validated quarterly with new data.

Growth Driver module

Once brand teams are clear on budget and have their brand plan in place, they plan the full mix of communication activity including media, experiential, sponsorship, consumer promotion, point-of-sale, value-added packaging, etc. in a Growth Driver module.

The system provokes the user to think about the impact of different choices on short- and long-term gross profit. It predicts the likely outcome of changes in real time using the saturation curves derived from econometric models specific to that brand, country, and type of growth driver.

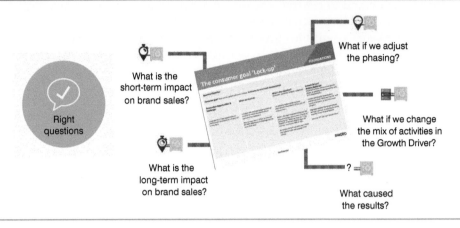

Figure 9: Growth Driver module – asking the right questions

Right questions

What is the short-term impact on brand sales?

What if we adjust the phasing?

What if we change the mix of activities in the Growth Driver?

What is the long-term impact on brand sales?

What caused the results?

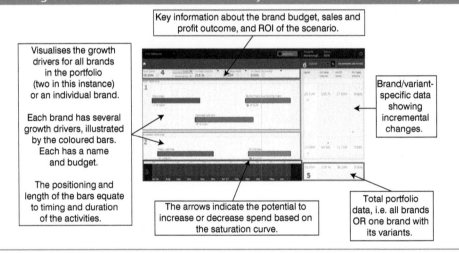

Figure 10: Growth Driver module – key features and functionality

Key information about the brand budget, sales and profit outcome, and ROI of the scenario.

Visualises the growth drivers for all brands in the portfolio (two in this instance) or an individual brand.

Each brand has several growth drivers, illustrated by the coloured bars. Each has a name and budget.

The positioning and length of the bars equate to timing and duration of the activities.

Brand/variant-specific data showing incremental changes.

The arrows indicate the potential to increase or decrease spend based on the saturation curve.

Total portfolio data, i.e. all brands OR one brand with its variants.

The module links directly into our media partners to create final media plans. Populated during the annual planning cycle, it acts as a living blueprint that updates with new data, and which the marketer can adapt when new information about brand performance or the external environment arises.

The system means we are able to use the best insights, in the moment, when high-value decisions are made. A 'star' rating enables users to judge the likelihood of the outcome, based on the quality of the underlying data.

This quality measure has been a critical component in deploying the approach worldwide, and overcoming the belief that if you couldn't model to the same standard as developed markets, it was not worth doing.

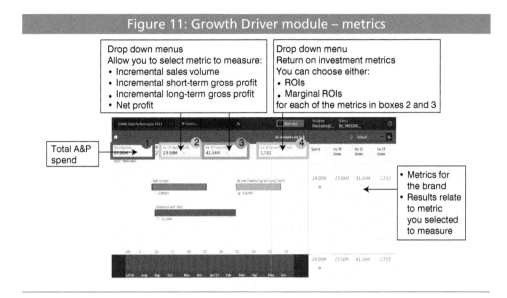

Figure 11: Growth Driver module – metrics

Across the world in markets as diverse as Colombia, Ethiopia, and Cameroon, we're now capturing data and running annual econometric modelling – a breakthrough in being able to apply locally relevant insight.

To achieve this, we tackled issues such as low data frequency, complexity, and coverage head on.

Macroeconomic factors also needed addressing, such as the impact of strikes, political uncertainty, health scares, and hyperinflation. These approaches enabled us to build models with 24 monthly data points, covering volume, value, spend, and seasonality.

In markets such as the US, we've increased coverage of models to our full portfolio and pushed boundaries to achieve excellent levels of prediction. Alongside models enabling us to plan future spend, new approaches such as geo-based attribute modelling give us tactical understanding of how communications are actually working at an individual execution/publisher/audience level.

Capability

To embed capability, we developed training called Peak Performance around the idea of 'marginal gains'. It covered those key elements of marketing theory underpinning our thinking and introduced the cognitive biases that affect decision making. Participants work on a simulated brand challenge before inputting their own plans.

Shorter versions were developed for different audiences – our executive team, general managers, and finance partners, helping to instil common understanding and language.

Figure 12: Peak Performance

DAY 1: WHAT IS PEAK PERFORMANCE AND HOW DO WE REACH AND SUSTAIN IT	DAY 2: PEAK PERFORMANCE IN ACTION
What is Peak Performance and why do we need it?	Hands on with the Marketing Catalyst Growth Driver Tool
Break	Break
Asking the Right Questions	Hands on with the Marketing Catalyst Growth Driver Tool Cont'd
Lunch (12.30-13.15)	Lunch (12.30-13.15)
How Marketing Catalyst Growth Driver helps	Hands on with the Marketing Catalyst Growth Driver Tool Cont'd
Making the Right Decisions- the impact of mental shortcuts	Action Planning
Break	Summary and Close – 17.00
Having the Right Data	
Getting started with the Marketing Catalyst Growth Driver tool	
Close – 17.00	

Creative Sparks

We know that distinctive and emotionally engaging creative is critical to effective marketing. Creative Sparks was developed in partnership with our agencies with the aim of deploying best-in-class ways of working worldwide. We saw five critical opportunities:

- powering creativity with media
- powerful insights
- brilliant briefs and briefings
- nurturing ideas
- measurement unlocks magic

Figure 13: Creative Sparks

In each area we explored how we could work most effectively with our agencies incorporating a range of illuminating case studies. The materials focused on tools and behaviours – for example: how to uncover and articulate insights, how to crack open and express a brand opportunity in a brief that would excite creatives, and how a learning mindset can improve creative impact.

Creative Sparks was deployed everywhere over an 18-month period. We combined interactive training with working sessions in which people applied the approaches to live work.

Each market appointed a champion to coach and improve capability. We also developed an inspiration programme, inviting experts into various offices to share best practice and new thinking. Filming the sessions ensured all markets could benefit.

Figure 14: Creative Sparks programme

Cultural change

These holistic changes were intended to create a major cultural shift, building belief and changing behaviours.

We thought about it like a marketing problem, considering different audiences, key messages, and channels. We considered the right language and how to appeal to people's emotions.

Figure 15: Cultural change

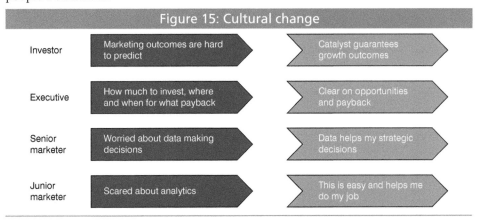

Investor	Marketing outcomes are hard to predict	Catalyst guarantees growth outcomes
Executive	How much to invest, where and when for what payback	Clear on opportunities and payback
Senior marketer	Worried about data making decisions	Data helps my strategic decisions
Junior marketer	Scared about analytics	This is easy and helps me do my job

So, for our executive and marketing leadership, we got their input in face-to-face sessions, using business language, not technical or marketing speak.

For investors, we presented our ambition at a Capital Markets Day, and then later, we updated on our progress.

For marketers, it was about building the approaches around deep understanding of their needs, their workflow, and using coaching to empower them. We sought to understand their concerns, especially around ensuring data was used in combination with judgement to make decisions. In many markets we continue to hold 'effectiveness weeks', and regularly communicate and share learning and progress.

We never lost sight of the critical business objective: to drive Diageo's long-term growth ambition and meet the commitment to £500m. This focus enabled us to unlock resource and ensure the target attached to the programme was owned by general managers as much as marketers – as part of our annual goals, we all had skin in the game.

To cement the change, we formalised Catalyst into our processes: marketing budgets are now signed off in the platform.

Results

Total business

The primary aim of this work was to achieve Diageo's ambitious transformation. So, how did we perform against our objectives (see Figure 16)?

Figure 16: Results against objectives
Business objectives
Deliver £500m in productivity
Overdelivered
Invest two-thirds back in the business
Achieved
Deliver 100 basis points (1ppt) organic operating margin
Overdelivered by nearly 2 times, 198pbs or almost 2ppt
Marketing objectives
Deliver £100m in incremental gross profit attributable to marketing
Overdelivered by over 2 times
Increase effective measurement of brands accounting for 30% of marketing spend to 80%
Overdelivered: 90%
Achieve an 8 times return on all investment for this project
Overdelivered 2 times, ROI of 16 times

Figure 17: Gross profit ROI of Marketing Catalyst programme

'The marketing effectiveness programme has had a profound effect on Diageo's results and its culture. Not only has it enabled us to realise significantly more profit from our marketing, but it has given us the confidence to increase marketing investment ahead of sales growth. We confidently know when, where, and how much to invest to grow our brands.'

Ivan Menezes, CEO

'Catalyst has been a game changer for Diageo in getting more bang for our buck on our brands. But the power of these analytics goes further – accurately predicting the short- and long-term impacts on profit of the future bets we make has given us conviction to invest ahead and meet our primary objective to deliver consistent growth.'

Kathryn Mikells, CFO

The programme gave Diageo confidence to increase marketing investment by almost £500m over three years. This is a 31% increase, and consistently ahead of sales growth (Figure 18).

Figure 18: Record levels of marketing investment

Diageo PLC reported marketing spend (GBP millions)

- 2016: 1,562
- 2017: 1,798
- 2018: 1,882
- 2019: 2,042

+31% increase in total marketing spend since 2016

Source: Annual reports.

133

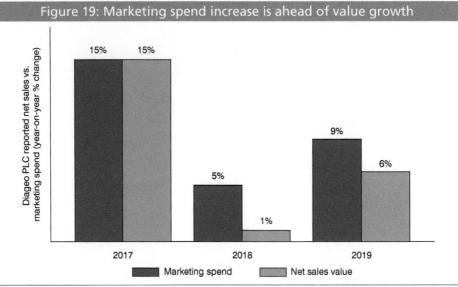

Figure 19: Marketing spend increase is ahead of value growth

Source: Diageo annual reports, F16–F19.

Profit growth and investor confidence also accelerated during the productivity programme.

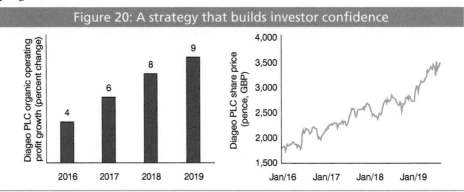

Figure 20: A strategy that builds investor confidence

Source: Annual reports.

Scale of implementation

Figure 21: Marketing Catalyst by numbers

Currently, Marketing Catalyst is used in 60 countries, by 1,200 marketers and all our media agencies. When we started, econometrics covered just 23 brands confined to Europe and North America. Now we don't just cover global giants such as Guinness and Johnnie Walker, but also local stars like Tusker in Kenya, Bundaberg in Australia, and YeniRaki in Turkey.

We sought to do more than demonstrate the relative performance of individual campaigns, looking to drive improvement in gross profit attributable to marketing across the world, unleashing creativity. With many markets and brands at different stages of maturity this was important – it was about more profit from our marketing, not better ROIs as an outcome in itself.

Results across our global giants

Let's look at results across our global giants, the core of our business and over 40% of net sales (Figure 22).

Figure 22: Global marketing effectiveness results – three-year percentage change

	JOHNNIE WALKER Keep Walking	GUINNESS	Captain Morgan	BAILEYS	SMIRNOFF	Tanqueray
Gross profit return on investment	5%	101%	6%	20%	–5%	6%
Marketing investment	76%	41%	27%	50%	14%	173%
Gross profit attributable to marketing	85%	183%	34%	81%	8%	190%

Source: Gain Theory and Data2Decisions enonometric modelling outputs. Based on latest available data at time of writing: F18–F16.

Numbers quoted for the change in gross profit attributable to marketing are all modelled numbers excluding any potential impact of changes in distribution, competitor activity, pricing and promotion, seasonality, and so forth.

We've seen improvements across all our global giants over this time frame. Understanding their future profit potential has led us to increase our marketing spend most on Tanqueray and Johnnie Walker, whereas Guinness and Baileys have shown most impact from improvements in their marketing, or ROI.

Let's highlight Baileys and Guinness briefly.

Baileys

Figure 23: Baileys advertising

Baileys has staged an impressive comeback post the 2008 financial crisis. We re-imagined the marketing model, shifting from operating as a classic liqueur with a big annual 'purpose'-driven Christmas TV campaign to operating as an adult treat – 'part cake, part booze'. We recognised the multiple opportunities in the year for adult treats, with a broader media mix, and many pieces of product-centric bite-size content leveraging the semiotics of treating.

These changes to strategy, creative, and media have increased ROI everywhere, most notably by 91% in Great Britain over a longer period of five years. The model has been successfully rolled out across all major Baileys markets.

Guinness

Figure 24: Guinness advertising

If Baileys is a story of reinvention, Guinness is one of committing to an idea and nurturing it. In the era covered by this paper, we'd already established strong ROI for 'Made of more', but were able to unlock more effectiveness through media optimisation – re-using and rotating copy in a way that maximised ROIs, using outdoor adjacent to pubs and stores, and being clear on the role of digital channels in creating year-round salience.

The Creative Sparks programme encouraged us to push ourselves creatively, celebrating the bravery of Gareth Thomas, the first openly gay man in rugby, daring to promote water with Guinness Clear, and toasting the courage of Japan's first female rugby team.

We also took this campaign beyond Europe, using the same core idea across Africa but leveraging football, with which the brand has a strong association. In the US, we've combined this with optimising our channel mix to be more present in the on-trade. Gross profit increased everywhere, and in Ireland targeting ROI improvements enabled us to weather the impact of an extraordinary summer in F18.

Results across regions

Gross profit attributable to marketing has improved in all regions, in different market types and on local jewels such as Bundaberg, Tusker, Crown Royal, and Bell.

In three regions this has been with increased ROI. In two of those it was accompanied by significant increased investment, while in Africa our business strategy was to enhance margin and therefore we eliminated ineffective spend. In the other two regions, our gross profit has increased, reflecting increased scope of investment across the portfolio (Figure 25).

Figure 25: Global marketing effectiveness results – three-year percentage change by region

Source: Gain Theory and Data2Decisions enonometric modelling outputs. Based on latest available data at time of writing: F19 vs. F17 for APAC, F18 vs. F16 for other regions.

Though space precludes us from sharing all results, let's look at a range of examples from markets with local jewels and significantly different environments.

US

The US started from a strong foundation, but we extended coverage of analytics from just five brands to the full portfolio. As intended, we have made more polarised choices in where to increase our marketing investment, for example increasing focus on brands such as Don Julio, Bulleit, and Crown Royal.

US: Crown Royal

Figure 26: Crown Royal

Crown Royal is our largest brand business in any single market – an established brand with a strong base where traditionally we would have seen limited opportunity to increase investment.

However, being able to see Crown in the context of all our brands changed our mindset: a pound invested in the brand would yield more in gross profit than in many other brands across the world, even if the ROI decreased.

We saw the opportunity to increase spend on TV by 257% in F18 and by 164% in F19. Gross profit soared, and ROI stabilised at a new level with our bold 'Generosity' campaign, and 'Water boys' moderation work. With an ROI of over £1, we can be confident of long-term payback.

Australia

Though data rich, Australia was a market where this capability was new. Understanding future profit has enabled us to make more polarised choices, keeping the budget for Bundaberg stable while increasing investment for Johnnie Walker, Captain Morgan, and Gordon's Gin where spend increased by over 16 times.

This has paid off with notable improvements, including a 231% ROI improvement on Gordon's with treble the spend.

Australia: Bundaberg

Figure 27: Bundaberg

Bundaberg improved effectiveness with its 'Unmistakably ours' campaign, which brought to life the Australian values of optimism, mateship, and pluck, which unite the brand and its drinkers. An increase of 45% on TV, the best-performing channel, drove incremental gross profit by 50%.

Comparing regional and metro TV at state level with subscription TV, we were able to prioritise regional Queensland and rebalance investment in under-served Victoria and New South Wales, reducing costly subscription TV.

African markets

In contrast, our effectiveness effort in Africa started from a blank sheet of paper in a more challenging environment.

Gaining real transparency enabled us to rapidly remove ineffective spend and make very different choices with many of our brands, developing better creative strategy with the help of Creative Sparks.

Kenya

Our biggest-spending Kenyan brand, Tusker, recognises that for the third generation post-independence, identity comes less from flag waving and more through a sense of community and shared passions. We increased our ROI by 116% and profit by 52% by activating our creative platform in national obsessions like Rugby 7s, Kenyan music, and NyamaChoma, the unofficial national dish. This has enabled us to fund other brands such as Balozi, which offers an inflation-busting beer positioned around natural ingredients.

Figure 28: Tusker

Figure 29: Balozi

Uganda

In Uganda, we've been able both to measure and drive significant incremental profit. Consumers had a strong emotional connection to mainstream lager Bell, but it lacked relevance to key occasions. Investing in experiential at scale with 'Bell jamz' was the right choice to achieve this objective while profitably increasing penetration by 4% (source: Kantar). With value lager Senator, we realised we could profitably expand our reach among hard-to-access C2DE consumers. The profit from highly effective premium-priced Guinness supported this portfolio expansion.

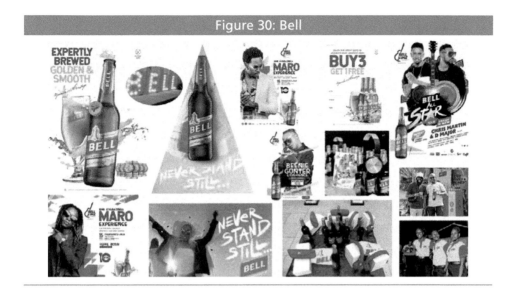

Figure 30: Bell

Creativity

Though we don't have a benchmark for a prior period, in 2020 we started to survey agency partners worldwide to understand the extent to which we were all living the aspirations of Creative Sparks.

Table 1: Agency perceptions of Creative Sparks	
	% who agree (top 2 box)
Diageo marketing teams have a deep sense of the role of their brand in their consumers / shoppers / customers' lives	91%
Activity briefs have a clearly articulated opportunity or challenge	74%
Diageo builds collaborative relationships with its creative agency partners	84%
Diageo teams are good at developing the potential of creative ideas	72%
Diageo teams are open to brave creative ideas	72%
Diageo teams have a 'learning mindset' and continuously strive to improve creative work	81%

Source: Diageo internal research. Sample: 50 worldwide agencies.

Learnings

The point of the programme was to impact all brands and the thousands of individual decisions affecting the development and deployment of an effective marketing campaign – strategy, creative idea, executions, and media.

Our ways of working now make this easier to implement at scale across the globe.

Scalable learning

Using our insight in aggregate uncovers new learning that we can apply in all Diageo brands and markets.

For example, serve and recipe content is consistently hard-working when used in the right channel and in combination with the right creative idea.

Figure 31: Recipe and serve-related content has been proven to deliver strong ROI for many brands

Baileys GB
Shifted focus to serve and recipe content in F17 with a 35% increase in ROI from latest iteration of the new strategy

Smirnoff GB
More recent shift in F19 for Smirnoff away from 'We're open' platform to focus on 'Soda Smash', which delivered a very strong TV ROI gain

F16 MEDIA ROI = 1.7   F19 MEDIA ROI = 2.3   F18 TV ROI = 0.6   F19 TV ROI = 1.2

J&B Spain
Shift to serve-related content since F18 with latest F18 H1 OOH campaign showing a 29% increase in ROI vs. the previous strategy

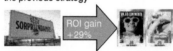

F17 H1 OOH ROI = 1.4   F19 H1 OOH ROI = 1.8

Note: All ROIs shown are long-term media ROIs.

We've also learned that the effectiveness of gifting can be improved with the right combination of ATL and in-store support.

Figure 32: Gifting as a growth driver requires coordinated ATL and BTL support

Zacapa Italy	**JW Spain**	**JW Greece**	**Talisker Germany**
1.58 long-term gross profit ROI	1.38 long-term gross profit ROI	1.25 long-term gross profit ROI	1.23 gross profit ROI
Why did it work?	**Why did it work?**	**Why did it work?**	**Why did it work?**
In-store VAP mechanic well supported by proximity OOH to drive footfall into stores at key time of year (Christmas)	Well-established brand with strong ATL media support with a gifting message during Christmas on higher-margin SKU (Black)	Gifting message on TV at Christmas supported strong in-store presence with Black VAP packs	Relatively low spend well focused on digital activations (display, search and social) driving to sale alongside in-store activations

Note: Based on average gifting ROIs in last 52 weeks modelled. Source: Data2Decisions.

We've seen how for the launch of a new variant like Gordon's Pink, the best results are achieved with a mix of trademark and variant spend versus advertising the innovation alone (Figure 33).

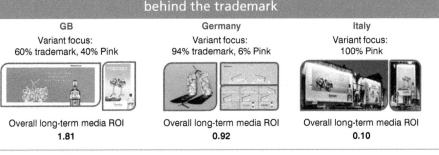

Figure 33: Trademark vs. innovation support – Evidence from Gordon's that it is vital when launching an innovation to retain some spend behind the trademark

GB	Germany	Italy
Variant focus: 60% trademark, 40% Pink	Variant focus: 94% trademark, 6% Pink	Variant focus: 100% Pink
Overall long-term media ROI **1.81**	Overall long-term media ROI **0.92**	Overall long-term media ROI **0.10**

Channel mix

We also appreciate how this kind of learning ladders up to shifting our spend profile across channels.

TV remains a critical part of our investment and we've increased spend and effectiveness. In place of bursts, we're on air more weeks with lower weights, leveraging more seasonal peaks and relevant cultural moments. We are also rotating copy, sometimes for three years or more as we have examples where ROI improves, instead of diminishing.

Sampling or experiential is key to driving trial on alcohol brands. We have improved our effectiveness by eliminating small-scale work in favour of scale and even paid-for events which have greater consumer relevance.

For outdoor, improvements have come from bringing serve to life with the right creative idea, and placing work close to restaurants, bars, and stores.

In other broadcast media, we've rationalised ineffective spend from cinema and print to fund other channels while improving our ROI on radio, which is a key channel in Africa.

The dramatic improvements in our social advertising come from the understanding and implementation of a range of learnings: placing our content in partner channels, not just our own, well-branded five-second content, focusing on occasion and serve, frequency capping, choosing afternoon/evening placements, mixing key seasonal peaks with 'always on' content, and using programmatic for hard-to-reach audiences.

Creativity and sales

There's been much discussion in the industry about the correlation between creatively awarded work and effectiveness.

Our datasets have enabled us to demonstrate the link between creative that cuts through with consumers and sales.

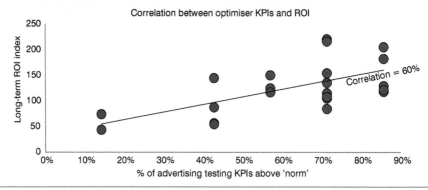

Figure 34: We have found a clear correlation between creative effectiveness score and ROI

- We tested a range of consumer measures for a correlation with TV campaign ROI
- Advertising testing KPIs tracked as above the 'norm' showed strongest correlation with ROI

Correlation between optimiser KPIs and ROI

Long-term ROI index (y-axis: 0, 50, 100, 150, 200, 250)

Correlation = 60%

% of advertising testing KPIs above 'norm' (x-axis: 0%, 10%, 20%, 30%, 40%, 50%, 60%, 70%, 80%, 90%)

Sources: Kantar and Data2Decisions.

We're now more confident in the key elements that have the strongest impact, proving the importance of distinctiveness and emotion.

Figure 35: Brand distinctiveness and brand appeal are the creative KPIs that drive strongest ROI

IS MY CREATIVE **GRABBING ATTENTION?**

Correlation with ROI

Engagement — 14%

Eye-catching — 41%

WILL THE CREATIVE **STAND OUT?**

Correlation with ROI

Creative distinctiveness — 45%

Brand distinctiveness — 58%

WILL IT BE **REMEMBERED FOR MY BRAND?**

Trademark recall — 36%

DO CONSUMERS **UNDERSTAND THE CREATIVE?**

Understanding — 29%

HOW WILL THE CREATIVE MAKE PEOPLE **FEEL ABOUT THE BRAND?**

Brand appeal — 51%

Sources: Kantar and Data2Decisions.

We've been able to apply this to drive ROI improvements in our creative. This example from Smirnoff shows how we made our most recent creative work three times more effective by focusing on emotion and distinctiveness while remaining just as engaging.

Figure 36: Case study – Smirnoff GB improvements in creative effectiveness mirror ROI gains					
ⓘ	IS MY CREATIVE **GRABBING ATTENTION?**	Engagement	6.06	6.96	6.70
		Eye-catching	3.21	3.24	3.41
⊕	WILL IT BE **REMEMBERED FOR MY BRAND?**	Trademark recall	3.82	3.78	4.14
⊗	WILL THE CREATIVE **STAND OUT?**	Creative distinctiveness	2.83	3.11	2.87
		Brand distinctiveness	3.49	3.75	3.66
⬚	DO CONSUMERS **UNDERSTAND THE CREATIVE?**	Understanding	3.11	3.24	3.40
👍	HOW WILL THE CREATIVE MAKE PEOPLE **FEEL ABOUT THE BRAND?**	Brand appeal	3.46	3.67	3.86
£	DID THE CAMPAIGN DRIVE SALES EFFICIENTLY?	Long-term ROI	0.51	0.64	1.26

Sources: Kantar and Data2Decisions.

Conclusion

Diageo over-achieved its productivity ambition and doubled its margin enhancement objective.

Not only that, we doubled our business case for marketing effectiveness, and exceeded our coverage target for analytics.

In over-delivering, we created a sustainable cultural change. We're seeing better results from our communications at scale, and consistently applying the best marketing principles. We've increased confidence in the marketing function and increased brand investments ahead of value sales.

We've combined creativity and coordination, risk and rigour, drama and data, magic and measurement. We've made every pound, dollar, and rupee count, 'every day, everywhere'.

Guinness

Guinness 'Made of more' 2012–2019: Consistency × creativity

By Lisa Stoney and Craig Mawdsley, AMV BBDO
Contributing authors: Andrew Geoghegan, Alison Falconer and Nanda Griffioen, Guinness, Diageo; Andrew Deykin, Data2Decisions
Credited company: Carat

Summary

Guinness has flourished under the 'Made of more' brand idea for eight years. This paper assesses its overall impact from 2012–2019, quantifying the value of the idea at £1 billion and highlighting increasing returns year on year. Extending its association with rugby, Guinness told the story of a mother's legacy to her rugby fan sons, and of a pioneering Japanese women's team. A PR and digitally-led idea, Guinness Clear, encouraged fans to moderate alcohol by drinking water. As a result, Guinness increased UK value share and protected it in Ireland. It is estimated 'Made of more' has returned a gross profit ROI of £4.81 per £1 since 2012.

Editor's comment

The judges thought this case was a masterclass in long-term brand building and the impact that you can have as a marketer on a brand, a business, society, and culture. Anyone involved in marketing should read it for the way it proves highly creative advertising was effective by using solid evidence and well-constructed arguments.

Client comment

Alison Falconer, Global Planning Director and Andrew Geoghegan, Global Consumer Planning Director, Diageo

This is our third 'Made of more' IPA paper. We considered not writing it, worrying that folk might be bored with more of the same. But it is not more of the same. This paper talks to how Guinness continues to change, to adapt to new contexts and drinkers, whilst keeping the DNA of the brand and the idea strong.

'Made of more' has powered Guinness since 2012, but it has evolved in execution with each iteration: shaped by culture, ensuring we remain relevant.

It is a story we find perpetually inspiring and important within Diageo beyond the marketing community. Guinness has always been a beacon for creativity. Now it is a beacon of creative effectiveness.

We have shaped a new culture of effectiveness at Diageo. Guinness sits at the very centre of that. A core proof-point and case study of the process of change, improving ROI with better work, better deployed. Stakeholders across the business are now understanding how rigour, creativity and curiosity generate growth. This has helped unlock investment for better effectiveness understanding throughout the business. We have supported significant increases in total marketing investment.

A case study based on this paper, and those that preceded it, is the central example within the 'Measurement unlocks magic' module of Diageo's marketing training programme. That training is delivered globally. We want everyone to be inspired by what Guinness has shown is possible; not just great creative, but a strong, open and honest relationship with the agency, and a drive to reach more people with more relevant and emotionally stirring work.

Meanwhile, the idea continues to grow and evolve in the hands of our Guinness teams and BBDO, driven by continual learning – the next chapter will be equally fresh and exciting.

It will be 'Made of more'.

Guinness has been powered by 'Made of more' for eight years.

Each year, creative has evolved, becoming more effective over time. The work has made an impact in culture beyond advertising, enabling Guinness to prosper in tough conditions.

It has now delivered the highest revenue and gross profit ROIs reported in a beer category IPA paper, beating our last two Gold-winning papers.[1]

Not only is the 2018–2019 ROI our strongest ever, we have proved that choosing to invest media money against 'Made of more', rather than previous ideas, delivered incremental sales of £1 billion since 2012.[2]

Consistency × creativity pays.

An idea made of more

When the world changes, it's tempting to change your idea.

This story carves a different path, delivering a highly creative *and* long-lasting, consistent, flexible and effective brand idea.

Ideas need an enduring core: but they shouldn't be static. To be consistently relevant and meaningful in culture, ideas need to evolve.

Through 'Made of more', we evolved short-term execution within our long-term strategy, producing extraordinary results for Guinness.

Eight years of data highlight the value of this approach; through econometric modelling we can compare 'Made of more' against our projected performance had we continued with Guinness pre-2012 communications ideas.[3]

In the face of new competition, we sustained our dominant value share in Ireland, and grew value share in Great Britain.[4]

Those ideas delivered ROI slightly above the beer category average; **'Made of more' delivers an ROI more than double the beer category average.**[5]

By evolving and committing to 'Made of more', we delivered an extra £1 billion in Guinness sales in GB and Ireland from 2012–2019.[6]

This is not the total effect of our advertising over that period (that figure would be much greater), £1 billion is simply the value of 'Made of more' as an idea.

This is the story of how we achieved it.

A bit about 'the black stuff'

Guinness is a dark stout beer originating from the brewery of Arthur Guinness at St. James's Gate, Dublin, in 1759.

Guinness does not look like a golden ale or lager; hence our comms traditionally focused on product truths (Figure 1).

Figure 1: Guinness advertising

(L-R) Guinness' first ever ad; Guinness' famous Gilroy work claiming 'goodness' in the drink; 'Good things come to those who wait' celebrated the 119.5 seconds it takes to pour the perfect pint.

But Guinness is not one product; available in different forms in different markets,[7] by 2011 we had five different global positioning statements. It was time to shift, merging the core markets of GB and Ireland with a single global strategy (Figure 2).[8]

Figure 2: Guinness global strategy

BRAND
Guinness is a brand with a bold outlook on life. The founder Arthur Guinness made a bold choice to sign a 9,000-year lease of his Dublin brewery, and chose to brew a dark stout when everyone else was brewing ale.

AUDIENCE
Rather than just follow the crowd, they make bold choices and carve their own path. They are people with more to them, who desire experiences and brands with more depth and substance.

PRODUCT TRUTH
Guinness is a unique drink: a black stout rather than a golden lager or ale. Guinness is bold in look, and because of the surge has more taste and character than other beers.

And present a united global platform idea:

Guinness is a beer made of more, for people made of more, and we tell stories of how unexpected character in people and beer enrich the world around us.

Since 2012 this idea has won two Gold IPA Effectiveness Awards (2016 and 2018), telling our story of learning and improvement, enhancing ROI.

First, we executed through metaphor ('Cloud', 'Clock', 'Surge'), then transformed ROI with true stories (from 'Sapeurs', onwards) (Figure 3).

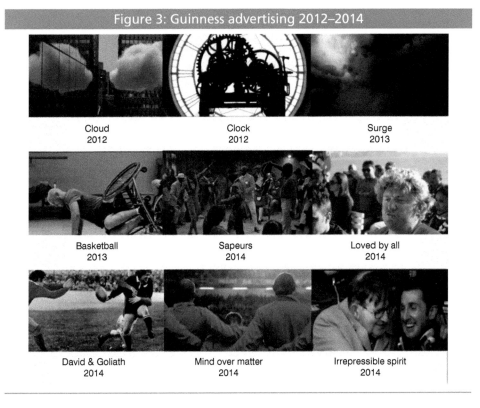

Figure 3: Guinness advertising 2012–2014

Cloud
2012

Clock
2012

Surge
2013

Basketball
2013

Sapeurs
2014

Loved by all
2014

David & Goliath
2014

Mind over matter
2014

Irrepressible spirit
2014

Then we elevated 'Made of more' to play a role in culture; by making work with a point of view, our stories went beyond advertising (Figure 4).

Figure 4: Guinness advertising 2015–2018

Gareth & Ashwin
2015

John Hammond
2017

Compton Cowboys
2018

The success of our idea was evidenced in our 2018 paper reporting a gross profit ROI (GP ROI) of £4.30 for every £1 invested (Figure 5).[9]

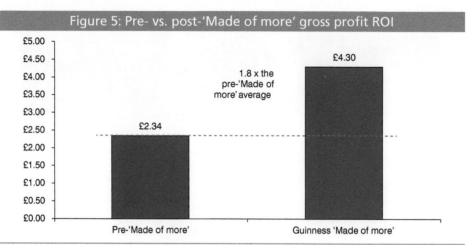

Figure 5: Pre- vs. post-'Made of more' gross profit ROI

1.8 x the pre-'Made of more' average

£4.30

£2.34

Source: Data2Decisions Econometric Modelling, 2012–2019

That paper told the story of 2012–2017, with escalating ROIs, ending with an estimation that our 'Compton Cowboys' campaign would continue this.[10] It did; delivering gross profit and revenue ROIs in Ireland and GB in excess of anything seen before (Figures 6 and 7).

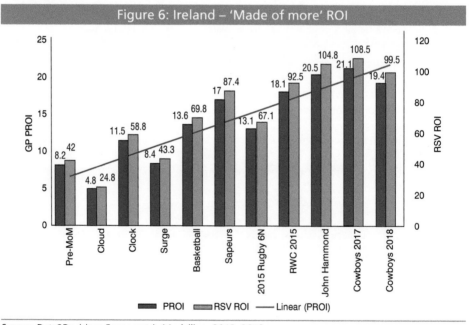

Figure 6: Ireland – 'Made of more' ROI

Source: Data2Decisions Econometric Modelling, 2012–2019

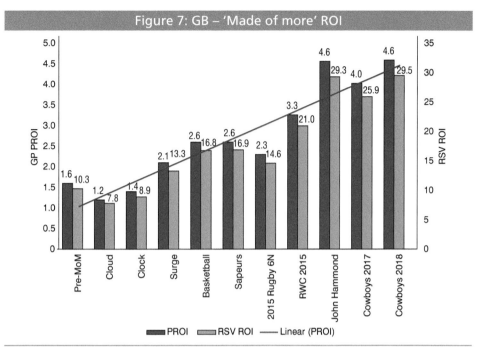

Figure 7: GB – 'Made of more' ROI

Source: Data2Decisions Econometric Modelling, 2012–2019

Since 'Cowboys', we have beaten that GP ROI, driving it up to £6.05 for every pound spent, making 2018–2019 the most profitable ever for 'Made of more' (Figure 8).[11]

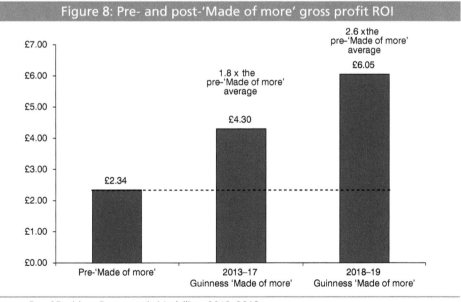

Figure 8: Pre- and post-'Made of more' gross profit ROI

Source: Data2Decisions Econometric Modelling, 2012–2019

Leading into 2018, market challenges were escalating

Beer market volume continued to decline (Figure 9).

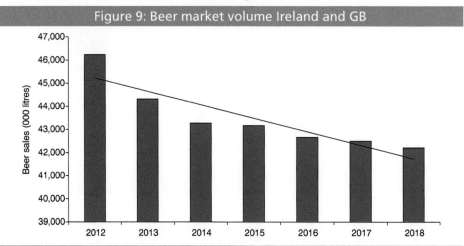

Figure 9: Beer market volume Ireland and GB

Source: Nielsen & CGA. Data are annual, running from January 2012 to January 2018; 'beer market' = all stout, lager, ale.

The pub trade was in decline.

Problematic, given Guinness is mostly enjoyed in the pub (Figure 10).

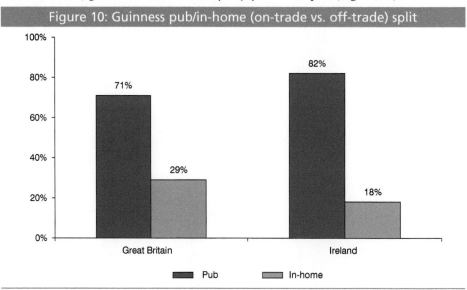

Figure 10: Guinness pub/in-home (on-trade vs. off-trade) split

Source: Data2Decisions Econometric Modelling, 2012–2019. Data based on 2018 fiscal.

Pubs kept closing their doors (Figures 11 and 12).

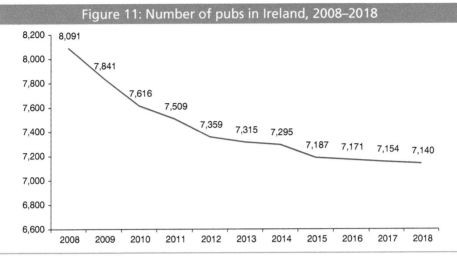

Figure 11: Number of pubs in Ireland, 2008–2018

Source: Drinks Industry Group of Ireland[12]

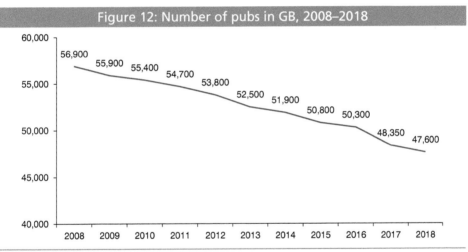

Figure 12: Number of pubs in GB, 2008–2018

Source: British Beer & Pub Association[13]

The beer market was increasingly competitive

A typical pub now has approximately 50 beers[14] to choose from (though it can be much higher), with 233 beer brands available in the UK and 86 in Ireland[15] by 2018 (Figure 13).

Figure 13: Range of brands in a typical pub

Source: Foodism

The number of breweries in GB and Ireland more than doubled from 2012–2018 (Figure 14).

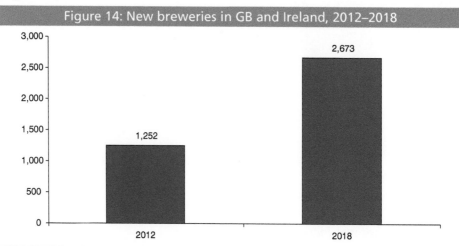

Figure 14: New breweries in GB and Ireland, 2012–2018

Source: Euromonitor, 2012–2018

Drinkers' repertoires grew (Figure 15).

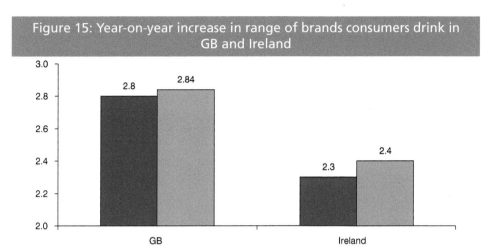

Figure 15: Year-on-year increase in range of brands consumers drink in GB and Ireland

Source: Nielsen 2017–2018

Established mainstream lager brands suffered the most (Figure 16).

Figure 16: Top 10 beer brands volume decrease in GB and Ireland, 2013 vs. 2018

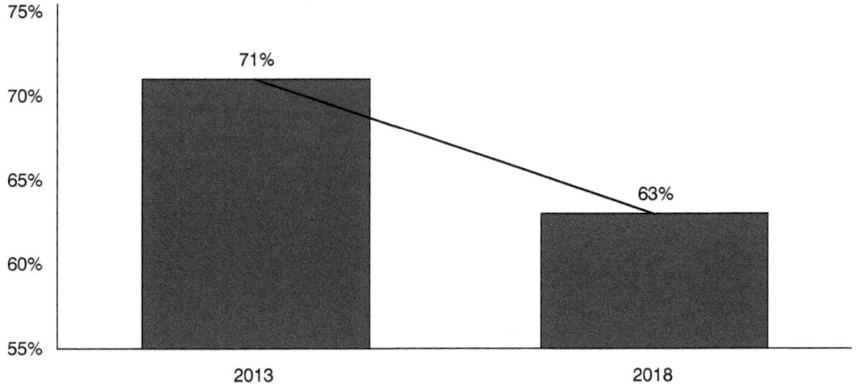

Source: Nielsen 2013-18

In GB, this shift was driven by the novelty and taste of craft beers *and* the growth of premium world lagers (Figure 17).

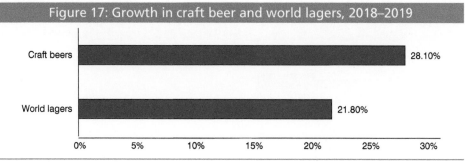

Figure 17: Growth in craft beer and world lagers, 2018–2019

Source: Nielsen 2018–2019

In Ireland, Guinness is a unique brand; the biggest player, with a big market share.[16] This means we're constantly defending our share as the main potential source of volume for category entrants.

The media landscape was shifting as we needed to reach a new audience

Over the period of this campaign, the IPA reported changes in media consumption, which accelerated dramatically – particularly amongst young adults (Figure 18).

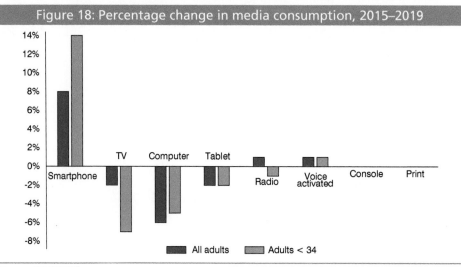

Figure 18: Percentage change in media consumption, 2015–2019

Source: IPA 2019[17]

The next generation of drinkers had a different relationship with brands – not built solely through broadcast, but augmented with participation and experience.

'Made of more' would need to evolve again.

Our objectives

Our focus has always been to ensure that every pound or euro spent on communication returns more to the business and brand.

Marketing objective

Drive and sustain distinctiveness and salience measures to lead the market and stand out in a sea of competition.

Communication objective

Produce highly creative communications to drive brand fame, make an impact in culture (in 2018–2019 this would mean making Guinness the number-one brand associated with the rugby and driving genuine responsible drinking behavioural change).

Commercial objective

Increase ROI every year (versus pre-'Made of more' and versus beer category), to deliver profit in the face of rising costs while sustaining value share in Ireland and growing in GB.

Brand learning and improvement

The story of 'Made of more' is of brand learning and improvement, rising to any challenge to achieve our objectives.

Our idea has always needed to flex.

We needed to deliver growth in a declining market.

Our favoured distribution channel was declining.

Innovative new entrants posed competition.

We needed to recruit new drinkers who live in a media environment far from familiar for the brand.

Thriving in these conditions would take extraordinary creativity.

A desire to never settle, and always use our experience to make our work better has helped us.

We didn't rely on the power of consistency alone, we teamed it with restless and bold creativity.

- In 2012–2014, we harnessed the power of true stories to add depth and meaning.
- In 2015–2017, we amplified the idea to play a role in culture, having a point of view to elevate societal issues.
- 2018–2019 was the third chapter of 'Made of more'.

'Compton Cowboys' had taken our idea to new heights, but in the spirit of constant learning we saw three opportunities to improve:

1. Amidst political and social upheaval in GB and Ireland, we would elevate Guinness' characteristic twinkle in the eye, bottling the joyful side of 'Made of more', which shone in 'Sapeurs'.
2. There was a shift in generational attitudes towards drinking, and an opportunity for 'Made of more' to drive genuine behavioural change.
3. At the heart of 'Compton Cowboys' was our culturally resonant message of carving your own path and inspiring those around you, which captured a new

generation of Guinness drinkers. We wanted to build on this through the lens of diverse representation and shifting gender dynamics.

The next era of 'Made of more' was our opportunity to capitalise on rugby's growing popularity.

The sport was becoming bigger and more mainstream,[18] giving us the opportunity to take our affinity with rugby and deploy it against a bigger audience, beyond diehard fans.

The connection between Guinness and rugby runs deep; their shared values are a perfect complement.

Figure 19: Guinness and rugby's shared values

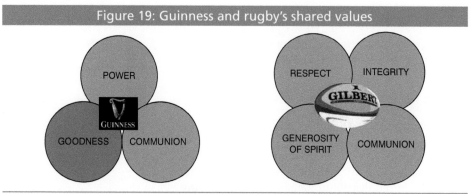

Left: Guinness' brand DNA is power, goodness and communion; right: rugby's core values.

Rugby events such as the Six Nations, Autumn Internationals, PRO14s and, every four years, the Rugby World Cup, create a seasonal sales effect for Guinness (Figure 20).

Figure 20: The seasonal sales effect of rugby

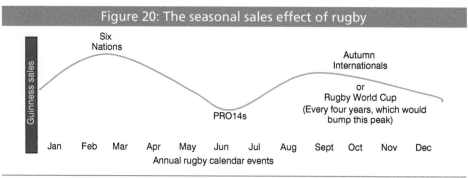

2019 was a bumper year for rugby – to make it ours, two decisions were taken:

- Become title sponsor of the Six Nations.
- Make the next epic 'Made of more' story a fresh take on the Rugby World Cup, which took place in Japan in October 2019.

'Made of more' would need to work harder than ever: to stretch from rugby into culture, drive a clear responsible drinking message and stand out in more places and spaces – from the bar to AV.

In a seven-month period we created and launched three new campaigns (the most in any single year of 'Made of more' to this point) (Figure 21).

Figure 21: 'Made of more' 2019 campaigns

Our Six Nations campaign wove together a ground-breaking responsible drinking activation with stories of rugby's unique spirit, to moderate consumption and ensure that when people chose to drink, more chose Guinness (Figure 22).

Figure 22: Guinness Six Nations (January–March 2019)

Together, this fuelled a powerful system of communication (Figure 23).

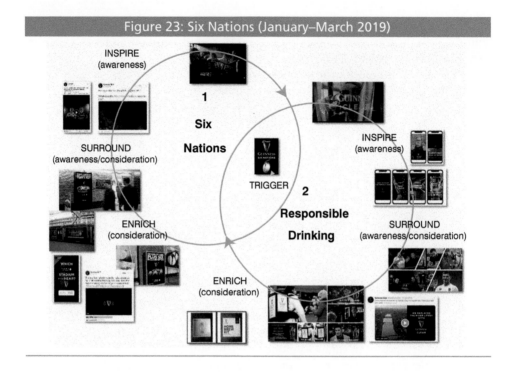

Figure 23: Six Nations (January–March 2019)

Step One: Winning the Six Nations

We would keep Guinness top of mind with our most joyful 'Made of more' story yet.

Turning our focus from stories of elite male players to fans, female players and amateurs, we celebrated the unique Six Nations blend of rivalry on the pitch and friendship off it. We used real stories that were universal in their appeal. This brought a stronger sense of joy and levity to 'Made of more' – celebratory, not sombre.

This spirit was encapsulated in two 'Made of more' stories.

'The purse' told the true story of two Welsh brothers and the unusual inheritance left by their mother. The brothers (played by the real Rees brothers) travel from city to city, enjoying rugby, friendships and the occasional Guinness (Figure 24).

Figure 24: 'The purse', 60"

THE PURSE – 60"

We open on two brothers carrying a coffin. The brothers in the solicitor's office exchange glances as they look over a will.

VO: **Our mam was different...**
In her will, she left us strict instructions...
To spend every last penny – on the Six Nations.

They break into a grin. The mother is in the stands at a rugby match, with fans of Wales and England also on their feet around her. She's an incongruous sight, amongst all these big, brawny blokes.

Mam loved the intensity, the rivalry.
And the way that rivalry was all forgotten afterwards...

Now we see the two brothers in Welsh rugby shirts squeezing through a packed bar. A little purse with a Welsh dragon on it is visible at the bar.

This was her purse. We keep the kitty in it.
It pays for our pints. Wherever we go, the purse goes.

We see the brothers after the game in the corner of a packed bar with some Irish musicians. They celebrate victory and dance along. Cut footage with stock footage from games.

We see the brothers in Rome, on their way to the game in the back of a taxi.

And every trip we make, every game we see, it's like mam's here
with us...
Love you, mam.

Title: **Guinness Six Nations logo**
Made of More

'Sisters' told the true story of Harriet and Bridget Millar-Mills, who were team-mates through their youth, until they became rivals (but always sisters): playing for the opposing England and Scotland national teams in 2013. This was a VOD partnership with ITV Sport (Figure 25).

Figure 25: 'Sisters'

VO: I started playing rugby when I was nine
To keep me company my sister came with me
To begin with, we'd only pass the ball to each other

VO: We got older
And we got better
Then one day I was picked for England
And I got picked for Scotland

VO: We didn't pass the ball to each other after that

Title: Harriet and Bridget Millar-Mills
Rivals. Always Sisters
Guinness. Made of More

These stories were the heartbeat of our Six Nations, but the campaign was surround-sound, touching everything from:

Our podcast 'House of Rugby', which launched in partnership with the website JOE in GB and Ireland (which is now ongoing) (Figure 26).

Figure 26: Panellists on the 'House of Rugby' podcast

Social channels, where we gave everyone the tools to celebrate friendships and rivalries (Figure 27).

Figure 27: Guinness social channels

The stadium, where we commandeered every branded surface (Figure 28).

Figure 28: Guinness stadium coverage

Pubs throughout Ireland and GB, which we decorated (Figure 29).

Figure 29: Guinness pub decoration

Bar takeovers, hosted at Flat Iron Square, a local London rugby hotspot, where every Six Nations game would be aired (Figure 30).

Figure 30: Guinness bar takeover

We partnered with app MatchPint to create 'Pint Predictor', a game that enabled everyone to predict the score to compete for free pints (Figure 31).

Figure 31: MatchPint 'Pint Predictor'

Step Two: Encouraging responsible drinking, in a 'Made of more' way

'Made of more' has always been about storytelling. Now we would turn it into behaviour.

A proven (and practical) way to moderate alcohol intake is to consume water, but people (especially men) are embarrassed to order anything non-alcoholic at the bar.[19] This is heightened during sporting events when the revelry is high; yet the confidence to carve your own path, not follow convention, is the heart of 'Made of more'.

To trigger genuine behavioural change, we needed people to feel comfortable ordering something other than alcohol – on a large scale.

We rebranded ordinary tap water as a cool 'new' product called Guinness Clear. Packaged with humour and wit, we turned ordering water from embarrassing to enjoyable (Figure 32).

Figure 32: Guinness Clear

We created a PR and online-led responsible drinking activation which turned our celebration of 'more' on its head with the idea: 'Sometimes, less is more'.

We promoted it just like a beer, with its own film (Figure 33).

Figure 33: 'Guinness Clear', 30"

Open on a man drinking water from a Guinness glass, savouring every drop of flavour.
Cut to sumptuous shots of water filling a pint glass and the master brewer admiring his creation.

VO: A flavour, unlike anything else.
        A look all of its own.
        Made to a time-honoured recipe.

A group in a bar all drink together as one, as the barman carefully pours a glass from the tap.
Cut to a final drop of water dropping into a brimming glass.

VO: What else tastes like it?
        Nothing.
        Make it a night you'll remember with new Guinness Clear.

Title: Sometimes less is more.
        Made of More

In social, we demonstrated how to master the Guinness Clear two-part pour (at home and in the pub) (Figure 34).

Figure 34: Pouring Guinness Clear

We introduced product extensions (extra cold, with ice) (Figure 35).

Figure 35: Guinness Clear product extension

Figure 35: Guinness Clear product extension

There were celebrity endorsements from influencers and Michelin star chefs (Figure 36).

Figure 36: Guinness Clear endorsements

(L–R) Taulupe Faletau (left) and Mako Vunipola (right); Tommy Brady (influencer); David Alorka (influencer); Brian O'Driscoll (left) and Lawrence Dallaglio (right); Owen Farrell.

We 'replaced' the River Liffey with Guinness Clear on St Patrick's Day (Figure 37).

Figure 37: Guinness parody Facebook post announcing the Liffey Stunt

We offered product sampling, such as 'hydration stations' at the games (Figure 38).

Figure 38: 'Hydration station' events and product sampling

And we created home brew kits – so you could make Guinness Clear at home (Figure 39).

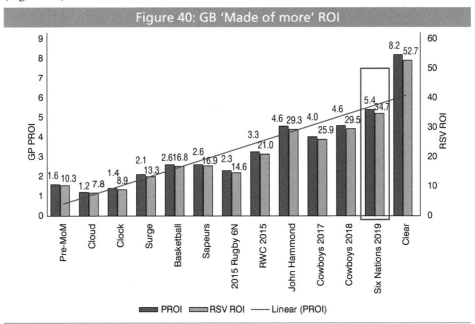

Figure 39: Guinness Clear home brew kits

Guinness Clear was encouraging people to drink a little less, but the power of the two campaigns ensured that when people chose to drink, more would choose Guinness.

We continued our run of growing ROIs

Stretching 'Made of more' beyond stories of elite male players delivered, using the power of our association with rugby, our strongest gross profit ROI in GB to date (Figure 40).

Figure 40: GB 'Made of more' ROI

Source: Data2Decisions Econometric Modelling, 2012–2019

In the thick of a tough trading environment in Ireland, the 'Six Nations' ROI dipped below the highs of 'Compton Cowboys' (although it beat our previous rugby work and was still more than twice as effective as our pre-'Made of more' ROI) (Figure 41).

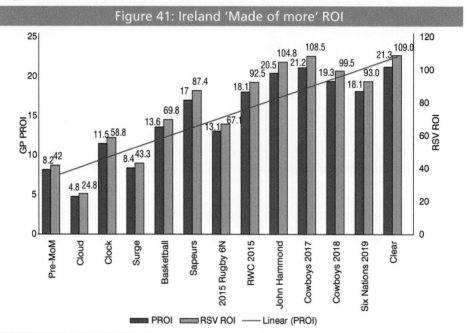

Figure 41: Ireland 'Made of more' ROI

Source: Data2Decisions Econometric Modelling, 2012–2019

The effect of sponsoring the Six Nations and the cost associated is accounted for elsewhere in our econometric model – these data are simply the return from media spend.

Additionally, this is not simply the effect of a seasonal Six Nations sales increase: the data show we have consistently increased the scale of the total volume uplift where 'Made of more' has been deployed in rugby (Figures 42 and 43).

We have also been able to isolate the specific effect of our responsible drinking initiative.

'Guinness Clear' delivered the highest gross profit ROI we had ever seen, in both markets.

Comparing the 'Guinness Clear' ROI with conventional advertising campaigns requires a caveat: this was a PR and digitally-led idea, with a lower budget and considerable risk attached. We could not guarantee that the idea would be picked up, and content shared.

These risks are mitigated when the idea is good, making the ROI remarkable.

Our shift into brand behaviour, rather than just brand storytelling, paid off.

This is the highest ROI we have seen for 'Made of more', and the highest ROI reported in an IPA paper for the beer category, by some distance (Figures 44 and 45).[20]

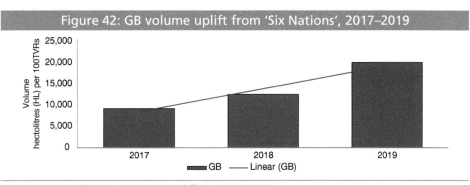

Figure 42: GB volume uplift from 'Six Nations', 2017–2019

Source: Data2Decisions Econometric Modelling, 2012–2019

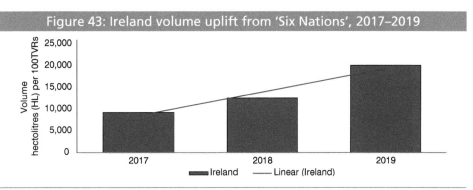

Figure 43: Ireland volume uplift from 'Six Nations', 2017–2019

Source: Data2Decisions Econometric Modelling, 2012–2019

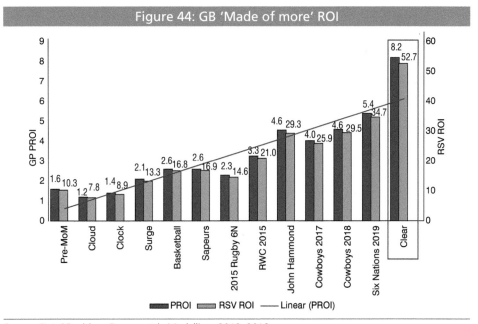

Figure 44: GB 'Made of more' ROI

Source: Data2Decisions Econometric Modelling, 2012–2019

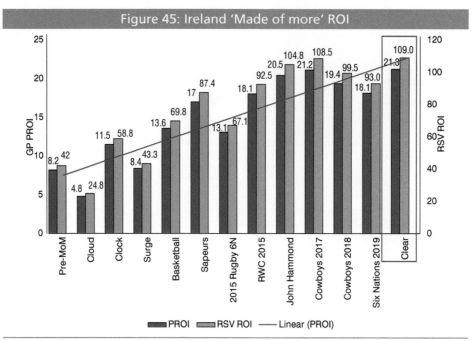

Figure 45: Ireland 'Made of more' ROI

PROI RSV ROI Linear (PROI)

Source: Data2Decisions Econometric Modelling, 2012–2019

Step Three: Winning the Rugby World Cup

The final 2019 campaign was an epic 'Made of more' story that captured the spirit of carving your own path against naysayers – 'Liberty Fields' (Figure 46).

Figure 46: Recreation of Liberty Fields celebrating their victory in Tokyo in 1989

Liberty Fields Rugby Club was the first women's rugby team in Japan. Their story is a joyful celebration of women who pursued their love of rugby in the face of naysayers and societal convention. It is a story of strength of character, love of team and self-belief, paving the way for women, and diverse representation in rugby (Figure 47).

Figure 47: 'Liberty Fields', 60"

We open on Tokyo's cityscape at night and a commuter train powers along carrying weary salarymen home. They look at the sight of a drenched woman, alone, in a strange part of town, straining every sinew to try and outsprint a train.

VO: **Some saw that as strange**

Title: **Tokyo 1989**

Cut to a woman at home doing squats with a heavy sack of rice on each shoulder. She is soaked in sweat as her mother-in-law looks on, mystified.

VO: **As troublemakers**

Cut to the interior of a corporate boardroom as grey-suited male managers sit around a long table.

An office lady tries to pour tea but two of her fingers are bound together with a tape and a splint. Much to the disapproval of one of the managers, she spills the tea, flashing a grin and a broken tooth.

VO: **As an embarrassment**

Cut to the Liberty Fields team in action, interspersed with documentary footage of the time. Despite the mud and fierceness, there are smiles all around. They pile on top of one another and gather in the bar after the game.

VO: **All we ever saw was a team**

We see the original photograph of the Liberty Fields team as the women gather together with a Guinness to celebrate joyously as one.

Title: **Pioneers of Women's Rugby**
              Guinness. Made of More

A documentary provided further detail of our group's story (Figure 48).

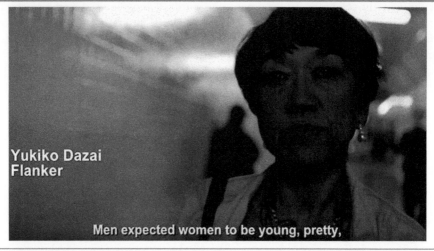

Figure 48: 'Liberty Fields' documentary

Social media enabled us to tell the story from every angle with GIFs, boomerangs and cinemographs (Figure 49).

Figure 49: 'Liberty Fields' social media

An ITV special saw former England players Maggie Alphonsi and Danielle Waterman travel to Tokyo, delving into struggles women face in sports (Figure 50).

Figure 50: Maggie Alphonsi and Danielle Waterman travel to Tokyo

We launched the Liberty Fields Fund with *Stylist* magazine, offering women's rugby teams the chance to win £15,000 (Figure 51).

Figure 51: Liberty Fields Fund

An all-female panel discussed the path forward for women and minorities in sport with Will Greenwood (Figure 52).

Figure 52: Discussion panel – Will Greenwood, Heather Fisher, Alex Danson and Ama Agbeze

We took over venues and transported attendees to Japan (Figure 53).

Figure 53: Flat Iron Square, London

Time zones meant matches were played in the early hours, so we inspired people with new servings (Figure 54).

Figure 54: Instagram – (left) Guinness and a burger, (right) Guinness collaboration with 232 Blend Coffee

Did this phase of 'Made of more' deliver the impact seen in previous years?

'Liberty Fields' should continue the trend of rising ROIs

As with 'Compton Cowboys' in 2018, we don't yet have the modelling for 'Liberty Fields'.[21] But as with 'Compton Cowboys', we believe it will at least be in line with the enhanced ROI performance reported elsewhere in the paper, because: [22]

- Media share of voice for Guinness remained approximately the same (or slightly less) for 'Liberty Fields' as it had been for previous campaigns.[23]
- Our Kantar post-testing showed that the campaign was highly regarded by drinkers (in fact, it's our highest-scoring ad ever).
- Our equity scores have remained strong.

The total effect of 'Made of more'

This paper isn't just about 2018 and 2019, it's the full eight years of our idea.

'Made of more' has been pushed forward by constant learning and a desire to improve. Combining creativity, effectiveness and longevity in a way matched by few other communications ideas.

This is unusual given all we know about the benefits of consistency and longevity. Most major beer players (including IPA Effectiveness Awards winners) have changed their brand idea whilst 'Made of more' has been running (Figure 55).

Figure 55: Brand ideas/taglines used by beer brands, 2012–2020							
	Guinness	Fosters	Heineken	San Miguel	Budweiser	Carling	Carlsberg
2012	Made of more	Good call	Open your mind	A life well lived	Made for music	Brilliantly British, brilliantly refreshing	That calls for a Carlsberg
2013							
2014				The best is to come	This Bud's for you		
2015							
2016		For the thirsty		Exploring the world since 1890	King of beers	Refreshingly perfect	Probably ...
2017							
2018			That's Heineken				
2019						Made local	
2020							

This consistency has paid back handsomely for Guinness' core objectives.

Marketing objective

Drive and sustain distinctiveness and salience measures to lead the market and stand out in a sea of competition.

By 2019, Guinness had the strongest brand equity in Ireland, and the second strongest in GB (based on Kantar's analysis of the entire beer category, quantifying brand impact based on distinctiveness, meaning and salience measures) (Figures 56 and 57).

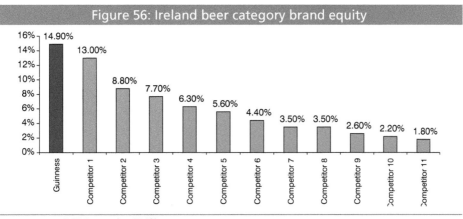

Figure 56: Ireland beer category brand equity

Source: Kantar BGS Perception F19[24]

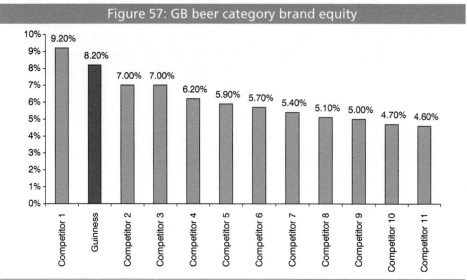

Figure 57: GB beer category brand equity

Source: Kantar BGS Perception F19

It was vital we maintained our distinctiveness and as we became more popular didn't start looking just like every other beer. Both markets saw an uplift (Figure 58).

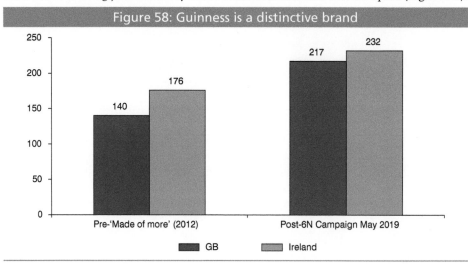

Figure 58: Guinness is a distinctive brand

Source: Kantar. Note these figures are measured as indices rather than percentages and are benchmarked against the category average.

In a more competitive environment, salience was key. Brand fame can be evidenced in improvements versus category average before and after 'Made of more' (Figures 59 and 60).

In the period 2012–2019, Kantar have tweaked their model. While these metrics are not precisely like-for-like, they are very much comparable and show the shift and impact that 'Made of more' has had on our marketing metrics.

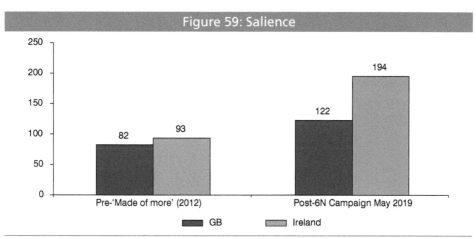

Figure 59: Salience

Source: Kantar. Note these figures are measured as indices rather than percentages and are benchmarked against the category average.

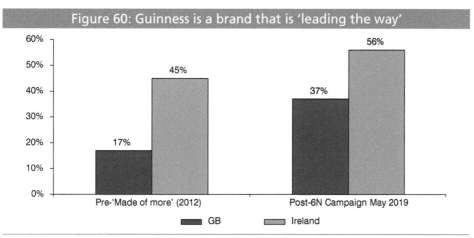

Figure 60: Guinness is a brand that is 'leading the way'

Source: Kantar. Note these figures are measured as percentages.

Communications objective

Produce highly creative communications to drive brand fame, make an impact in culture (in 2018–2019 this would mean making Guinness the number one brand associated with the rugby and driving genuine responsible drinking behavioural change).

The 'Made of more' work in this paper has received 180 creative awards including wins at all major international award festivals.[25]

It has won 20 Cannes Lions, including Gold in the illustrious Glass Lions for Gareth's 'Never Alone', and last year received the new addition of Gold in Brand Experience and Activation for 'Guinness Clear', as we drove 'Made of more' into behavioural change.

'Made of more' work has created growing waves in culture since 2012 (Figure 61).

Figure 61: 'Made of more' campaigns

'Surge' was covered in surf magazines; half a million people watched our 'making of' film.

'Basketball' had the Huffington Post 'utterly captivated'.

Rugby in 2014 had 66% of people claiming they would tell their friends about it, including England's captain Dylan Hartley, who tweeted about it.

Rugby in 2015 earned 38m video views; Gareth Thomas presented a BBC documentary about homophobia in sport; we were the brand most associated with the 2015 RWC; and it won a Gold Lion at Cannes.

John Hammond's story was championed by Lianne LaHavas; shown at the Manchester Film Festival; connected to coverage of racism at the Grammy's and Oscars; 80% of those who saw the ad online also explored our documentary on the topic.

'Compton Cowboys' sparked an immense social media reaction; despite little paid-for support, people spent over two minutes watching Cowboys content; the story has since been commissioned as a Hollywood movie.

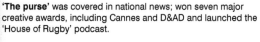

'The purse' was covered in national news; won seven major creative awards, including Cannes and D&AD and launched the 'House of Rugby' podcast.

'Clear' resulted in a new bar call; Guinness Clear at any pub or game; 74% positive sentiment in social media; doubling the Diageo video view-through rate;[25] *Forbes* magazine dubbed us 'masters of the head fake'; it won a Gold Lion at Cannes.

'Liberty Fields' sparked a debate about the role of women in sport across international news outlets, and, with Stylist, set up a £15k prize grant available to women's rugby teams in GB and Ireland.

In terms of our specific 2018–2019 objectives:

- Guinness, within our first year of investment in the Six Nations, became the number-one brand associated with rugby. [26]
- Attribution jumped to 25% in GB and Ireland (12 percentage points higher than the Royal Bank of Scotland in their final year of sponsorship). [27]
- Guinness became the beer brand most associated with responsible drinking (Table 1).

Table 1: Guinness became the beer brand most associated with responsible drinking

Ireland			Great Britain		
Brands	Prompted awareness	Spontaneous awareness	Brands	Prompted awareness	Spontaneous awareness
Guinness	56%	52%	Guinness	18%	9%
Heineken	36%	33%	Heineken	17%	5%
Carlsberg	17%	11%	Carlsberg	12%	3%
Budweiser	15%	9%	Budweiser	12%	4%
Stella Artois	11%	0%	Stella Artois	11%	5%
Carling	7%	0%	Carling	11%	0%
Coors Light	5%	0%	Coors Light	11%	0%
Fosters	3%	0%	Fosters	9%	3%

Source: Kantar GB and IOI Responsible Drinking Behaviour, 2018

The majority agreed 'Guinness Clear' made it acceptable to drink water in a pub (an effect amplified amongst rugby fans) (Figure 62). [28]

Figure 62: Percentage agreeing that 'Guinness Clear' made it acceptable to drink water in a pub

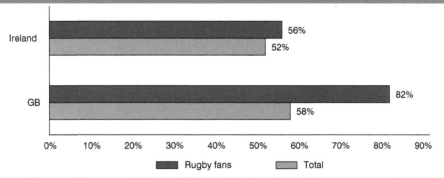

Source: Kantar, April 2019

'Guinness Clear' contributed to genuine behavioural change (Figure 63).[29]

Figure 63: Percentage moderating their alcohol intake by choosing to drink more water, and others drinking less altogether or a soft drink

Ireland	82%
GB	80%

Source: Kantar, April 2019

Commercial objective

Increase ROI every year (versus pre-'Made of more' and versus beer category), to deliver profit in the face of rising costs while sustaining value share in Ireland and growing in GB.

Market share

Most other beers our size suffered market share decline during this period. But Guinness market share grew (Figure 64).

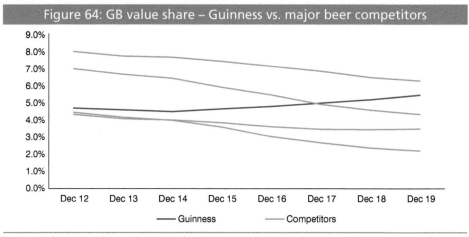

Figure 64: GB value share – Guinness vs. major beer competitors

Guinness —— Competitors ——

Source: Nielsen December 2012 – December 2019

Guinness has held dominant market share in Ireland for years and is the main potential source of volume for beer brands seeking to grow. Thanks to 'Made of more', we've sustained our position (Figure 65).

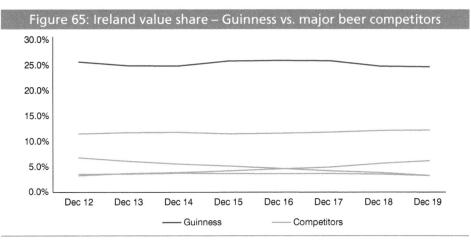

Figure 65: Ireland value share – Guinness vs. major beer competitors

Source: Nielsen December 2012 – December 2019

This share performance has actually been achieved with a marginal *decrease* in Guinness' share of voice in GB and Ireland.[30]

Data2Decisions has conducted econometric modelling on the effect of the campaign. Our ROI has built with every 'Made of more' campaign in GB, and almost all work in Ireland. This has been achieved by learning from the performance of our work and adapting creative to remain culturally resonant – but always being backed by the same idea (Figures 66 and 67).

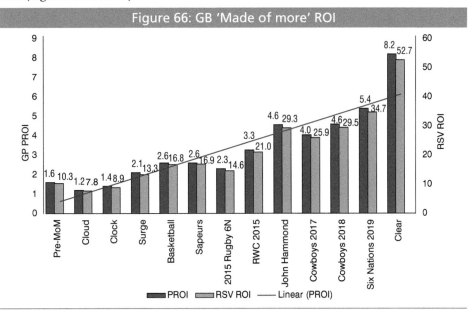

Figure 66: GB 'Made of more' ROI

Source: Data2Decisions Econometric Modelling, 2012–2019

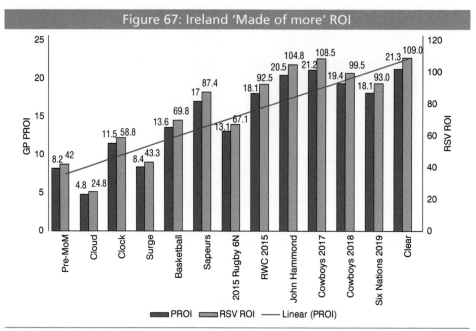

Figure 67: Ireland 'Made of more' ROI

Source: Data2Decisions Econometric Modelling, 2012–2019

Revenue ROI

We increased our return on investment versus pre-'Made of more' work with a more profitable return than competitors, growing sales and share. Over eight years, 'Made of more' revenue ROI is £24.56 per £1 spent, doubling the pre-'Made of more' revenue ROI (Figure 68).[31]

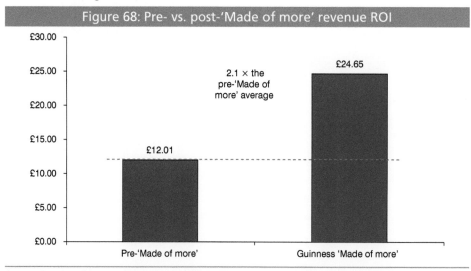

Figure 68: Pre- vs. post-'Made of more' revenue ROI

Source: Data2Decisions Econometric Modelling, 2012–2019. Note: This is a blended GB/Ireland figure.

Our most recent campaigns delivered 2.6 times the pre-'Made of more' revenue ROI (Figure 69).

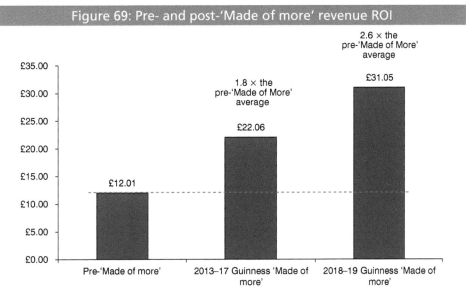

Figure 69: Pre- and post-'Made of more' revenue ROI

Source: Data2Decisions Econometric Modelling, 2012–2019

We achieved our highest revenue ROI in GB with our most recent 'Made of more' work (Figure 70).

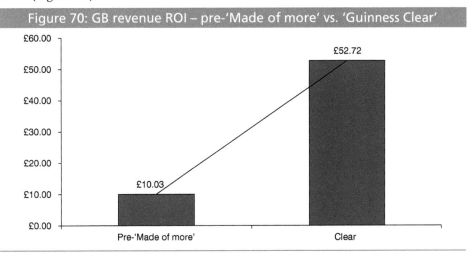

Figure 70: GB revenue ROI – pre-'Made of more' vs. 'Guinness Clear'

Source: Data2Decisions Econometric Modelling, 2012–2019

This is now the highest recorded revenue ROI for a beer brand in the IPA awards – comfortably ahead of the Grand-Prix-winning ROI from 2014 (Table 2).

Table 2: Revenue ROI from previous IPA awards		
Brand	**Year**	**Revenue ROI**
Guinness (Clear, GB)	**2020**	**£52.70**
Fosters	2014	£32
Guinness	**2020**	**£24.65**
Guinness	**2018**	**£22.06**
Guinness	**2016**	**£19.90**
Coors Light	2016	£17
Stella Artois	2000	£12
Budweiser	2002	£6
Bud Ice	1998	£5
Stella Artois	1996	£5
Marston's Pedigree	1994	£4
Stella Artois	1992	£2
Budweiser	2018	−£0.85

Source: WARC/IPA. Budweiser's 'Light up the nation' media ROI was 1.52 Canadian dollars, which has been converted to GBP, where 1 GBP = 1.79 CAD. No ROI was noted for Heineken's Silver-winning 2018 paper, 'A game changer: How Heineken reinvented its Champions League communications'.

Profit ROI

The total 'Made of more' gross profit ROI is £4.81 per £1 spent: we have more than doubled the pre-'Made of more' gross profit ROI. 'Made of more' has now delivered a gross profit ROI 85% higher than previous campaigns (Figure 71).

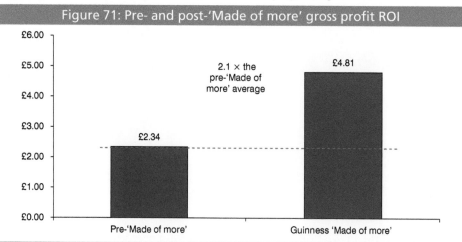

Figure 71: Pre- and post-'Made of more' gross profit ROI

Source: Data2Decisions Econometric Modelling, 2012–2019

Our most recent campaigns delivered 2.6 times the pre-'Made of more' gross profit ROI (Figure 72).

Figure 72: Pre- and post-'Made of more' gross profit ROI

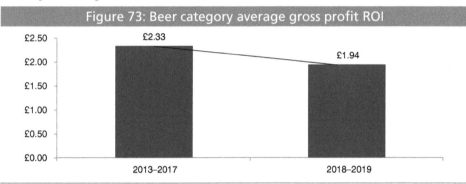

Source: Data2Decisions Econometric Modelling, 2012–2019

This is impressive considering the beer category average gross profit ROI declined in this period (Figure 73).

Figure 73: Beer category average gross profit ROI

Source: Data2Decisions Econometric Modelling, 2012–2019

'Made of more' is the most profitable beer campaign in the history of the IPA awards (Table 3).

Table 3: Beer campaigns from previous IPA awards

Brand	Year	Gross profit ROI
Guinness	**2020**	**£4.81**
Guinness	**2018**	**£4.33**
Coors Light	2016	£4.13
Guinness	**2016**	**£3.88**
Carling	1996	£2.08
Stella Artois	1992	£1.92
Marston's Pedigree	1994	£1.64

Source: WARC/IPA

The cumulative effects of these profit ROI figures is **£518m** in profit for the brand over the life of 'Made of more'.[32]

The power of our idea is evidenced below: our advertising outperforms other brands of comparable size and level of spend (Figure 74).

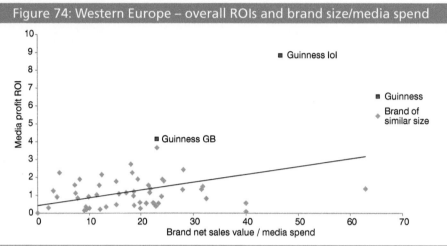

Figure 74: Western Europe – overall ROIs and brand size/media spend

Source: Data2Decisions Econometric Modelling, 2012–2019[33]

Can we define now how much 'Made of more' is worth?

Our modelling enables us to compare the results of 'Made of more' with the likely performance of that media spend had we continued with previous advertising ideas. Those ideas delivered ROI just above the beer category average; 'Made of more' delivers an ROI more than double the category average (Figure 75).

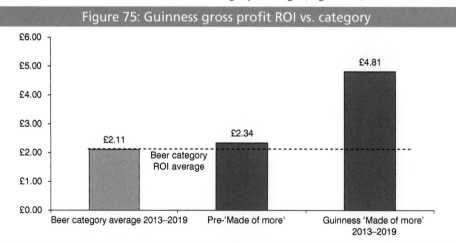

Figure 75: Guinness gross profit ROI vs. category

Source: Data2Decisions Econometric Modelling, 2012–2019

Choosing 'Made of more' and sticking with it delivered an estimated extra £1 billion in sales for Guinness in GB and Ireland over those eight years 2012–2019[34]

(versus the hypothetical scenario of investing the same media money in the pre-'Made of more' work and the lower ROI associated with it) (Figure 76).[35]

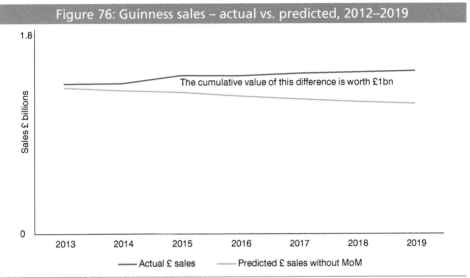

Figure 76: Guinness sales – actual vs. predicted, 2012–2019

The cumulative value of this difference is worth £1bn

Sales £ billions

—— Actual £ sales   —— Predicted £ sales without MoM

Source: Data2Decisions Econometric Modelling, 2012–2019

This is not the total effect of our advertising over that period (that figure is much greater), it is the difference in the effect of the ROI we achieved versus the effect of the pre-'Made of more' ROI.

It is the likely value of 'Made of more' as an idea.

Discounting other factors

Econometric modelling conducted by Data2Decisions has isolated the effect of the communications when calculating the ROI. This section demonstrates how none of the other key sale drivers could have been responsible for the continued success in commercial results for Guinness.

Price

Our econometric modelling accounts for the effect of price, so we can be confident that the results are due to the effect of our marketing communications. And in fact, there has been little change in the price index of Guinness versus the rest of the market since the start of the 'Made of more' campaign in both markets.

Price promotions

In this paper we have focused on the impact of our campaign on draught Guinness sold in pubs and bars (the on-trade), as this channel accounts for at least 80% of Guinness sales. We have excluded a detailed examination of the off-trade in this paper, partially due to the complexity of the range of products and pack sizes sold through this channel and the vast array of price promotions that inevitably increases the complexity. Price promotion in the on-trade of alcohol is minimal and therefore not a factor.

In-outlet activations

Guinness has invested in a number of in-outlet activations in the on-trade over the analysed period, with marketing materials distributed to pubs around key events, including major rugby tournaments and matches. The impact of these activations on sales has been captured in the econometric models.

Product

Guinness launched a range of new products over the period in question, including a range of new porters, a golden ale and a new lager. We have not included sales from these new products as part of our volume sales, value share or ROI calculations; even though the 'Made of more' campaign will have driven additional sales for these products.

Distribution

Distribution in Ireland has remained steady at a very high level, but declined in GB. If anything, distribution has applied negative pressure on sales and market share in that market (Figure 77).

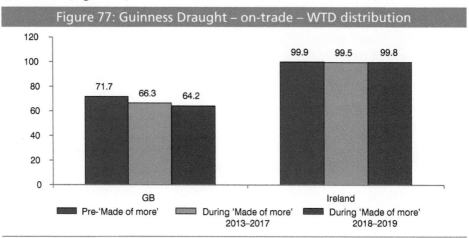

Figure 77: Guinness Draught – on-trade – WTD distribution

Source: Nielsen/CGA, 2013-19

Number of pubs

Success cannot be attributed to a growth in the number of pubs. As evidenced earlier in this paper, pub numbers continued to decline in both markets.

Economy

The effect of any economic growth (and beer trends driven by the economy) has been captured in the econometric models. We have also shown that market share has turned around for Guinness in both markets since the start of 'Made of more', which accounts for any change in overall beer consumption driven by macroeconomic factors.

Spend level

Media spend levels for Guinness have remained relatively consistent across the full 'Made of more' period. There was no sustained share-of-voice advantage for Guinness during the campaign compared to the pre-campaign period (Figure 78).

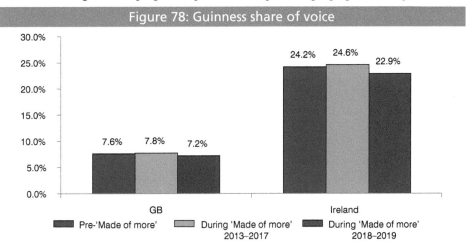

Figure 78: Guinness share of voice

Source: Carat Nielsen Addynamix, 2013–2019

Weather

Weather does influence Guinness sales over time. Perhaps unsurprisingly, colder weather drives an increase in Guinness sales whilst warmer weather dampens them as consumers tend to switch to other options like lager. On average, over the period, temperatures were slightly higher in GB and slightly lower in Ireland. So these temperature shifts would have had a small negative impact on GB sales and a small positive impact in Ireland. Each effect has been controlled in the econometric models (Figure 79).

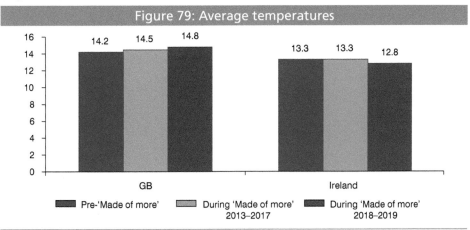

Figure 79: Average temperatures

Source: World Weather Online

Conclusion

Campaigns as powerful as 'Made of more' don't come along often.

The chance to document the evolution of an idea over an eight-year period and isolate the reasons for success are rare. And they are the reason why the IPA Effectiveness Awards exist.

More than anything else, it is an illustration of the power of the long term.

Ideas get better and better over time, with increasing returns for each new iteration, if they are kept fresh, interesting and culturally connected.

It's a simple formula: consistency × creativity.

It has produced an idea that has delivered an extra £1 billion over eight years than would have been achieved had the media been invested in less effective ideas.

The story of 'Made of more' is a story that any brand could have achieved.

Any brand with the rigour to define an idea that reaches to the heart of their brand meaning and unites it with a powerful truth about their consumers.

Any brand with the creative flair to turn that idea into world-class executions that win creative awards each time.

Any brand with the discipline to stick with that idea when times were tough and to understand the difference between idea and execution.

But of course, Guinness isn't any brand.

It is 'Made of more'.

Appendix: 'Made of more' campaigns 2012–2019

'Basketball': https://www.youtube.com/watch?v=iiB3YNTcsAA
'Sapeurs': https://www.youtube.com/watch?v=66HuFrMZWMo
'Jonny Wilkinson': https://www.youtube.com/watch?v=lJhw0FeKaU0
'David & Goliath': https://www.youtube.com/watch?v=JyE56rF6mU8
'Mind over matter': https://www.youtube.com/watch?v=wHu6ZM7gDbs
'Irrepressible spirit': https://www.youtube.com/watch?v=oK9ioFs1i20
'Never alone': https://www.youtube.com/watch?v=xFTUTfiUMeM
'The right path': https://youtu.be/534aGB00VC4
'Intolerant champion': https://www.youtube.com/watch?v=S4y6kBYF084
'Compton Cowboys': https://youtu.be/9HWnO5XZf2M
'Purse':https://www.youtube.com/watch?v=W4ao5033FfY
'Sisters': https://www.guinness.com/en-gb/advertising/sisters/
'Guinness Clear':https://www.youtube.com/watch?v=907B0pAed_k
'Liberty Fields': https://www.youtube.com/watch?v=HJQDto9pSUI

Notes

1   Data2Decisions Econometric Modelling, 2012–2019.
2   Data2Decisions Econometric Modelling, 2012–2019.
3   Assuming we had the same level of media spend.
4   Great Britain = GB; Ireland = Republic of Ireland and Northern Ireland.
5   Data2Decisions Econometric Modelling, 2012–2019.

6   Data2Decisions Econometric Modelling, 2012–2019; the difference in the effect of the ROI we did achieve versus the scenario of sticking with the pre-'Made of more' communications idea and associated ROI.

7   In Europe and the US, it is mainly Guinness Draught (the famous pint with the creamy head), also available in can form; while in Africa and south-east Asia, Guinness is bottled as Foreign Extra Stout.

8   'Made of more' runs globally. This paper tells the story of the effect of the idea in our key markets, GB and Ireland.

9   Data2Decisions econometrics, cited in IPA 'Guinness "Made of More" 2012–2018' *Advertising Works 24*, London: IPA 2018.

10 Data2Decisions econometrics, cited in IPA 2018.

11 Data2Decisions Econometric Modelling, 2012–2019.

12 The Drinks Industry Group of Ireland: http://www.drinksindustry.ie/news/news-and-press/almost-1500-less-pubs-in-ireland-last-year-than–2005-a-17-1-decrease/

13 British Beer & Pub Association: https://beerandpub.com/statistics/pub-numbers/

14 Diageo Internal Data, 2019.

15 Global Data Database: No. of Trademark Beer Brands by Market.

16 Nielsen, 2018.

17 IPA *Making Sense: The Commercial Media Landscape*, London, IPA, 2019.

18 79% of the available TV audience would tune in to ITV to watch England play South Africa in the World Cup Final: https://www.theguardian.com/sport/2019/nov/03/rugby-world-cup-final-tv-figures-yearly-best-12m-peak–2019

19 Diageo qualitative research 2018.

20 Data2Decisions Econometric Modelling, 2012–2019; IPA/ WARC.

21 Our econometric analysis is completed by Data2Decisions at the end of our financial year, every year, which runs from June to July. We will receive the next wave of data in August 2020.

22 All of these statements are backed by Nielsen data, Kantar Millward Brown data and Data2Decisions across the 2018-19 period.

23 Carat / Nielsen Addynamix, 2018-19.

24 Competitor brand names anonymised for publication in compliance with Diageo corporate data policy.

25 AMV BBDO collation of all global creative awards.

26 Kantar Six Nations Post-Campaign Analysis, 2018.

27 Combined evaluation from Diageo C&E agencies, March 2019.

28 Kantar – Guinness: Responsible Drinking Fast Forward Lab – Omnibus, April 2019.

29 Kantar – Guinness: Responsible Drinking Fast Forward Lab – Omnibus, April 2019.

30 Carat / Nielsen Addynamix, 2018-19.

31 Data2Decisions Econometric Modelling, 2012–2019.

32 Data2Decisions Econometric Modelling, 2012–2019.

33 Brand size is a key determinant of ROI and that ROI can diminish as spend increases. This chart plots media profit ROI vs. net sales value divided by media spend for brands modelled in the last year. It shows how ROI increases in line with net sales value/media spend and how ROI performance varies for different brand and country combinations. Guinness delivers an ROI far beyond what we would expect given brand size and media spend.

34 Data2Decisions Econometric Modelling, 2012–2019.

35 Data2Decisions Econometric Modelling, 2012–2019.

John Lewis & Partners

John Lewis: An amazing decade

By Charlotte Wood, adam&eveDDB
Contributing authors: Tom Roach, Les Binet, Saima Vohra and Martin Beverley, adam&eveDDB; Matthew Philip, Manning Gottlieb OMD; Amy Warwick, Neustar Econometrics

Credited companies: Manning Gottlieb OMD, System1

Summary

John Lewis ads are almost synonymous with UK Christmas advertising. This paper covers the creative and media principles and learnings drawn from the brand's Christmas campaigns from 2010 to 2019. It estimates that, over that period of time, Christmas TV advertising, increasingly supported by other touchpoints, helped the group grow 4.4 times faster than the average across the non-food retail category. Modelling calculates advertising drove £1.2bn incremental sales and £411m net profit, with a profit ROI of up to £10 per £1 invested. The paper details the client and agency partnership and creative choices behind the brand's distinctive and effective emotional storytelling.

Editor's comment

By producing consistently memorable and effective Christmas advertising year after year, John Lewis has demonstrated to the retail category the business value of emotionally impactful advertising and encouraged other advertisers to raise their games. The judges thought this case set out with impeccable clarity how John Lewis worked in partnership with its agencies to balance consistent creative and media principles against the need to evolve and keep audiences engaged for a decade.

Client comment

Emma Wood, Senior Marketing Manager, Brand, John Lewis & Partners

We couldn't be prouder of what we've achieved together over the last decade with our agency partners adam&eveDDB and Manning Gottlieb OMD. Everything we've achieved with this campaign is testament to the power of that partnership.

Being part of the John Lewis Partnership means everyone who works here owns the business. So it's essential that we treat every pound as our own, and that every pound spent on advertising is paid back several times over. And every year for 10 years the campaign has done exactly this – every year it works harder and harder for us commercially.

The fact that we're a Partnership also means we have a very distinctive culture, driven by a strong belief in doing right by our customers. Which means that just as important as the campaign's commercial results is the way those results are achieved. And we're hugely proud of how those commercial results are achieved.

The ads reflect and reinforce the esteem in which the John Lewis & Partners brand is held. They give every Partner an enormous sense of pride in the Partnership. They mirror the way we go about retailing – always respecting the customer, never resorting to the hard sell, and everything made to the highest possible standards.

We relish the challenge we face each year to bring new 'creative magic' to this important moment in our marketing calendar. The way it has evolved for us over the years is something we could never have foreseen when it started a decade ago.

Becoming part of the signalling of the start of Christmas is a privilege we hold very dearly. Seeing the happy faces of children clutching a new Monty, Buster or Edgar toy in our stores is just the icing on the cake.

Introduction

From the vantage point of 2020, it's hard to imagine Christmas without the John Lewis ads. To the public they've become a much-loved part of Christmas. And to ad land, they're amongst the most written about, dissected, and awarded in the history of UK advertising. But much, much more important of course is the far greater impact the ads have had in the real world.

This paper tells the full, and as yet untold, story of the campaign throughout the entire 2010s, from 'Remember the feeling' at the start of the decade to 'Excitable Edgar' at its close. It demonstrates its full commercial impact, including the incremental £1.2bn sales and £411m profit it has generated with a profit ROI of up to £10, the 4.4 times faster growth than UK non-food retail and the 10-point market-share growth it helped John Lewis achieve over the decade. It will outline the lessons the industry can learn from a decade of consistent creative excellence. And it will reveal the secrets behind how we did it.

Introducing John Lewis

Founded in 1864, John Lewis[1] is a UK department store with 51 shops and a strong e-commerce business. Unusually, the John Lewis Partnership[2] is mutually owned, making it the UK's largest employee co-operative.

A tough time for UK retail

The 2010s: the UK's 'lost decade'

Our story covers 2010 to 2019. This period has been called Britain's 'lost decade': a decade of low growth, low wages, low consumer confidence, a weak housing market, and economic austerity. For high street retailers and department stores, the pressures were acute and intensifying (Figure 1 and Table 1).

2009: a tough market

In 2009, the pressures facing John Lewis were huge. After years of solid growth, like-for-like sales were −3.4% and operating profit had dropped by 26%. Like-for-like sales had been negative for 16 months and were below the British Retail Consortium's average.

Andy Street, the then Managing Director said in 2009:

'Last year was probably the most tricky in my time at the Partnership … the year ahead is going to be equally difficult, if not harder.'

It's often forgotten, but in 2009 the brand had a low profile and was respected but not loved. For many it seemed expensive, aloof and out of touch with the times.

Figure 1: A tough time for retail

Table 1: UK retail failures

	Retail companies failing	Stores affected	Employees affected
2019	43	2,051	46,506
2018	43	2,594	46,014
2017	44	1,383	12,225
2016	30	1,504	26,110
2015	25	728	6,845
2014	43	1,314	12,335
2013	49	2,500	25,140
2012	54	3,951	48,142

Source: Centre for Retail Research

In 2009, *Marketing* magazine said of incoming Head of Brand Communications Craig Inglis:

'Whether Inglis has inherited a poisoned chalice is open to debate. He certainly faces a considerable challenge, given that sales at the upmarket department store have been sliding.'

2009: the Christmas campaign is born

Every year, The John Lewis Partnership awards a bonus to all employees ('Partners'), depending on profits. Christmas is vital for generating those bonuses as it accounts for around 40% of profits. A successful Christmas can set the trajectory for good trading the following year.[3]

So Christmas matters a lot to the Partners at John Lewis. In 2009, adam&eve were appointed to create a Christmas campaign that would boost John Lewis' ailing sales.

No one could possibly have predicted what happened next.

An amazing decade

Ten years of amazing Christmas advertising

Far from the 2010s being a lost decade or Craig Inglis inheriting a poisoned chalice, John Lewis[4] subsequently produced 10 years of acclaimed Christmas advertising, contributing to a decade of outstanding growth (Figure 2).

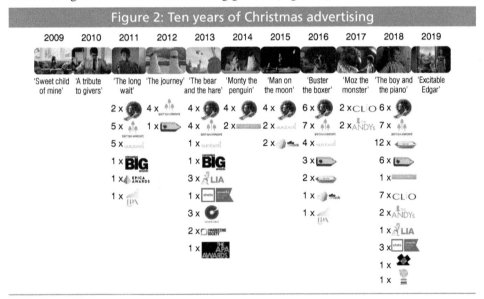

Figure 2: Ten years of Christmas advertising

Sustained creative 'purple patches' are exceptionally rare in advertising. Many brands can create a single great campaign, but few are able to achieve a full decade of consecutive 'hits'.

John Lewis' advertising success has inspired other brands and Christmas has now become the UK's Super Bowl. We're proud of the shot in the arm our campaign has given to the UK ad industry (Figure 3).

Figure 3: John Lewis-inspired Christmas advertising

Iceland	Sainsbury's	Sainsbury's
Boots	M&S	Aldi
Argos	Very	M&S

Ten years of success for John Lewis

This period of unparalleled commercial creativity kick-started and drove a period of unparalleled commercial success for John Lewis, during British retail's worst decade in history.

Many factors influenced John Lewis' performance, however advertising was a key contributor to success. From the moment our advertising began, John Lewis began to outperform its competitors, and has done so ever since. Over the decade, John Lewis has grown 4.4 times faster than competitors (Figure 4).[5]

This happened when department stores were suffering more than most retailers, due to fierce competition from online retailers like Amazon. No one weathered the storm like John Lewis, which gained 10 points in market share since the new advertising began (Figure 5).

The most consistently effective advertising of the early 21st century?

'In every marketing decade there are a couple of brands that everyone follows. Not just because the brand is brilliant, but because those in charge of it are so far ahead of everyone else that you have to keep an eye on what they do next.

Three decades ago we all looked to Levi's, then to Boddingtons, and to Tango, then Gillette, on to ŠKODA, and First Direct, and then spectacular work at Stella Artois, and Häagen-Dazs, and Cadbury, to Dove, then Tesco and most lately John Lewis.

The John Lewis work is the very epitome of contemporary brand work. It is creative. It is mass-marketed. It is emotional. It is long feeding short. It is highly distinctive. It dominates both paid and organic media. It uses TV as a platform to integrate across to other media.

And it has taken a long-term, multi-campaign approach and built the John Lewis brand into something far greater than it has ever been before.

It is among the best and most effective work of the early 21st century. And it also has Elton John.'

Mark Ritson, marketing professor, 2019

Figure 4: John Lewis sales vs. UK retail sales

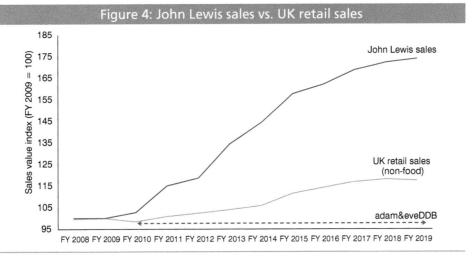

Source: ONS and John Lewis company reports

Figure 5: John Lewis sales/market share

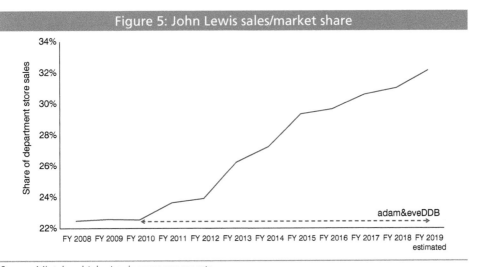

Source: Mintel and John Lewis company reports

Five big lessons

There are many ways we could choose to tell this story, but we've focused on five lessons we think the industry could learn from:

1. The power of consistency: consistency is rare and undervalued in creative agencies
2. The value in the irrational: things that don't appear to make sense can be hugely powerful
3. The power of popular: nothing matches populism when you need to make a big impact
4. Short and long: all long-term success is dependent on short-term
5. Make data your servant: use data to measure success, not to replace creativity

Lesson 1: The power of consistency

Consistency vs. innovation

Advertising people are often obsessed with the new. They worry campaigns will 'wear out' before they've even worn *in*. They mistake creativity with discontinuity, originality with total reinvention, choosing to start from scratch every time with a completely new strategy, idea or line.

With John Lewis, we may *appear* to reinvent our creative approach every year, but this belies our obsession with strategic consistency.

Consistent objectives

Since 2009, our Christmas campaigns have shared the same objectives (Figure 6).

Figure 6: Christmas campaign objectives
Commercial objectives Increase share of department store market By increasing sales during the Christmas period **Marketing objectives** Get more customers spending more By increasing store traffic By increasing propensity to shop at John Lewis for Christmas gifts **Communications objectives** Increase brand salience and emotional connection By creating Britain's most loved, shared and talked about advertising

Strategic consistency

The Christmas strategy was born in 2009, when brand, business and consumer insights suggested John Lewis shoppers wanted to be seen as *thoughtful* gift-givers, and that John Lewis – a retailer with something for everyone – could claim that space.

This led to the strategic proposition: 'John Lewis is the home of thoughtful gifting', and our first Christmas campaign 'Remember the feeling' (Figure 7).

Figure 7: Insights that led to the 'thoughtful gifting' strategy

Business insight	**Brand insight**	**Customer insight**
John Lewis makes around 40% of its profits over Christmas, and has more products than anyone on the high street. So, no matter who you are buying for, you will find the perfect gift at John Lewis	John Lewis is a calm, understated brand in all that it does. At a time of glitz and celebrities, John Lewis is more considered and thoughtful in everything that the brand does	John Lewis appeals to an affluent customer base, who like to buy well, and be seen to do so. When it comes to buying presents, they like to think more carefully and choose more thoughtfully

John Lewis is the home of thoughtful gifting

The following year, we returned to the same strategy. The creative brief has remained the same ever since – it's tight enough to focus the mind, and expansive enough to excite it.

Whilst we explore new creative expressions and different stories of 'thoughtful gifting',[6] every ad is rooted in the same enduring strategy.

Executional consistency – developing our 'brand handwriting'

Over time, we've developed 'brand handwriting' – consistent elements that make the campaigns feel unmistakably 'John Lewis': small children; lovable characters; a 'rug-pull' twist; an emotional soundtrack. This handwriting is no accident: it's been honed by failure and success over a period of ten years. The evolution of the campaign's DNA is creative Darwinism in action.

In 2009, John Lewis' first ever Christmas ad, 'Remember the feeling', featured vignettes of children opening gifts, set to a cover of 'Sweet Child O' Mine' (Figure 8).

Figure 8: 'Remember the feeling', 2009

In 2010, we followed a similar approach with 'For those who care', set to 'Your Song' (Figure 9).[7]

Figure 9: 'For those who care', 2010

Research showed we had many strong 'ingredients' in place, but people weren't as emotionally engaged as we expected. This proved to be a vital lesson and we adapted our approach, moving from vignettes to a single narrative. 'The long wait' featured a small boy who couldn't wait to *give* his gifts on Christmas morning. It was a roaring success with the public (Figure 10).

Figure 10: 'The long wait', 2011

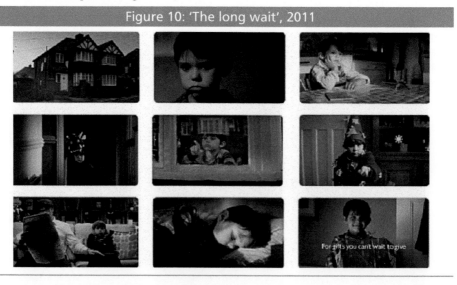

All three ads exhibit similar creative elements, but the key difference was the narrative structure. We learnt that individual stories were more powerful than vignettes. That viewers loved a plot twist. That the heart-warming moments (often involving children or characters) delighted viewers and made them talk about the ads. We also learnt a big lesson – not to spoil the magic with overt selling. In 'The long wait', the gift is never revealed. We realised the ads shouldn't be about selling specific products, they should be about the *feeling of giving*.

Over the next decade, we steadfastly applied these learnings and found that committing to consistency actually made us more creative, as TS Eliot said:

'When forced to work within a strict framework, the imagination is taxed to its utmost – and will produce its richest ideas. Given total freedom, the work is likely to sprawl.'

Balancing consistency and freshness

The challenge with consistency is maintaining freshness. We do this by flexing the story, setting, character and song, but keeping the basic premise the same. It's a bit like the James Bond franchise.

The John Lewis 'brand handwriting' – our take on distinctive brand assets

It's crucial that John Lewis ads are instantly recognisable. Most brands achieve this with rigid brand guidelines, but we've been more subtle. Our 'distinctive brand asset' is our stylistic handwriting and storytelling.

Little details matter: casting, lighting, colour grading, performance, so we over-invest in production (over the 90:10 rule of thumb) to ensure everything looks and feels like a John Lewis ad. We also use the same directors again and again – Dougal Wilson has directed half of the ads (Figure 11).

Figure 11: We ensure everything looks and feels like a John Lewis ad

Over time, the stylistic 'handwriting' has become branding in itself. Branded recognition improves every year and despite our many copycats, 80% recognise and correctly attribute a John Lewis ad (Figure 12).

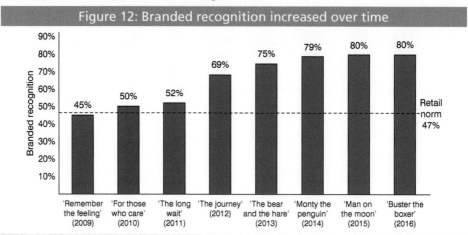

Figure 12: Branded recognition increased over time

Sources: Millward Brown (2009–2012); John Lewis Image Tracker (2013–2016); no data available after 2016.

Lesson 2: The value in the irrational

Many of the creative decisions we make seem irrational – they don't appear to make immediate business sense and only appear to have commercial logic behind them retrospectively, if at all.

Everything we do is driven by the belief that intangible creative magic is disproportionately responsible for tangible commercial impact. We make decisions that other brands might not, for fear of not being able to justify them to their CFO.

We've become accustomed to uncertainty, learnt to trust instinct over logic and allow space in the process for 'magic' to happen. We have faith in the creative process and embrace risk to generate even bigger rewards.

The power of emotion

A decade ago, emotional storytelling in retail was rare. Retailers used rational messages in their advertising to persuade shoppers to purchase from them.

John Lewis took a profoundly different approach. Instead of telling people what to *think*, we created emotional stories that made people *feel*.

People's reactions to the ads were irrational – they didn't derive any rational meaning from the ads or what they implied about John Lewis, but they were moved by them and more affectionate towards the brand as a result.[8] This emotional approach was ahead of its time, as the subsequent prevailing narrative is now that we prefer 'System 1' emotional storytelling to rational selling (Table 2).[9]

Table 2: Emotional ads condition our responses					
Time-pressured agreement	UK finished film norm	'The journey' 90" (150)	'The bear and the hare' 90" (150)	'Monty the penguin' 90" (178)	'Man on the moon' 90" (160)
Famous brand	82%	83% (+1%)	85% (+4%)	90% (+9%)	93% (+13%)
High quality	76%	86% (+13%)	86% (+14%)	87% (+14%)	86% (+13%)
Trustworthy	78%	90% (+15%)	83% (+7%)	83% (+7%)	87% (+12%)
Distinctive	69%	79% (+14%)	73% (+6%)	78% (+12%)	78% (+13%)
Different	61%	64% (+5%)	72% (+18%)	73% (+20%)	75% (+23%)

Q: In this section we're going to show you a series of words in quick succession. All you need to do is tell us whether you feel the words describe [advertised brand] by saying 'yes' or 'no' … but be quick, you only have three seconds to make your choice!
Source: Brainjuicer implicit characteristics test.
Note: Figures in brackets show deviation from norm. Ads after 'Man on the moon' have not been monitored.

Market research company System1 rates emotional intensity, which predicts long-term growth. Our ads consistently score above the norm (Figure 13).[10]

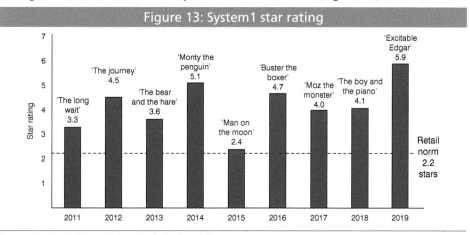

Figure 13: System1 star rating

Source: System1. Note: Only 1% of all ads get 5 stars.

John Lewis has by far and away the most emotional advertising of any retailer (Figure 14, Table 3).[11]

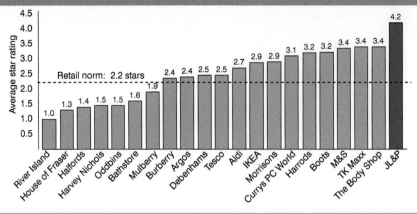

Figure 14: On average, John Lewis has the most emotional advertising of any retailer

Source: System1. All retailer ads tested by System1.

Table 3: John Lewis has six of the top 10 retail ads ever tested by System1

Advert	Brand	Star rating
'Excitable Edgar'	John Lewis & Partners / Waitrose & Partners	5.9
'Monty the penguin'	John Lewis	5.1
'Buster the boxer'	John Lewis	4.7
'The journey'	John Lewis	4.5
'Rediscover the joy of the kitchen'	IKEA	4.5
'Moz the monster'	John Lewis	4.0
'Special Because'	Boots	3.8
'Seanytunes'	Harrods	3.8
Christmas TV advert 2013	Boots	3.7
'The bear and the hare'	John Lewis	3.6

Source: System1.

Small moments and scenes stuck in people's minds vividly[12] and evoked emotions such as surprise, delight, sadness and joy. This helped gain attention, engagement and harness the motivating power of emotion that's essential for effective communication. Phil Barden noted:

'The most commercially successful ads convey the right motivational link in an emotionally engaging way. It's a rare combination but one that John Lewis has delivered perfectly and consistently; the message of the ad and the driver of the emotion are fundamentally and credibly rooted in unique truths of the

brand – the certainty that John Lewis provides of finding exactly the right gift for Christmas that will make your loved ones happy.'

Phil Barden, 2013[13]

The power of rule breaking

So much of what we do conflicts with industry best practice:

1. There's very little explicit branding (the brand only appears at the end, not throughout)
2. We feature hardly any products (and if we do, only at the end)
3. We communicate no claims, reasons to believe or news
4. We ignore the 90:10 media-spend-to-production-cost ratio (every frame must be perfect so we overspend on executional precision)
5. We don't create short time lengths for short attention spans (we're yet to see any evidence human attention spans are 'shortening' – our ads are over one minute long).

The power of creative democracy

Each Christmas campaign takes a year to develop from start to finish. The brief is open to the entire agency and anyone can submit an idea.[14] We receive around 400 stories each year and present a handful to clients. It's a costly, but essential, process generating a quantity of ideas from which we pick the best quality[15]. We're simply looking for the best story of thoughtful gifting.

The selection process is swift, based on instinct and experience from the agency and client team. We go into production around May, launch in November and get ready to do it all over again (Figure 15).

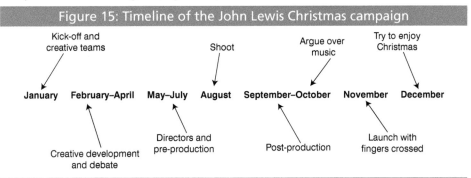

Figure 15: Timeline of the John Lewis Christmas campaign

The power of experimentation

In parallel to production, we develop the campaign's 360 communications architecture, amplifying the story in entertaining ways across multiple channels. Our aim is making as much 'noise' around the ad as possible, for as long as possible, across three key phases: 'Tease', 'Launch' and 'Sustain' (Figure 16).[16]

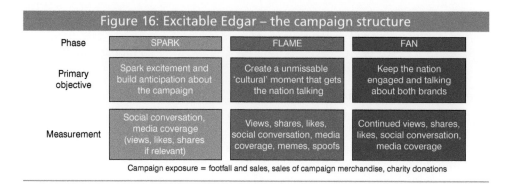

Figure 16: Excitable Edgar – the campaign structure

Phase	SPARK	FLAME	FAN
Primary objective	Spark excitement and build anticipation about the campaign	Create a unmissable 'cultural' moment that gets the nation talking	Keep the nation engaged and talking about both brands
Measurement	Social conversation, media coverage (views, likes, shares if relevant)	Views, shares, likes, social conversation, media coverage, memes, spoofs	Continued views, shares, likes, social conversation, media coverage

Campaign exposure = footfall and sales, sales of campaign merchandise, charity donations

In 'Tease', we excite the nation about the upcoming ad, hinting at what's to come.

In 'Launch', we create a huge 'surge' of interest that gets the ad trending on Twitter and the news. We launch as early as possible (now 6am), and via partners:[17] they're given the ad to release on their own social media accounts, despite the risk that it may be 'leaked' (Figure 17).

Figure 17: Partner launch

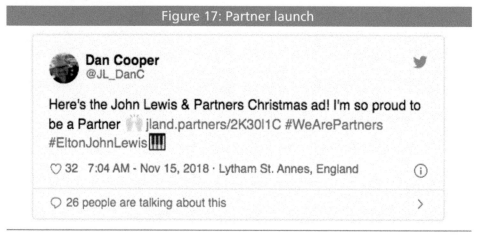

In 'Sustain', we prolong excitement and engagement. People love the characters, so we create ways to interact with them and their worlds, on social and in-store. In 2016, we recreated Buster's trampoline in-store where, with VR headsets, shoppers could bounce along with the characters. In 2019, we created an Edgar emoji and Snapchat filter that enabled people to 'breathe' fire like Edgar (Figures 18, 19 and 20).

Figure 18: In 'Sustain', people interact with the characters and their worlds

Figure 19: Campaign assets for 'Excitable Edgar', 2019

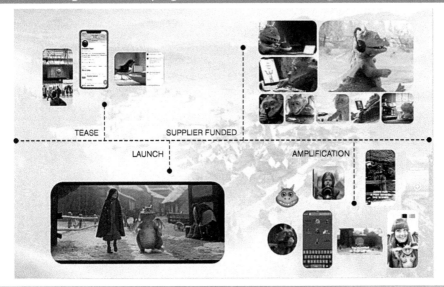

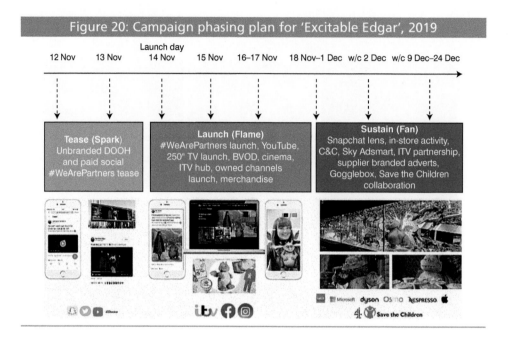

Figure 20: Campaign phasing plan for 'Excitable Edgar', 2019

Every year we experiment with new media platforms.[18] If they work, we adopt them into the following year's plan, which grows our campaign (Figure 21).

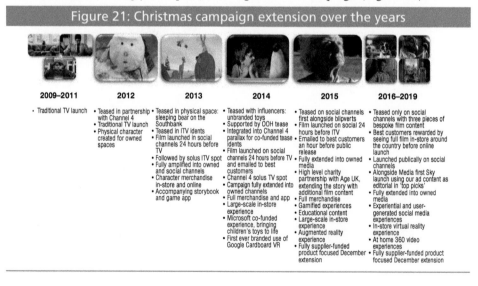

Figure 21: Christmas campaign extension over the years

The power of music

The right music can generate an incredible emotional response and is a prime example of why 'little details' matter so much. Music increases attention, recall and purchase intent, and can increase sales effects by 20%–30% (Figure 22).[19]

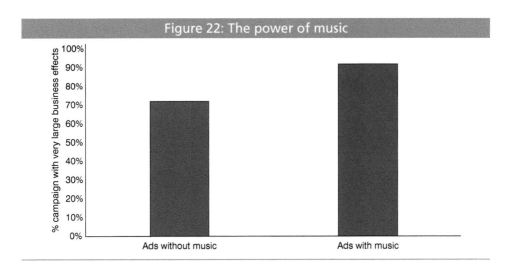

Figure 22: The power of music

People not only love the ads' songs, they Google (Figure 23), stream, Shazam and buy them. Thousands of people globally search for them and the ads become the most Shazamed in the UK.[20]

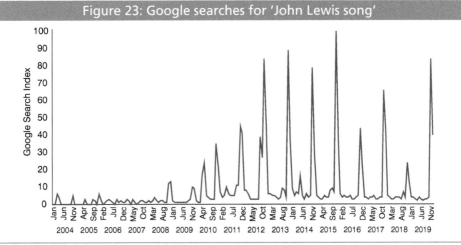

Figure 23: Google searches for 'John Lewis song'

Source: Google Trends

The songs receive millions of Spotify plays[21] and generate millions in royalties for featured artists (Table 4).

Table 4: John Lewis songs are streamed millions of times

John Lewis Christmas advert	First aired	Featured song	Artist	Streams (Spotify)	Earnings
'The bear and the hare'	2013	'Somewhere Only We Know'	Lily Allen	189,638,000	£647,312
'For those who care'	2010	'Your Song'	Ellie Goulding	142,774,000	£487,346
'Man on the moon'	2015	'Half the World Away'	Aurora	69,548,000	£237,396
'Monty the penguin'	2014	'Real Love'	Tom Odell	41,438,000	£141,445
'The journey'	2012	'The Power of Love'	Gabrielle Aplin	37,626,000	£128,433
'Remember the feeling'	2009	'Sweet Child O' Mine'	Taken by Trees	34,053,000	£116,237
'Moz the monster'	2017	'Golden Slumbers'	Elbow	11,086,000	£37,841
'Buster the boxer'	2016	'One Day I'll Fly Away'	Vaults	3,307,000	£11,288
'The long wait'	2011	'Please, Please, Please'	Slow Moving Millie	1,778,000	£6,069

Source: Spotify

Masses buy the songs and they creep up the charts; we've had two 'Number Ones'. Interest in the songs[22] make ads more effective, creating additional exposure (Table 5).

Table 5: John Lewis songs in the UK charts

John Lewis advert	First aired	Featured song	Artist	Weeks in UK charts	Peak position
'The long wait'	2011	'Please, Please, Please'	Slow Moving Millie	7	31
'The journey'	2012	'The Power Of Love'	Gabrielle Aplin	12	1
'The bear and the hare'	2013	'Somewhere Only We Know'	Lily Allen	15	1
'Monty the penguin'	2014	'Real Love'	Tom Odell	14	7
'Man on the moon'	2015	'Half the World Away'	Aurora	8	11
'Buster the boxer'	2016	'One Day I'll Fly Away'	Vaults	3	53
'Moz the monster'	2017	'Golden Slumbers'	Elbow	7	29
'The boy and the piano'	2018	'Your Song'	Elton John	–	–
'Excitable Edgar'	2019	'Can't Fight This Feeling'	Bastille	39	5

Source: Official Charts Company

The uplifting, emotive songs became 'musical handwriting' for John Lewis. As a result, the song is an important decision – often the most contentious part of the creative process.[23] We pick songs which intensify the story, and 'test' their emotional power on colleagues, family and friends.

Things that don't make sense

It's hard to make the case that a dog jumping on a trampoline or a fantastical dragon will sell gifts, yet over the last decade, we've learnt the power of things that don't make sense. We've broken rules and gone against logic, trusted our instincts and embraced risk in the creative process. So much of the campaign's 'magic' is born from our steadfast belief in doing what *feels* right rather than what makes sense – and it works. As Orlando Wood says:

> *'People, human connection, humour, monsters, music and metaphor; the John Lewis Christmas campaign offers an important lesson to any advertiser looking to elicit an emotional response in their audience. For these are the things that attract and sustain attention, that get campaigns noticed and remembered, and that drive market share growth.'*
>
> Orlando Wood, Chief Innovation Officer, System1

Lesson 3: The power of popular

The release of the John Lewis Christmas ad has become a 'cultural moment' in the UK, signalling the start of the Christmas season. It gets talked about on breakfast TV, in the papers, at the school gates. We ignore the industry's obsession with efficiency and micro-targeting, and aim for universal awareness. We're as obsessed with showing off our ads as we are with creating them – we aren't building 'cathedrals in the desert'.

Nothing sells like populism

Adland seems to have lost touch with the British public and become too self-referential, caring too much about industry approval and too little about whether ordinary people like (or even see) our ads.

Our intention is to make ads that ordinary people love, rather than ads that are revered within Adland. ARF research suggests that likeability is the metric with the strongest power to predict effectiveness in advertising.[24] A surefire way to sell stuff is populism.

The huge popularity of 'The long wait' proved the power of populist work, so we kept doing it. And our ads have been Britain's favourites, year after year.

Table 6: Britain's favourite Christmas ads									
	2011	2012	2013	2014	2015	2016	2017	2018	2019
Netmums / Channel Mum	1st	1st	1st	1st	1st	2nd	1st	1st	n/a

Source: Netmums / Channel Mum (Netmums became Channel Mum in 2015)

Targeting is overrated

We need to be populist in our creative work, and we need to be populist in our targeting too. Many marketers – especially marketers in retail – think loyalty is the key to success. We could have focused exclusively on existing customers, and tried to grow by extracting more value from them. But marketing theory tells us the most effective campaigns talk to all category buyers,[25] which for department stores means nearly anyone.

We could also be exclusive in our targeting, because John Lewis is an upmarket department store. Yet YouGov and TGI data show John Lewis shoppers are only *slightly* more upmarket. They may value high quality and service, but the newspaper they're most likely to read is the *Daily Mail.*[26] So our audience is pretty much *all* adults, with a slight upmarket skew.

A million is a small number

Populist creative work is useless if people don't see it. We need to talk to a very broad audience, and we need to talk to them multiple times over the Christmas season to get them to shop with us.

When you're trying to move Britons en masse, a million exposures is not much more than a rounding error. Our ads get over one billion exposures each Christmas (Figure 24).

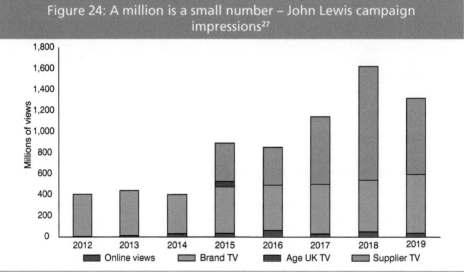

Figure 24: A million is a small number – John Lewis campaign impressions[27]

Source: Manning Gottlieb OMD

Digital is not the answer

True emotional impact requires video. Online video is a no-brainer – cheap, efficient and shareable – we get millions of exposures online every year (Table 7).

Table 7: Millions of online exposures every year

	'Man on the moon'	'Buster the boxer'	'Moz the monster'	'The boy and the piano'	'Excitable Edgar'
Facebook views	7,800,000	35,700,000	14,578,666	13,362,212	14,432,102
Twitter views	969,889	4,060,000	4,853,302	24,040,000	12,970,000
YouTube views	23,700,000	24,600,000	9,049,146	12,812,734	10,988,690
Total views	32,500,000	64,360,000	28,481,114	50,214,946	38,390,792

Source: Manning Gottlieb OMD

But that's still not enough. We need *hundreds* of millions. That requires TV. Despite changes in the media landscape, and the cries of 'TV is dead', TV remains a crucial medium to deliver emotion at scale. TV is the most effective medium for John Lewis, driving over 60% of media-driven sales (Figure 25).[28]

Figure 25: Media contribution to revenue

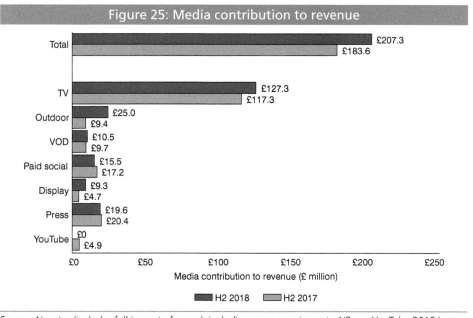

Source: Neustar (includes full impact of spend, including carry-over impacts. NB: no YouTube 2018.)

TV effectiveness has increased over time. TV gets the bulk of the budget, but digital is an important, low-cost amplifier. Indeed, most of our online views come for free (Table 8).[29]

Online and offline work in synergy. TV views stimulate online views and vice versa (as everyone has a device in their hand these days).

The power of fame

Creativity, emotion, reach and scale all enhance effectiveness, but the best campaigns have something else: fame. When ads are seen, loved and talked about by everyone, efficiency rises dramatically, by a factor of four.

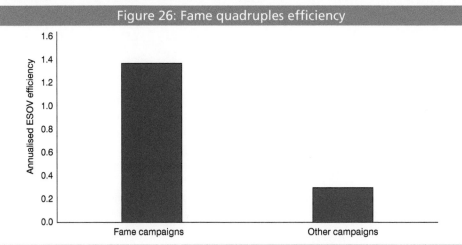

Figure 26: Fame quadruples efficiency

Source: Binet and Field (2013)[30]

Our campaigns create tremendous fame. Ordinary people, who don't normally care about ads, love ours, talk about them and share them, giving us extra exposure for free (Figures 27 and 28, Table 8).

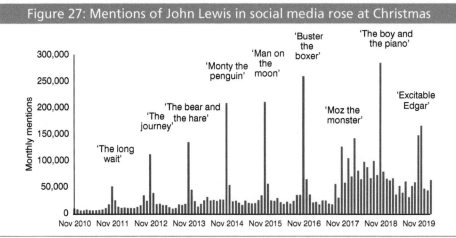

Figure 27: Mentions of John Lewis in social media rose at Christmas

Sources: Crimson Hexagon (2010–2017); Netbase (2017, 2020)

Table 8: John Lewis became the most talked about retailer

	2013	2014	2015	2016	2017	2018	2018
1	John Lewis	John Lewis	John Lewis	John Lewis	Marks & Spencer	John Lewis	John Lewis
2	Marks & Spencer	Marks & Spencer	Marks & Spencer	Marks & Spencer	John Lewis	B&M Bargains	B&M Bargains
3	Boots	Boots	B&M Bargains	B&M Bargains	B&M Bargains	Home Bargains	Marks & Spencer
4	Debenhams	Poundland	Boots	Home Bargains	Home Bargains	Primark	Home Bargains
5	Lakeland	Lakeland	Home Bargains	Boots	Boots	Boots	Primark

Source: YouGov BrandIndex 2013–2019

Figure 28: A small fan's drawing of Excitable Edgar the Dragon, 2019

People make parodies of our ads,[31] which have become a 'searched for' sub-genre in their own right. We don't mind; it's a sign we've become part of culture, and gives campaigns further exposure. A 'Buster' spoof was viewed 113m times and shared 1.64m times – higher engagement than our competitors' official Christmas ads (Figure 29).[32]

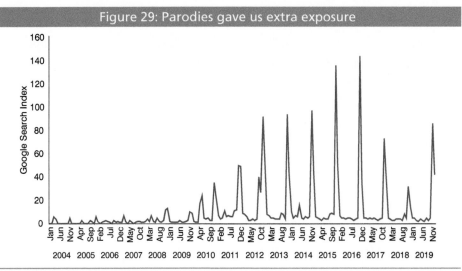

Figure 29: Parodies gave us extra exposure

Source: Google Trends

Press pick up on campaign buzz, and their coverage gives us billions of extra exposures for free (Figure 30).

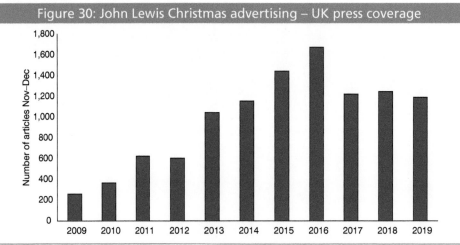

Figure 30: John Lewis Christmas advertising – UK press coverage

Source: Factiva

In 2019, press coverage generated three billion exposures, double the OTS from TV and online video. When you include coverage from TV and radio,[33] PR gives us greater exposure than we actually pay for.

The number of exposures in the national press for 'Excitable Edgar' was 3,736,472,091, according to ABC and Factiva (Figure 31).

Figure 31: Edgar in the papers, 2019

This buzz increases anticipation. People actively search for the new ad (Figure 32).

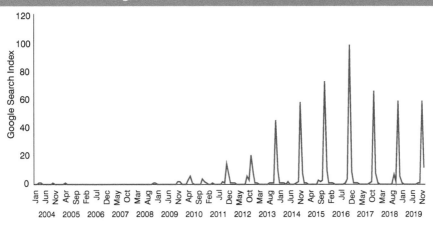

Figure 32: People searched for the ads before and after they launched –
Google searches for 'John Lewis advert'

Source: Google Trends

Over time, the ad launch has become a national 'event' (Figure 33).

Figure 33: Newspapers anticipate the launch of the advert

Figure 33: Newspapers anticipate the launch of the advert

John Lewis Christmas ads 2007 to 2015: from humble roots to national event

Countdown to Christmas: John Lewis Christmas advert

When is the John Lewis Christmas 2019 advert coming out?

HOME » FINANCE » NEWS BY SECTOR » RETAIL AND CONSUMER

It's funny how John Lewis Christmas Advert is now part of our Christmas countdown

A perverse sign of popularity

Not everyone loves advertising, and not everyone loves our ads. As campaign fame has grown, we've gained a few trolls online and in tabloid newspapers – ironically, this increases campaign buzz (Figure 34).

Figure 34: Perverse sign of popularity

John Lewis becomes more salient

All this buzz means John Lewis is front of people's mind at Christmas. That's worth its weight in gold. As Byron Sharp notes, the main reason people don't buy a brand (or visit a store) is because it slips their mind. But nobody can forget John Lewis.

Punching above our weight

Our advertising is fantastically efficient, but we face incredibly tough competition. In this environment, just standing still is an achievement – yet every year, we receive higher ad awareness and recall than competitors (Figure 35).

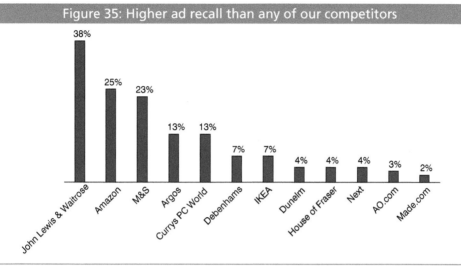

Figure 35: Higher ad recall than any of our competitors

Source: JL&P Brand Image Tracker 2019 QGI

In particular, we beat Amazon. An incredible achievement, given Amazon spends 3.5 times more on media at Christmas than we do (Figure 36).

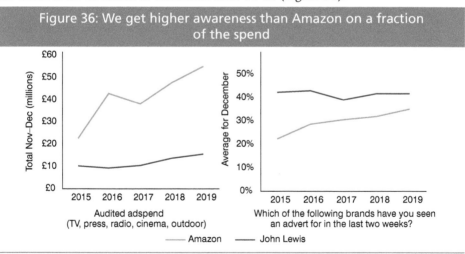

Figure 36: We get higher awareness than Amazon on a fraction of the spend

Sources: Nielsen; YouGov

225

Lesson 4: The short and long of it

You might think our ads are designed solely for long-term brand building. Wrong. John Lewis ads are engineered for *immediate* success. We want people to *do* something as a result of seeing, and being moved by, our advertising. We want people to *buy* stuff in the run-up to Christmas. And they do.

Immediate success online

We release our ad in early November. Within *seconds*, people rush to watch it online, causing an immediate surge in web traffic (Figure 37).

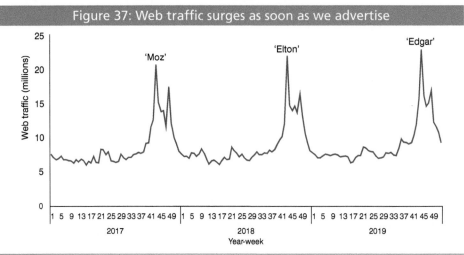

Figure 37: Web traffic surges as soon as we advertise

Source: John Lewis

Many visitors stay on to buy something. Online sales start rising within *minutes* of the ad going live (Figure 38).

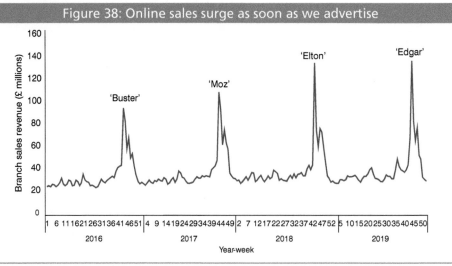

Figure 38: Online sales surge as soon as we advertise

Source: John Lewis

Immediate success on the high street

Within a day or two, people start coming into our shops. Our ads come out on a Thursday or Friday. By the weekend, footfall is up dramatically (Figure 39).[34]

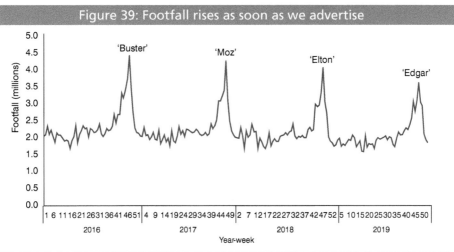

Figure 39: Footfall rises as soon as we advertise

Source: John Lewis stores with cameras installed

Within a week, we're seeing the results in branch sales. That sets us up nicely for Black Friday,[35] a few weeks later (Figure 40).

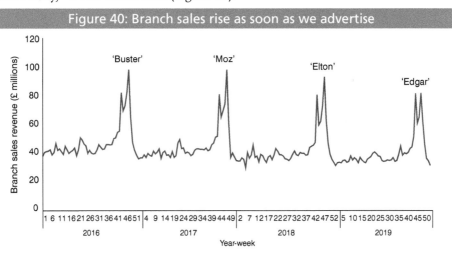

Figure 40: Branch sales rise as soon as we advertise

Source: John Lewis

Our ads sell product directly

Some sales come directly from campaign merchandise. Starting with 'The bear and the hare' storybook in 2013, we've created ad-themed products each year, and they're surprisingly profitable. Sales of penguins almost paid for the making of 'Monty' (Figure 41).

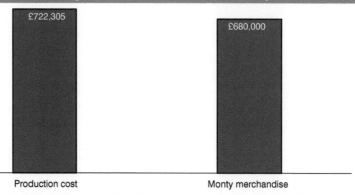

Figure 41: Sales of Monty merchandise covered 94% of production costs

£722,305 — Production cost

£680,000 — Monty merchandise

By 2019, campaign merchandise accounted for 13% of online sales. On launch day, Edgar toys sold at 100 a minute.[36] In total, campaign merchandise generated £1m profit (Figure 42).

Figure 42: Excitable Edgar merchandise generated £1 million profit

FESTIVE FLOGGING Excitable Edgar £15 toys already being flogged on eBay for £50 just hours after John Lewis releases Christmas advert

But it's not all about penguins or dragons. Sales surge across the *whole* product range. Suppliers realise this, and pay to be associated with the campaign. We feature their products in films alongside our characters – in 2016, a badger snuffled a Nespresso coffee machine, in 2019 Edgar tried out Beats headphones. In 2019, suppliers paid several millions to have products featured alongside Edgar.[37] These ads sell their products *and* double our exposure, at zero cost (Figure 43).[38]

Figure 43: Suppliers pay to be associated with the John Lewis campaign

Immediate payback

Our Christmas ads really do sell products, surprisingly quickly. Our 'sentimental' ads pay for themselves in a matter of weeks (Figure 44).

Figure 44: Short-term effect of John Lewis ads on total sales

Weekly sales contribution (£ millions)

Week ending

Base   Other   Christmas (TV, VOD, YouTube)

Source: Neustar

Long-term success, immediately

Some retailers can be sniffy about brand advertising. They prefer offers that sell stuff now. But our ads sell short *and* long term.[39] They kick-start sales in minutes, and keep sales growing through Christmas and beyond. As Jeremy Bullmore says of all great ads, they sell *'both immediately and forever'*.[40]

Broad reach is key to this. Many retailers focus on existing customers, offering discounts to keep them loyal. We talk to everybody, expand our customer base, and get people paying *more* (Table 9).

	2009	2010	2011	2012	2013	2014	2015	2016	2017	2018	2019
Table 9: We recruited more customers, who spent more											
Number of customers	100	105	106	115	118	123	126	132	133	140	138
Average spend per customer	100	106	110	117	121	125	127	128	132	131	126
Total sales	100	112	117	134	144	154	160	170	176	185	175

Source: John Lewis GCI detailed customer dashboard full year. Data indexed (2009 = 100).

That means durable growth, firmer pricing and revenues that beat the market every year, on and offline (Figure 45).

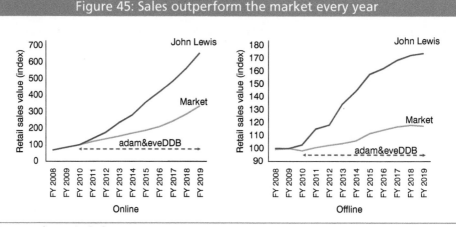

Figure 45: Sales outperform the market every year

Sources: John Lewis; ONS

Lesson 5: Make data your servant, not your master

Too many marketers play it safe, attempting to de-risk creative decisions by delegating them to mechanical pre-testing systems. This can lead to goodish, but rarely great, advertising. John Lewis takes a different approach: risk, refinement and reward. Our winning formula uses judgement to inform creativity, but meticulously evaluates business results over the medium to long term. Those learnings inform the next wave. Short-term data isn't followed slavishly, it's interpreted with an understanding of its limitations and an eye on the long term.

Trust your instincts

Long before we found our Christmas advertising formula, we learnt to trust our creative judgement with a highly emotive ad called 'Always a woman'.[41] At the time, Millward Brown were sceptical about how effective it would be, but we stuck with it and it was a huge success, both with the public and commercially. To this day, it remains one of the UK's most loved ads. We learned that when it comes to commercial success, instinct is an undervalued indicator.

It's our job to decide

In 10 years, John Lewis hasn't pre-tested a single Christmas ad. When choosing the final story, it refuses pre-testing and script research. The clients say: 'It's our job to decide'.

When reading potential scripts, we look for 'moments that get you'. Small, simple moments within the storyline that make us *feel* something. Those moments are incredibly hard to pre-test because it's impossible to research an expression or convey nuances effectively, yet subtleties are disproportionately important. People have episodic memories, they only remember key scenes, images or moments – which would be missed by pre-testing, or impossible to plan for.

Campaign magazine's review of 'The boy and the piano' noted this, *'It's phenomenally well done. Especially the little "look up" Top of the Pops Elton gives to the camera'* (Figure 46).[42]

Figure 46: Elton looks to camera on 'Top of the Pops', 2018

We create space for magic and serendipity within the production process. In 2018, the little boy playing Elton loved pandas. His expression on Christmas morning was caused by a man on set surprising him dressed as a panda. It makes the film. We had the idea the day before (Figure 47).

Figure 47: The little 'Elton' surprised by the panda suit, 2018

Real creativity can't come from data, machines or systems. As Rory Sutherland[43] says, *'A spreadsheet leaves no room for miracles'*.

Measure and learn

But that doesn't mean we're reckless. We rigorously measure results in hard business terms. We look at what drives sales and profit, repeat what works and lose what doesn't. Exactly as Booz and Company recommend:

> *'Be creative and measure what happens. If it works, do more of it. If it doesn't work, go back and be creative again.'*
>
> Moeller and Landry, 2009[44]

We use econometrics to measure the precise impact of each element in our marketing mix. This enables us to judge and refine creative work where it matters: in the real world.

This approach helped John Lewis sales outperform the market every year (Table 10):

Table 10: Christmas sales, year-on-year									
	2009	**2010**	**2011**	**2012**	**2013**	**2014**	**2015**	**2016**	**2017**	**2018**
John Lewis	+12.7%	+7.6%	+6.2%	+14.8%	+6.9%	+4.8%	+5.1%	+2.7%	+3.1%	+1.0%
M&S	+1.2%	+3.8%	−1.8%	−3.8%	−2.1%	−5.8%	−5.8%	+2.3%	−2.8%	−2.2%
Debenhams	+0.1%	−1.3%	0.0%	+5.0%	+1.5%	+2.4%	+1.8%	+5.0%	−2.6%	−6.2%
Argos	+0.1%	−4.9%	−8.8%	+2.7%	+3.8%	+0.1%	−2.2%	+4.0%	−1.4	−2.3%
Comet	−3.9%	−7.3%	−14.5%	Closed	Closed	Closed	Closed	Closed	Closed	Closed
Mothercare	n/a	n/a	−3.0%	−5.9%	−4.0%	+1.1%	+4.2%	+0.6%	−7.2%	−11.4%

Like-for-like sales, Christmas period (non-food). Year-on-year sources: published financial information.

Econometrics help us to maximise effectiveness. Over the decade, our ads have delivered a staggering £1.2bn in extra revenue and £411m in extra profit.[45] That's enough to pay for the advertising many times over.

As you can see, there is no sign that this profit-generating machine is running out of steam. 'The boy and the piano'[46] delivered a ROMI of over 1,000%, our highest yet. That's nearly five times higher than a typical IPA Effectiveness Awards case (Table 11).

Table 11: John Lewis ads are unusually profitable		
	Net profit per £1 spent	**ROMI**
John Lewis Christmas ads	£8.83	883%
Average for all other IPA cases	£1.74	174%

Source: IPA Effectiveness Awards Databank (median of all verified ROMIs, 1998–2016)

Postscript: The next 10 years

The Partnership also includes supermarket chain Waitrose. In 2019, it was decided to bring both brands into the Christmas campaign, featuring an excitable dragon named Edgar (Figure 48).

Figure 48: 'Edgar the Dragon', 2019

Edgar preliminary results

The campaign had a phenomenal response with the public, generating 38m online views and becoming the UK's most recalled Christmas ad.[47] Sales of campaign merchandise delivered £1m in profit,[48] paying for campaign production. System1 awarded Edgar a score of 5.9, the highest star rating for a Christmas ad they've ever recorded.[49]

John Lewis became the strongest brand in Britain in any category, for the third year running (Table 12).

Table 12: The strongest brand in Britain in any category			
Rank	2017	2018	2019
1	John Lewis	John Lewis	John Lewis
2	BBC iPlayer	BBC iPlayer	IKEA
3	Sony	Marks & Spencer	Marks & Spencer
4	Amazon	Heinz	Heinz
5	BBC One	IKEA	Visa
6	Samsung	Samsung	Samsung
7	Heinz	Amazon	Royal Mail
8	BBC Two	Cathedral City	Boots
9	Boots	BBC One	Cathedral City

Source: YouGov BrandIndex 2017–2019

Until now, our ads have helped John Lewis[50] to keep growing every year, despite phenomenally tough conditions in British retail. Last Christmas, the headwinds were too strong. We still outperformed the market, but department store sales fell slightly in absolute terms.[51]

But that's not the whole story. Because Edgar promoted Waitrose alongside John Lewis, the campaign will have influenced a much broader sales base, boosting payback. Whilst we are awaiting econometric analysis of the campaign, given Edgar out-performed every other measure available, it's likely that profit ROI will be at the level of 'The boy and the piano', i.e. at around £10[52] (perhaps even higher), and that the campaign remains as profitable as ever.

Summary of the decade

Table 13: Summary of key highlights from the decade	
Advertising	**Performance**
TV/video impressions	6.8bn (2012–2019)
Branded recognition	Increased from 50% to 80% (2010–2016; retail norm 47%)
Emotional impact	The most emotional retail advertiser overall (average 4.2 star rating vs. 2.2 retail norm); Edgar's 5.9 star rating the highest ever recorded Christmas ad
Likeability	Britain's favourite Christmas ads 2011–2018
Shareability	6.8m video shares (2011–2017)
Cannes Creative Awards	27 Cannes Lions (2010–2019)
Brand	
Brand talkability	'Most talked about retailer' six out of seven years 2013–2019
Brand health	Strongest brand in the UK in any category 2017–2019
Commercial	
Incremental media-driven revenue	£1.2bn (2010–2018)
Incremental media-driven profit	£411m (2010–2018)
Profit ROMI £	£7.54–£10.20
Profit ROMI vs. IPA average	Five times IPA average of £1.74
John Lewis growth	22%–32% value market share growth (2010–2019); 4.4 times faster sales growth than UK non-food retail (2010–2019)

Learnings

The power of consistency

Stick to what works and refine it gradually. Small incremental improvements are an unrivalled learning exercise in creativity, and more powerful than total reinvention.

The value in the irrational

Creativity, by its very nature, is an unexplainable, chaotic and risky process. Embrace it, trust it and question blanket rules or techniques that claim to have 'decoded' it.

The power of popular

Waste isn't wasteful; it's the waste that works. Go big on media. Really big. Aim for popularity.

Short and long

Enduring, long-term success is dependent on short-term sales. Engineer campaigns to achieve both simultaneously.

Make data your servant, not master

Use rigour to measure reward, not mitigate risk. And use rigour in the right places – with what sells, in the real world, with real people who've seen the work and the conversation around it.

Conclusion

In the last decade, the industry has shifted further and further away from human insight and human judgement. In a way, it's become fearful of creativity – outsourcing decision-making to machines, data and systems in an attempt to reduce risk.

John Lewis have stayed firm believers in the power of creativity, and firm protectors of the messy, intangible elements of the creative process that can't be explained logically or quantified neatly.

We've relied on human instincts to create work that moves a nation. We've stuck to our guns, taken huge risks and made room for magic. We've applied rigour in the right places – in the real world, where our ads are seen, judged and loved by people who matter. At the end of these 10 years, it's our immense privilege to have created work that's made a historic dent in the fabric of British society and delivered £1.2bn sales and £411m profit to the business.[53]

The human, creative magic on display in our advertising – and the data in this paper – are clear evidence that our approach works.

We hope this case inspires a return to believing in creativity, believing in magic and ultimately, believing in a human approach to advertising, in an industry, and world, that's becoming increasingly less human.

Notes

1   In 2018, John Lewis evolved their name to 'John Lewis & Partners' to reference their partner workforce. For the purpose of this paper, we will refer to the company simply as 'John Lewis'.
2   The John Lewis Partnership includes department store, John Lewis & Partners, and supermarket, Waitrose & Partners.
3   John Lewis econometrics.
4   In 2019, John Lewis and Waitrose partnered for a joint Christmas campaign.
5   UK non-food retail; calculation of John Lewis growth: 74/17 = 4.4.
6   The gift of acceptance, a gift that unlocks someone's talent.
7   'Your Song' was re-recorded by Ellie Goulding.
8   Consumer qualitative research following 'The bear and the hare', 2013.
9   The psychology of emotional, System 1 vs. rational, System 2 thinking, was outlined by Daniel Kahneman *Thinking, Fast and Slow*, London: Allen Lane, 2011.
10 System 1 star rating predicts the potential for ads to drive market share based on the intensity of positive emotion it evokes in viewers. Their star rating norm is 2.2 but our Christmas advertising scores far above this.
11 On average, John Lewis ads have the highest average star rating of all the ads by retailers tested by System 1.
12 Consumer qualitative research following 'Buster the boxer', 2016.
13 Phil Barden, *Decoded: The Science Behind Why We Buy*, Chichester, John Wiley, 2016.
14 This means that anyone could come up with that year's Christmas ad, from the ECD to an intern.

15 This is similar to the process that used to be used on the famous *Economist* and Guinness campaigns, which may not be a coincidence.

16 For Edgar, we named these Spark, Flame, Fan.

17 Partner launch started in 2018.

18 Often these platforms are so new they're commercially untested in terms of likely payback.

19 Les Binet, Daniel Müllensieffen, and Pal Edwards, 'The Power of Music', *Admap*, October 2013.

20 Shazam 2013 to 2015.

21 Spotify plays create big profits for John Lewis Christmas ad songs, Prolific London: 2019.

22 Popular radio stations play them, 'Pop Idol' contestants sing them on Saturday night TV and celebrity Goggleboxers hum along to them.

23 We start thinking about music in March. Come October, we're still arguing about it.

24 Advertising Research Foundation's Copy Research Validity Project. Lars Bergkvist and John R. Rossiter, 'The role of ad likability in predicting an ad's campaign performance', *Journal of Advertising*, 37(2008): 2.

25 Les Binet and Peter Field, *Media in Focus: Marketing Effectiveness in the Digital Era*, London: IPA, 2017. Byron Sharp, *How Brands Grow*, Melbourne: Oxford University Press, 2010.

26 *The Daily Mail* is a UK tabloid newspaper.

27 Supplier ads are supplier-funded films featuring their products alongside our characters.

28 Neustar econometric modelling, H2 2017 and H2 2018.

29 In fact, for the SOV we receive, our ad spend is far lower than you'd imagine.

30 Les Binet and Peter Field, *The Long and the Short of It: Balancing Short- and Long-Term Marketing Strategies,* London: IPA, 2013.

31 Rival retailers and people on the internet.

32 YouTube analytics.

33 From plays of the ads song.

34 Over the last seven years, footfall for high street retailers in general has fallen 10%, making our achievements even more remarkable. Source *Retail Gazette*, 2019.

35 Black Friday changes the market every year, and every year we evolve our approach accordingly to maximise sales.

36 Edgar cuddly toys were sold at £15, and listed half an hour later on eBay for £50. Nobody on the team could get their hands on one!

37 Apple, Google, Dyson, Nespresso, Lego, Microsoft, Bose, Sage each paid £350k in production and media costs.

38 Viewing figures, Manning Gottlieb OMD.

39 All great brand campaigns do this. As Professor John-Philip Jones argued many years ago, there are no long-term sales effects without short-term sales effects. But great brand ads keep selling for much longer. See Binet and Field (2013), *The Long and Short of It*.

40 Jeremy Bullmore, 'A 20th century lesson for 21st century brands', WPP Annual Report and Accounts 2017.

41 One of our first ads for John Lewis (April 2010).

42 *Campaign* magazine, Christmas Adverts review, 2018.

43 Rory Sutherland, *Alchemy: The Surprising Power of Ideas that Don't Make Sense*, London: Penguin, 2019.

44 Leslier H. Moeller and Edward C. Landry, *The Four Pillars of Profit-Driven Marketing*, New York: McGraw Hill, 2009.

45 These figures (£1.2bn incremental revenue and £411m profit) are derived from combining the analysis of two different econometric modelling companies (Brand Science 2010–2012 and Neustar 2013–2018).

46 Most recent ad to be fully evaluated.

47 Public sentiment analysis, Manning Gottlieb OMD.

48 Waitrose created a special Edgar Christmas pudding and food range.

49 System1 internal study of Christmas ads.

50 The department store, not full Partnership.

51 Gross sales were down 2%. Christmas trading statement for the seven weeks from 17 November to 4 January 2020.

52 We are still awaiting full econometrics results, to be released in June 2020.

53 Econometric modelling by Brand Science (2010–2012) and Neustar (2013–2018).

SECTION 3

Silver winners

Baileys

From forgotten icon to global treat

By Jack Carrington and Neasa McGuinness, Mother; Venya Wijegoonewardene, Carat

Contributing authors: Sheila Cunningham and Vicki Holgate, Diageo; Andrew Deykin, Data2Decisions; Chantal da Fonseca and Robin McGhee, Kantar; Mark Linford, VMLY&R; Philip Price, Carat; Katie Mackay-Sinclair, Mother

Summary

The global 'Don't mind if I Baileys' campaign revived the cream liqueur from a cultural irrelevance with declining sales volumes to a versatile treat for adults, comparable to eating cake. Combining consistent semiotics for creative elements and greater use of shorter, digital media formats and content partnerships, the new approach also emphasised optimisation and mid-campaign learning. This paper outlines evidence that communications activity helped reframe the brand and increase its usage. Between 2014–2019, global volume sales grew 32% and Baileys recovered 1.6 percentage points of global volume share.

Client comment

Jennifer English, Global Brand Director, Diageo

I would pick out five learnings that have changed the way I work:

- Product and purpose must meet. In 2015, when this journey began, finding a meaningful social purpose was the go-to solution for brands. Baileys chose to focus instead on the product truth as the source of its purpose. Baileys' purpose to be 'your co-conspirator in the pursuit of pleasure' turned out to be more resonant for consumers than anything loftier.
- Brands have an intrinsic meaning but you must find their modern cultural relevance. Highly distinctive brands can become encumbered by their truths. Are cream and sugar over? What is a liqueur anyway? Redefining Baileys as a treat opened our eyes to a world of indulgence, exciting sources of insight, new partners and endless inspiration.
- The long- and short-term goals can be achieved in one communication. Baileys shows that with the right kind of communication, rooted in a clear product

truth, you can build both long-term memory structures and drive immediate purchase.

- Too often measurement is seen as the enemy of magic when, in fact, it can release the magic. If a group of posts have higher engagement rates, find out why and make more content in that image. If a social platform is performing particularly well, spend more money there. If pre-testing shows consistently strong or weak performance on a measure, resolve it.
- Media is as important as creative. Short content (3-20 seconds), new platforms and rigorous M&E have multiplied the effectiveness of the work. We set out to find the consumer in their adult treat moment before we set out to create the work.

Baileys

Central Coast

Building a big billion dollar tourism brand through 'Little adventures'

By Luke Brown and Angela Smith, AFFINITY

Summary

Domestic tourism to Australia's Central Coast in New South Wales had fallen significantly over four years, largely due to negative perceptions of the region. This paper outlines how the area won back tourism revenue and increased market share in a multi-phase brand campaign that targeted Gen X and 'empty nesters'. The approach used novel data analysis to distinguish claimed from actual behaviour (purchase behaviour), with insights gleaned informing the brand platform and a campaign spanning digital, TV, PR and outdoor. By inspiring 'little adventures' across the Central Coast, tourism revenues grew 22.7% in 2017–2019 (compared to a target of 5%), contributing AUD240m of additional tourism revenue over two years.

Client comment

Russell Mills, Director, Industry Services and Partnerships, Tourism Central Coast

Tourism plays such an important role in creating healthy economies for most of Australia's regions. This is very much the case for the Central Coast. We had a big responsibility to make a real difference, to help start the process of reinvention for the entire region.

The Coast's poor reputation meant it was not somewhere you wanted to go to spend your precious holiday time. We knew we only had one shot at changing people's minds about the Central Coast as a holiday destination and we didn't have the budget to produce a mass-media campaign. Plus, after a five-year decline in tourism, our local operators were less than optimistic we could bring about a change of fortune. So, we definitely had some big hurdles to overcome.

To get the industry on board we needed to adopt a more evidence-based approach from the outset. With data at its core, we were able to build a bullet-proof business case which gave operators the confidence to contribute more than we'd targeted for.

Importantly, this groundwork also meant we had identified a brand positioning that would go on to deliver the very real perception change we needed and incredible growth in tourism for the region.

Thinking about specific learnings from this campaign, I'm struck by the realisation that we're in an industry obsessed with big one-off ideas, almost to the exclusion of anything else. We found that by applying the same degree of rigorous thinking to each and every aspect of a campaign, we were able to deliver exponential outcomes. We learned very much that the small details matter, and can make the difference to produce huge impacts – the legacy of which will help the region for years to come.

Gordon's Gin

Legacy brand turned challenger: Doubling the size of a legacy brand by thinking like a challenger

By Vicki Holgate, Mark Jarman and Emiliana Vidali, Diageo; Stuart Smith, Anomaly London

Contributing authors: Ronan Beirne, Sri Shan, Anita Robinson and Jessica Lace, Diageo; Andrew Deykin, Data2Decisions; Jessica Collings, 1000Heads; Ant Harris and Shai Idelson, Anomaly London; Harriet Mansfield, CGA; Jessica Walsh, Kantar; Venya Wijegoonewardene, Carat

Credited companies: Data2Decisions, CGA, Kantar, Carat, 1000Heads

Summary

New gin launches had chipped share away from Diageo's market-leading brand, Gordon's. Adopting a challenger mindset, Gordon's relaunched with a new positioning, '… Shall we?', emphasising sociability, and a new premium berry variant, Gordon's Pink. Investment was split 60:40 between the main brand and the new product. TV, posters and digital were used, as well as smart targeting. Between 2017 and 2019, Gordon's value sales more than doubled and Gordon's Pink became the UK's number-two gin brand. The relaunch attracted drinkers new to the brand and to gin. It is estimated the relaunch generated £843m of incremental revenue in 2017–2019.

Client comment

Mark Jarman, Global Head of Gordon's Gin, Diageo

There are three things that we have embedded into our campaign planning as a result of the Gordon's success story:

- Belief in the scale of change possible. Diageo has the privilege of owning over 200 brands; many, like 250-year-old Gordon's, with long histories. The transformative change that we achieved with Gordon's over the last three years of its history has been a valuable lesson for us in what is possible. Gordon's had a 38% share of the market, established competition and literally hundreds of new entrants to the market. Yet, we proved it is possible to more than double the size of the brand in three years. That is the scale of what is possible.

- The importance of the right 'mindset'. Many legacy brands these days are under pressure from new entrants to their markets. In this situation, it is easy to become defensive. But what Gordon's shows us so clearly is that legacy brands can benefit enormously from adopting a proactive 'challenger brand mindset'. More specifically, this case has inspired us as an organisation to embrace entrepreneurial principles such as looking for ways to save in some areas in order to invest in others and how to zag when others are zigging.

- How to use new product development (NPD) strategically. The creation and launch of Gordon's Premium Pink has also thrown a spotlight on the importance of NPD that is strategically aligned to the brand. And our experimentation with the balance of brand versus NPD advertising support levels has been revelatory. In this case, the right balance was a 60:40 split of brand comms / NPD comms. This learning has been fed into the Diageo Marketing Catalyst campaign planning tool which is used throughout Diageo to plan future campaigns worldwide.

Gordon's Gin

Heinz [Seriously] Good Mayonnaise

How Heinz [Seriously] Good Mayonnaise overcame the 'difficult second stage of launch' syndrome

By John Harrison, BBH

Contributing authors: Lucy Cooke and Ash Anzie, Kraft Heinz

Credited companies: Wonderland, Starcom

Summary

After a successful launch, the performance of Heinz [Seriously] Good Mayonnaise (SGM) reached a plateau. A more nimble, challenger-style approach was sought. To revive mental availability and consideration, the brand changed its TV strategy to increase frequency. A nationwide poster and print campaign took the market leader head on, whilst celebrating the 'Heinzeness' of the challenger. Following a Twitter campaign to assess interest, a new product, Heinz Saucy Sauce, was quickly launched. Another PR and social media-driven innovation, the Heinz Mayo Creme Egg, generated further interest. After the strategy shift in 2018, Heinz SGM grew UK value sales and share, outperforming the brand's other European markets. According to two different models, incremental sales were estimated at between £12.3m and £16.1m in 2018–2019.

Client comment

Lucy Cooke, Brand Manager, Kraft Heinz

The impact we have seen as a result of the activity on Heinz [Seriously] Good Mayonnaise, in terms of both commercial and brand growth, has already provided valuable learning across Kraft Heinz. It has provided an invaluable case study on different ways to achieve the common key objectives of talkability and saliency, especially:

- How embracing a challenger mindset ensures you don't fall into the tropes of the category in how and what you communicate
- The potential of earned media to cut through in an extremely disruptive and engaging way
- The role of channel selection, and how taking the battle to a different media can drive cut-through and give the appearance of dominance

From a Heinz SGM-specific point of view, sharing the positive consumer engagement and reaction to the comms with the trade has helped us gain traction with growing the brand in store, as this continues to be a key strategic priority for our sauces business.

Heinz [Seriously] Good Mayonnaise

SickKids

SickKids vs. Conventional fundraising

By Denika Angelone and Cat Wiles, Cossette; Louise Cook, Holmes & Cook

Contributing authors: Lori Davison and Heather Clark, SickKids Foundation; Craig McIntosh, Jaimes Zentil, Peter Ignazi, Courtney Mulock, Carolyn Khoo, Emma Sleeper and Carlos Morena, Cossette; Cathy Collier, OMD Canada

Summary

Toronto's Hospital for Sick Children (SickKids) embarked on an ambitious fundraising journey to raise over CAD1bn to build a new hospital. It needed to broaden its donor base and dramatically increase contributions, without alienating existing supporters. A radical revamp repositioned the charity as a performance brand with a fresh identity that jolted people off the sidelines. Over four years, communications drove urgency, making audiences feel personally and locally connected by transforming donors into partners and asking them to join the fight. Research showed dramatic growth in both awareness of the charity and in share of wallet versus the competitive set.

Client comment

Lori Davison, VP, Head of Brand and Communications, SickKids Foundation

The SickKids VS campaign has been transformational for both the business and the culture at SickKids Foundation and The Hospital for Sick Children itself. It has galvanised SickKids by articulating a sense of purpose that was always in the DNA of the organisation but never before brought to life in a full and enduring expression.

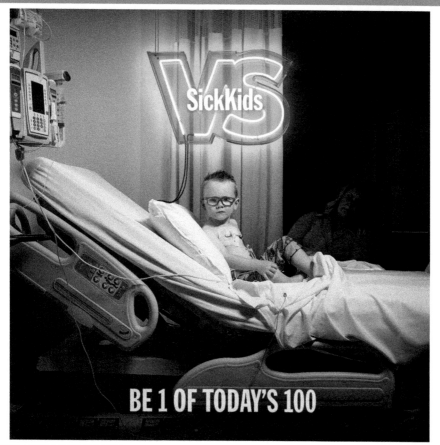

Volvo

A defiantly human success story

By Matt Gladstone and Gilliam Caldwell-Dunn, Grey
Contributing authors: Liam Hannan, Mindshare; Mark Stockdale, The Effectiveness Partnership
Credited company: Mindshare

Summary

Volvo UK moved upmarket by rediscovering the human purpose behind its famous safety positioning and the 'defiant pioneers' who would embrace it. An innovative approach to sponsorship of the Sky Atlantic TV channel was developed using short, emotionally involving films and idents about individuals trying to make the world a better place. Films were amplified on social media and well recalled. Research showed a shift in brand perceptions and sales uplifts coinciding with phases of media activity. Volvo UK outperformed other European Volvo markets where activity did not run. It is estimated that communications generated a net profit of between £8.9m and £12.7m.

Client comment

Georgina Williams, Head of Marketing, Volvo Cars UK

Our partnership with Sky Atlantic celebrates the human-first values that have always been at the heart of Volvo. Bringing these campaigns together in an IPA paper has highlighted our success in using idents and branded content to work in concert. Despite having challenged the traditional TV sponsorship model, we now have a robust set of evidence in favour of this new approach. Confident in the power of investing in this communications model, we are excited at the possibilities of branded storytelling in this space and how we could use such partnerships to drive effectiveness for the Volvo brand in the future.

SECTION 4

Bronze winners

Aldi UK

Aldi 2010–2019: How taking an alternative path took Aldi from shame to pride

By Jamie Peate and Marie Koropisz, McCann Manchester

Contributing authors: Darren Hawkins and Andrew Houghton, McCann Manchester

Credited companies: Gain Theory, Universal McCann

Summary

After 20 years of UK trading, the German discount supermarket, Aldi, still only had 2% value share of the UK market. From 2010 to 2019, Aldi employed communications to turn attributes – such as its lack of big brand products – from perceived negatives into positives. Humorous campaigns, including 'Like brands' and 'Kevin the Carrot', increased brand consideration and affinity, persuading more shoppers to use Aldi for a range of needs from weekly shops to special occasions. Penetration, frequency, and basket size rose. By the end of the period, sales had grown to £9.49bn and value share was 7.9%.

Client comment

Sean McGinty, Marketing Director, Aldi

Anyone who works in retail knows you have to define and stay true to your long-term vision and goal whilst attending to the short-term issues in the day-to-day. The tricky thing is doing them both at the same time.

That is just what we did at Aldi; we were able to find the truth of our brand and communicate it in a way that connected with shoppers, and that connection has endured over the last ten years. It has meant we were able to flex this truth across the many communication tasks we faced and channels we needed to use, whilst giving us a north star to guide us and a yardstick to measure against. As a business, we learnt to resist the temptation to follow everyone else, instead choosing to stay true to who we are and the role we could play in our customers' lives.

Once we had defined this role, we needed to ensure that everything we did helped to reinforce it. We also learnt that it's not just what you have to say that matters: the way you say it is just as important. Your tone of voice can make you distinctive and get you noticed. It can get you liked and therefore listened to and believed. In a world where everything seems to be about shorter and shorter time frames, with an expectation of immediate results, it was the setting of a big, audacious goal over a realistically long time frame that delivered us success.

Campaign Against Living Miserably

Breaking the silence: How an image, not an ad, transformed the way the UK treats male suicide

By Will Grundy, adam&eveDDB

Contributing authors: Tom Roach, Martin Beverley, Sarah Carter, Nic English and Luke Williams, adam&eveDDB; Ben Hawley and Dipika Saggi, CALM; Dr Grace Kite, Gracious Economics

Credited companies: ITV, Harry's Grooming Company, W Comms

Summary

Project 84 demonstrates how the Campaign Against Living Miserably (CALM) transformed the way the UK treats male suicide, by placing 84 statues on top of the ITV Tower for the whole world to see. Despite growing awareness of its prevalence as the single biggest killer of men under 45, male suicide rates were increasing. This was in no small part a result of the deafening silence surrounding the issue; the less suicide was discussed, the more stigmatised and virulent it became. Despite a total budget of £100,000, Project 84 pierced this silence, sparking widespread media coverage and social conversation. The intervention led to the prevention of 283 suicides, the appointment of the UK's first Minister for Suicide Prevention, and delivered a societal payback of £5,119 per £1 spent.

Client comment

Simon Gunning, CEO, Campaign Against Living Miserably

There's one word we've always used to describe Project 84, ever since the idea was first presented: watershed.

It was a watershed moment for our sector – proving with great effect that it wasn't just acceptable, but necessary, to tackle suicide head on.

It was a watershed moment for CALM – allowing us to significantly increase and diversify our service capabilities, as well as widen our broader efforts to instigate a populist movement against suicide.

Most importantly, it was a watershed moment for anyone and everyone in this country who has ever felt vulnerable, scared, alone, depressed, and – yes – suicidal.

When those statues appeared on the ITV tower, we weren't just visualising the scale of male suicide. We were standing against it. We were standing in solidarity with all those – victims, survivors, families and friends – affected by the menace of suicide, refusing to let it go unnoticed for one second longer.

The results, as this paper demonstrates, speak for themselves.

But our work is far from done.

As the UK re-emerges from the medical, social, psychological and economic catastrophe of COVID-19, it will likely be met by a perilously embattled charity sector, and the beginnings of a long-term national mental health crisis.

Make no mistake: we will need another watershed.

Thanks to Project 84, we've found the blueprint and the bravery to meet this challenge head on.

Campaign Against Living Miserably

Cotswold Co.

A leap beyond optimisation

By Andrew Gibson and Catherine Owen, Creature London

Summary

With a reduced marketing budget available and slowing growth, online furniture retailer Cotswold Co. committed to more brand-led TV advertising to grow awareness and alter unfavourable perceptions. Print inserts, direct mail, digital and social amplified TV creative. The brand experienced an 8% revenue increase – its biggest ever annual rise – and grew household penetration. Research showed the brand became more appealing to audiences exposed to its TV ads. Brand building also made the retailer's search marketing more effective. It is estimated that marketing returned a short-term profit of £2.69 for every £1 invested.

Client comment

James Birtwhistle, Co-Founder, Marketing Director, Cotswold Co.

The Cotswold Company was born and raised in the era of sophisticated online optimisation, but as competition in the sector increased, we worked with Creature to take a creative leap. The campaign shows that by taking a creative leap, you can generate the kind of step change in effectiveness that cannot be achieved through optimisation alone. More than that, by taking a page out of the brand-first book, we dramatically improved the performance of our search-first activities – and all with a reduced budget.

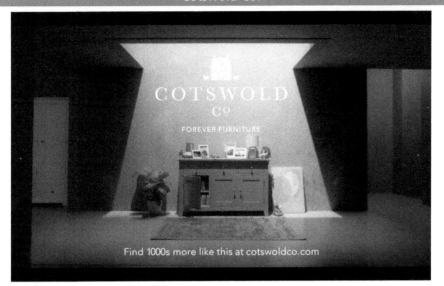

Formula 1

Unlocking the value of direct-to-fan for Formula 1

By Jackson Russ, Martin Delamere and Frank Duck, Ogilvy UK

Summary

Following an ownership change in 2017, Formula 1 (F1) aimed to transform direct digital interactions with fans and unlock new revenues. The challenge was F1's previous focus on deals with broadcasters and circuits left a dormant database and little or no direct contact with the fans. F1 created a new direct-to-fan relationship, recasting eCRM as a fast-paced, brand-building, global entertainment channel. This was built on magazine-style editorial emails with results regularly analysed and optimised, measured against a control group. Fans receiving the programme outperformed the control set on engagement, retention and commercial metrics, exceeding targets. The fan-first strategy is estimated to have returned its investment fourfold in two years.

Client comment

Ellie Norman, Director of Marketing and Communications, Formula 1

Since we started our partnership with the agency two years ago, they have helped us build up our direct-to-fan ecosystem. They are the lead with both fans and business direct acquisition for F1 and have been key to driving our F1 TV OTT service across the globe. This has transformed the way we do things and made fans more valuable to F1 with impressive returns on our audience investment. We have done this all at the speed of F1 and the agency is delivering commercial value as well as awards in creativity and effectiveness.

Formula 1

Heineken 0.0

Taking Heineken 0.0 to the parts other beers cannot reach

By Ed Booty, Publicis Groupe; James Moore, Publicis Italy; Javier Galindo Jimenez and Els Dijkhuizen, Heineken

Credited companies: Publicis Worldwide, Starcom Worldwide

Summary

Heineken wanted to launch 0.0 globally as a premium brand in the growing non-alcoholic beer category. Research showed consumers were sceptical about the image, role and taste of non-alcoholic beer. The 'Now you can' proposition sought to frame 0.0 as a positive choice rather than as a compromise. Communications created a new role for the category, showing consumers drinking it at work, the gym or whilst parking. Targeted social was directed at the 'active parents' and 'health conscious' segments, along with mass sampling. This paper mainly covers rapid sales growth and other results from the seven launch markets, from 2017 to 2019. The brand has subsequently expanded into another 51 countries.

Client comment

Els Dijkhuizen, Director Global Communication & Innovation, Heineken

With the Heineken 0.0 'Now you can' campaign we have targeted new beer occasions to expand our Heineken footprint. With this consistent approach we have been able to attract new consumers, and inspire Heineken consumers to drink our beer on new occasions all across the globe. A great result for a great tasting beer, with almost no cannibalisation and a positive halo effect on Heineken.

TAKING HEINEKEN 0.0 TO THE PARTS OTHER BEERS CANNOT REACH

How Heineken defied convention to build the world's largest non-alcoholic beer brand in under 4 years.

Authors:

Els Dijkhuizen, Heineken NV
Javier Jimenez, Heineken NV
James Moore, Publicis Worldwide Italy
Ed Booty, Publicis Groupe APAC

NOW YOU CAN.

KFC

Michelin Impossible: How an Aussie underdog took on the food establishment

By Toby Harrison and Ryan O'Connell, Ogilvy Australia

Contributing authors: Hamish Hartley and Charlotte Jones, Ogilvy Australia

Credited companies: KFC Australia, Ogilvy PR Australia, Infinity Squared

Summary

To unlock faster growth driven by Australia's growing appetite for quick dining, KFC needed to recruit more of the category's new and 'light' buyers. However, KFC's biggest barrier was the nation's long-held scepticism of its food's quality, which was stymying trial. After previous failures to convince the nation with rational communications, the brand took a different approach – by tapping into a highly emotional, and uniquely Australian, version of national pride. Following the underdog story of an outback KFC's quest for a Michelin star, the brand achieved an entirely earned-media-led campaign, sparking widespread national and international coverage and social conversation that lasted for an entire month. Post-campaign research showed seismic shifts in brand perceptions, which generated significant incremental revenue and doubled category sales growth.

Client comment

Sally Spriggs, Marketing Director, KFC SOPAC

Every three months, KFC Australia has a formal quarterly review session with all of its agencies, where each of the previous quarter's communications campaigns are reviewed in detail. Each campaign is analysed, dissected and discussed amongst the group, with the objective of learning from the work we produce; this is arguably the best kind of 'advertising research' there is.

After each review, a robust list of learnings is documented and then circulated to every individual who works on the KFC business; from the internal marketing department, to all agency teams. These learnings can be as 'upstream' as product naming and pricing, all the way down to the miniature of granular executional learnings, like font size and lighting.

This documented list of learnings is then applied to the next quarter's work, ensuring we are always learning, always evolving, and always understanding which campaigns (and individual elements) are effective, and which are not. These open sharing sessions, and the application of their learnings, are the greatest manifestation of how KFC Australia and its agency partners build a culture of effectiveness.

For the 'Michelin Impossible' campaign, the lessons learnt were, of course, documented and shared with the wider team, and we have already applied many of the learnings in subsequent campaigns. Given that it was the first time we had attempted an idea where the media strategy was to gain earned PR traction, the lessons were certainly new, and have proved vital in the designing of similar campaigns thereafter.

Lloyds Bank

Lloyds Bank: The power of pure brand

**By Benjamin Worden, adam&eveDDB;
Matt Delaney, MediaCom; Craig Palmer,
Lloyds Banking Group**
Contributing authors: Ricky Watson and
Catherine Slingsby, Lloyds Banking Group

Summary

After the financial crisis, while other banks focused on rates and offers or trust-driving initiatives, Lloyds Bank focused on using the power of brand. Believing that driving spontaneous awareness would deliver the greatest commercial benefits, from 2015 to 2019 Lloyds consistently ran creative with prominent branding and a promise to be 'by your side'. There was a relentless focus on putting the message in iconic British TV and outdoor placements, and 80% of budget was spent on brand. Awareness, perception of the bank's expertise and share of searches all rose. This paper details how the strategy contributed to customers putting more money into Lloyds' accounts and products, and recruited new users.

Client comment

Richard Warren, Director, Marketing and Communications, Lloyds Banking Group

Pure brand is a strategy that goes from strength to strength. It has enabled us to consistently create the most distinctive, effective and efficient communications in the category.

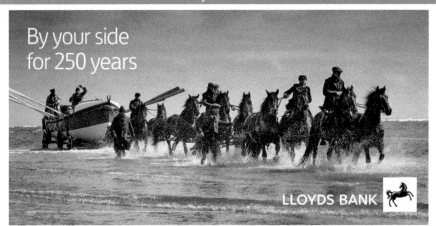

NHS England

We are the NHS

By James MacAskill, MullenLowe; Jane Dorsett, MullenLowe Group; Fran Griffin, MullenLowe Open; Sabina Usher, Mediahub UK

Contributing author: Jo Arden, MullenLowe

Summary

In 2018, when this paper begins, NHS England faced negative publicity, and a staffing crisis, with one in 10 nurses leaving every year and 34,000 unfilled vacancies. Communications needed to increase recruitment, encourage ex-nurses to return, and improve staff retention and career perceptions of the NHS. Over two years, emotive 'We are the NHS' and 'We are nurses' creative ran on TV, radio, social and outdoor among other channels. CRM recruited A-level teenagers and potential career switchers. Research showed NHS staff satisfaction and applications rose after the media activity. It is estimated communications drove 10,000–14,000 extra applicants and reduced cost per applicant.

Client comment

Ian Hampton, Lead Campaigns Manager, NHS England

Working with MullenLowe on the 'We are the NHS' campaign has changed the way I think about advertising and specifically recruitment advertising. Year 1 of the campaign was delivered at breakneck speed with the imperative to coincide with the NHS's 70th anniversary on 5 July 2018. This necessitated extremely speedy audience selection, insight generation and media planning. We didn't get it all right, but what we did do was deliver a compelling advertising campaign that resonated with the British public and, perhaps more importantly, with current nurses. We knew when we received initial feedback that we had something special. This was confirmed by being voted the nation's favourite campaign of 2018.

Year 2 was spent converting our learnings into a truly effective campaign – and this is what I am most proud of and thankful to MullenLowe for achieving – combining

Year 1 insights with world-class research to form customer journeys that will shape our advertising for years to come. We tightened our strategies, and crucially created an approach that was relentlessly audience-focused, evidence-based, and single-mindedly concentrated on delivering what we required – applications to nursing degree courses.

We didn't lose sight of the emotional engagement we'd managed to obtain, highlighting how wonderful a career in nursing can be, and our creative is a testament to that. With less budget, we targeted audiences with precise media and a keen eye on conversion. We then used that conversion to create a meaningful relationship with our audience, helping them over the line into a wonderful career.

I can simply say that this is the campaign I am most proud of from my 30 years in public communication and that working with the world-class professionals throughout MullenLowe has been the highlight of my career.

PPI Deadline

Billions to millions

**By Steve Parker and Richard Storey,
M&C Saatchi; Matthew Philip, Manning
Gottlieb OMD**

Summary

It was estimated 36m potential claims of payment protection insurance (PPI) mis-selling were not yet lodged when this paper begins. By setting a deadline for final claims and investing in advertising, the Financial Conduct Authority (FCA) aimed to bring PPI redress to 'an orderly end'. Communications was needed to motivate consumers to make a decision on claiming. A PR-generating animatronic head of Arnold Schwarzenegger was used in video, audio, print and outdoor. Results showed a step change in awareness, searches and claims after advertising began. This paper details evidence that communications drove relevant web traffic and claims referrals during the period.

Client comment

Emma Stranack, Head of Business and Consumer Communications, Financial Conduct Authority

Across the two-year campaign, Arnie helped raise awareness of the PPI deadline and return billions to millions. By investing in comprehensive measurement and continually reviewing performance against our objectives, we were able to make evidence-based improvements to the campaign to ensure clarity of communications, fair and consistent outcomes, and crucially that the campaign reached the more vulnerable and hard-to-reach consumers. The success of the campaign also resulted from the FCA's rigorous focus on evidence and effectiveness at every stage – from initial consultation, to creative development and ongoing optimisation. The insight and experience gained from this campaign will shape the way the FCA uses marketing as a key tool for behaviour change in the future.

Royal Navy

Building a brand fit for the biggest decision of your life: Made in the Royal Navy

By Elizabeth Baines, ENGINE; Ruth House, Wavemaker

Contributing authors: Zoe Whelehan and Susanna Cousins, Wavemaker

Credited companies: Gain Theory, Jigsaw, Great State

Summary

After years where recruitment meant replacing leavers in a shrinking headcount, the Royal Navy needed to attract 34% more annual entrants over five years. Marketing's objective was to increase short-term applicants by sustaining long-term consideration of the Navy as a career option. The 'Made in the Royal Navy' brand platform was developed to build the salience and emotional connection needed to support this life-changing career choice. Digital tools were also introduced to remove barriers to expressing interest in applying. This paper describes how communications exceeded targets over five years, whilst reducing the media cost per expression of interest.

Client comment

Paul Colley, Head of Marketing and CRM, Royal Navy

At 474 years old, the Royal Navy is the UK's oldest armed force, but without manpower its ships, submarines, helicopters and aircraft are rendered impotent, so recruitment is critical. In 2014, our recruitment challenge was substantial and we knew that we were going to have to make tough decisions – both in what we changed and in what remained. Key to this process was working in a truly symbiotic way with a range of specialist agencies, with the mutual respect needed to have honest and frank debate to get to the heart of the Royal Navy experience.

Together we identified the need to build a long-term brand approach that could be both consistent and adaptable. And over the last five years we have done just that. Stewards and submariners, ratings and apprenticeships, Carlisle to Portsmouth ... all 'Made in the Royal Navy'.

What we're becoming more and more aware of is that one of the great strengths of 'Made in the Royal Navy' lies in its being true to the lived experience of so many.

This means that every single person's own 'Made in the Royal Navy' story – whether told through an ad, at a recruiting event or over a beer – can be the inspiration for someone else to begin their very own 'Made in …'

Royal Navy

Tango

Rescuing Tango from a sticky situation

By Rachel Walker and Lucy Allen, VCCP

Contributing author: James Lomax, Britvic

Credited companies: m/SIX, Nielsen, Kantar, Movement Research

Summary

Tango was struggling behind its rival Fanta, which dominated the category. Fanta's relaunch precipitated the rapid delisting of Tango, which had to relaunch to survive. Parent company Britvic invested £0.75m in media for one year, making future backing conditional on proven success. Tango needed greater distinctiveness to justify its category role. It developed a new brand platform, rooted in the insight that 16–24-year-olds often suffer excruciating awkwardness, and lack the skills to style it out. This led to disruptive brand-building communications, attracting 1.4m extra households, stealing share from Fanta, and growing brand value by £11.6m in the year leading up to March 2020.

Client comment

James Lomax, Brand Manager, Britvic

At the start of this campaign, Tango stood at a crossroads – the simple option was to consign Tango to the history books. Instead, we took the riskier path: to invest in an audacious turnaround plan. This is the remarkable tale of how Tango's advertising rescued the brand from the edge of extinction, and restored it to its former glory.

The biggest lesson we learnt on our advertising journey is that when you operate in a large, busy category with many established brands (that you can't outspend), being brave and bold is critically important.

First, this bravery manifested itself in refusing to be a follower and adopt the same category norms as everyone else. The need to be different and cut through the noise was one of the principle ingredients for success – contributing to Tango's extraordinary value growth of 38% year on year.

Second, having a communications idea which is rooted in solid consumer insight ensures your campaign will go beyond simply being entertaining and have cultural relevance (which is crucial when speaking to younger audiences). Teens actually ended up telling us that 'Tango is a brand that understands [them]' – a phenomenal result for a notoriously tricky audience. As a result, we have now invested in upfront strategic research for several other Britvic brands' campaigns.

Third, ensuring that the brand turns up in the right way and at the right moments for the audience ensured that we drove quality mental availability, and we are now looking at how this 'cherry-picked' approach may help other brands.

Internally, the campaign has built huge belief in the Tango brand and its future potential – transforming Tango from a brand on a declining path, to one that sets an example of what can be achieved with the right approach.

Tango

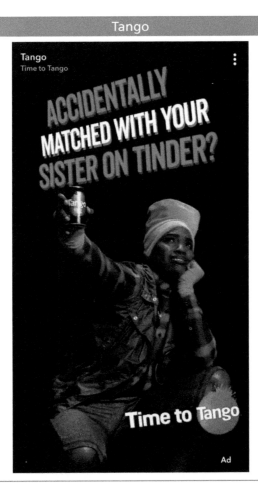

Truth Project

Making the unspeakable speakable

**By Sandy Doran and Jo Arden,
MullenLowe; Jane Dorsett and
Annabelle Butler, MullenLowe Group;
Tom Barlow, Bray Leino**

Summary

This is a paper about the power of advertising responsibly. The challenge was to raise awareness of the Truth Project, part of the Independent Inquiry into Child Sexual Abuse, which encourages adult survivors of child sexual abuse to share their personal experiences. This paper outlines the steps taken to ensure creative and media deployment were sensitive to avoid retraumatisation of survivors. It details evidence that communications was effective and efficient in conveying the Project was a safe space, leading to a four-fold increase in survivor experiences shared over a two-year period.

Client comment

Fatim Kesvani, Head of Marketing, Independent Inquiry into Child Sexual Abuse (IICSA)

Shockingly, child sexual abuse is more endemic than you'd think. As a result of our work, the ONS has now been able to estimate that nearly 3.1 million adults have suffered child abuse in England and Wales; equating to nearly 1 in 13 people.

The government set up the Independent Inquiry into Child Sexual Abuse (IICSA) in 2014. A vital part of the inquiry is the Truth Project, where survivors can share their experience in writing, by phone or in person in a supportive and confidential setting. This can be an important, restorative step in a survivor's recovery journey. Importantly they are also invited to make recommendations for consideration by the inquiry to keep children safe in future.

We knew that we needed to address society's reluctance to discuss child sexual abuse to help survivors feel more comfortable coming forward. We were reminded of the powerful behavioural economics principle of 'social norming' delivered via mass communications. This could help normalise the behaviour of coming forward to share stories of sexual abuse, minimise stigma and provide implicit support.

However we found ourselves with a careful balancing act to perform. A stretching target, led by the need to drive more testimonies to support real change, meant that a large campaign was necessary. But there was a real risk of re-traumatisation, resulting in a dereliction of our duty of care. Deployment of every element of the campaign, from creative development to media buying, needed to be considered sensitively. Managing this balance became the core challenge.

Truth Project

wagamama

Stirring souls and selling bowls the wagamama way, through the secret power of cinema

By Becky Geiringer, MullenLowe; Maria O'Connor, the7stars; Jane Dorsett, MullenLowe Group

Contributing authors: Ross Farquhar, wagamama; Annabelle Butler, MullenLowe Group; Simon Harwood, the7stars; Louise Cook, Holmes & Cook

Summary

With consumer confidence falling and closures in the casual dining sector, wagamama responded by focusing on brand building over price promotions. It targeted younger diners ('urban butterflies') with distinctive cinema ads, expanding the approach after a successful test to London, where wagamama earns 45% of its revenue. In 2019, TV was added as a secondary channel. Sales in control outlets near cinemas rose, as did brand metrics and purchase intent. It is estimated that the activity delivered 440,000 incremental customers in 2019, with penetration growing among the targeted group. Advertising's return is calculated at £10.80 per £1 invested.

Client comment

Ross Farquhar, CMO, wagamama

We've written this paper at a time where the very future of the hospitality industry is under threat, with no guarantee that guests will return to eat at restaurants in the aftermath of COVID-19. For an industry that has historically built its brands through great experience once through the door, rather than communications before it, we sincerely hope that this paper persuades operators sceptical of the relevance of brand communication and 'traditional' paid media to the sector to look again.

For wagamama specifically, this paper is a key milestone in cementing the role of marketing communications as a primary growth lever that began with the econometric study that it features. The extreme turbulence we're all experiencing means that the knowledge accumulated amongst people in the business is not enough – we simply must document what we've learned in a way that can live beyond any one individual.

The econometric study and this IPA Effectiveness paper are the recipe for recovery that we hope those tasked with resuming wagamama's growth story will take heed of.

To that end, the intention remains to re-run the econometric study at an appropriate interval to bolster our learning with a view of how the effectiveness of our approach changes over time, and in particular to review whether the success of cinema as a channel grows as it becomes an increasing focus for media spend. wagamama's second piece of cinema creative was released shortly before the pandemic hit, and we hope to air it again afterwards, so the learnings we've taken are already being embedded in our mix.

We sincerely hope that the tremendous results we saw over the time period covered by this paper are replicated and enhanced after it, and a sequel is submitted in the years to come.

wagamama

WaterAid

A partnership that has saved five million children's lives and built a new model for fundraising

By Mike Colling, The Kite Factory

Contributing authors: Will Richardson, The Kite Factory; Dominic O'Kane, WaterAid

Summary

This paper describes a 16-year client/agency partnership that has saved the lives of an estimated five million children and built a distinctive model for charities to use paid advertising to create value for, as well as from, regular donors. Three strategy phases are described, starting with a focus on performance before moving on to brand response and then finally, engagement. Metrics evolved accordingly. Initially, TV was the sole media channel, with digital and print added later. This paper presents evidence that the total marketing spend of £63.4m generated £448.8m in net income during the period. And, as a result of funds raised, millions of people gained access to clean water and decent toilets.

Client comment

Marcus Missen, Director of Communications and Fundraising, WaterAid

Over the past 16 years, we have worked with The Kite Factory to revolutionise our fundraising. We have moved from a model that focused purely on transactional measures, to one that also values interactions, engagement and supporter benefit. We no longer simply measure our supporters' value to us, but also our value to them. This new, integrated approach truly connects people with the cause, making them partners in our mission.

WaterAid

How to access the IPA Effectiveness Awards Databank

The IPA Databank represents the most rigorous and comprehensive examination of marketing communications working in the marketplace, and in the world. Now in its fortieth year, the IPA Effectiveness Awards competition has collected over 1,500 examples of best practice in advertising development and results across a wide spectrum of marketing sources and expenditures. Each example contains up to 4,000 words of text and is illustrated in full by market, research, sales and profit data.

IPA Effectiveness Awards Search Engine (EASE)

You can use the EASE search engine at www.ipa.co.uk/ease to interrogate over 1,500 detailed case studies from the IPA Databank. You can search the case studies by keywords and/or filter by any parameter from questions asked in the Effectiveness Awards Entry Questionnaire. EASE is free to use and is the first search engine on the web which allows you to do this. IPA members can also contact the Insight Centre directly, where more complex searches can be commissioned and the results supplied by e-mail.

Purchasing IPA case studies

Member agencies can download case studies from https://ipa.co.uk/knowledge/case-studies/ at a discounted rate of £25 per case study. Alternatively, members can sign up to WARC.com (see overleaf) at a beneficial IPA rate and then download case studies as part of that subscription. Non-IPA members can purchase case studies from the IPA website at £50 per copy.

Further information

For further information, please contact the Insight Centre at the IPA,
44 Belgrave Square, London SW1X 8QS
Telephone: +44 (0)20 7235 7020
Website: www.ipa.co.uk
Email: insight@ipa.co.uk

WARC.com

WARC is the official publisher of the IPA Effectiveness Awards' case histories. All IPA case studies are available at WARC.com, alongside thousands of other case studies, articles and best practice guides, market intelligence and industry news and alerts, with material drawn from over 50 sources across the world.

WARC.com is relied upon by major creative and media agency networks, market research companies, media owners, multinational advertisers and business schools, to help tackle any marketing challenge.

IPA members can subscribe at a 10% discount. To find out more, request a demo at www.warc.com/demo.

www.ipa.co.uk/effectiveness

On our dedicated Awards website you can find out everything you need to know about the annual IPA Effectiveness Awards competition, including how to enter, and who's won what since 1980.

As well as viewing case study summaries and creative work, you'll also find a series of over 30 brand films from over three decades of the Awards including:

- Audi
- L'Oréal
- The Economist
- Direct Line Group
- HSBC
- John Lewis
- Marmite
- Yorkshire Tea
- Cadbury Dairy Milk
- Walkers
- PG Tips

IPA Databank cases (A–Z)

*   Denotes winning entries
**   Denotes cases published in *Area Works* volumes 1–5
S   Denotes cases published in *Scottish Advertising Works* volumes 1–4

NEW ENTRIES 2020

2020	Aldi Ireland
2020	Aldi UK*
2020	Anusol
2020	Audi*
2020	Baileys*
2020	Barclaycard
2020	Birds Eye
2020	Brighthouse Financial
2020	Burger King UK
2020	bwin
2020	Campaign Against Living Miserably*
2020	Central Coast*
2020	Confused.com
2020	Cotswold Co.*
2020	Dairy Milk
2020	Diageo portfolio*
2020	Fidelity Stocks & Shares ISA
2020	Formula 1*
2020	Gala Bingo
2020	Galaxy S9
2020	Glider
2020	Gordon's Gin*
2020	Gousto
2020	Great Western Railway
2020	Guinness*
2020	Haig Club
2020	Heineken 0.0*
2020	Heinz [Seriously] Good Mayonnaise*
2020	Help for Heroes
2020	Hollyoaks
2020	ITV & Veg Power
2020	John Frieda
2020	John Lewis & Partners*
2020	KFC*
2020	L'Oréal Paris
2020	L'Oréal Paris
2020	L'Oréal Paris UK
2020	Libresse
2020	Lloyds Bank*
2020	National Trust for Scotland
2020	NHS England*
2020	O₂

2020	PPI Deadline*
2020	Refinitiv
2020	Royal Navy*
2020	Sambito S.A
2020	Samsung
2020	SickKids*
2020	Smart Energy GB
2020	Soreen
2020	Sudocrem
2020	Tango*
2020	Tesco*
2020	The United Nations
2020	Truth Project*
2020	TUI
2020	Vimto
2020	VitalityHealth
2020	Volvo
2020	Volvo*
2020	wagamama*
2020	WaterAid*
2020	Which?
2020	Whiskas

NUMERICAL

2016	5 Gum
2018	32Red*
2003	55 Degrees North**
2006	100.4 smooth fm
2000	1001 Mousse*
2012	2011 Census

A

2004	AA Loans*
1982	Abbey Crunch
1990	Abbey National Building Society
1980	Abbey National Building Society Open Bondshares
1990	Aberlour Malt Whisky*
2004	Ackermans (SA)
2008	Acquisition Crime*
2006	Actimel*
2012	Admiral
1996	Adult Literacy*

1998	Batchelors Supernoodles*
2005	Baxters Soup^S
2008	BBC iPlayer
2004	Beck's Bier (Australia)
2005	Belfast City
2001	Belfast Giants**
1998	Bell's Whisky
2002	Benadryl*
2006	Bendicks
2009	Benecol
1986	Benylin*
2010	Berocca*
2006	Bertolli
2007	Big Plus, The (Improving Scotland's adult literacy and numeracy)
1990	Billy Graham's Mission 89
2020	Birds Eye
1986	Birds Eye Alphabites*
1992	Birds Eye Country Club Cuisine
1994	Birds Eye Crispy Chicken
1982	Birds Eye Oven Crispy Cod Steaks in Batter*
1999	Birmingham, City of**
1988	Birmingham Executive Airways
2010	Bisto*
1990	Black Tower
1996	Blockbuster Video
2005	Blood Donation*
2014	Blue Dragon
1982	Blue Riband
2000	Bluewater*
2005	bmi baby
1994	BMW*
2004	BMW Films – The Hire*
1994	Boddington's*
2016	Bolia.com
2018	Bolia.com
2012	Bombay Sapphire
2008	Bonfire Night
2003	Bonjela**
1994	Book Club Associates
2012	Boots*
1998	Boots Advantage Card
1988	Boots Brand Medicines
2004	Bounty (paper towels)*
1994	Boursin
1998	Boursin
1986	Bovril
2000	Bowmore
2008	Bradesco
1986	Bradford & Bingley Building Society*
1990	Bradford & Bingley Building Society
2006	Branston Baked Beans*
1980	Braun Shavers
1982	Bread Advisory Council*
1982	Breville Toasted Sandwichmaker
2020	Brighthouse Financial
2002	Britannia Building Society*

1994	British Airways*
1996	British Airways
2004	British Airways*
1984	British Airways Shuttle Service
2018	British Army*
1994	British Diabetic Association*
1980	British Film Institute*
2012	British Gas*
1994	British Gas Central Heating
1988	British Gas Flotation*
2006	British Heart Foundation*(Anti Smoking)
2009	British Heart Foundation – Watch Your Own Heart Attack*
2009	British Heart Foundation – Yoobot*
2014	British Heart Foundation – Stayin' Alive*
1988	British Nuclear Fuels
1988	British Rail Young Person's Railcard
1982	British Sugar Corporation
1980	British Turkey Federation
2005	Broadband for Scotland*^{S}
2006	Brother
2007	Brother*
1992	BT
2008	BT
2009	BT
2010	BT
2012	BT*
2014	BT
2018	BT
2004	BT Broadband*
2005	BT Broadband (Consumer)
1994	BT Business
1996	BT Business*
2000	BT Business
1992	BT Call Waiting*
2002	BT Cellnet*
1986	BT Consumer*
2001	BT Internet (Northern Ireland)**
1999	BT Northern Ireland**
1986	BT Privatisation*
2002	BT Retail*
2007	BT Total Broadband
2010	BT Total Broadband*
1998	Bud Ice
1988	Budweiser
2002	Budweiser*
2018	Budweiser
2006	Bulldog 2004
1980	BUPA
2000	BUPA
2002	BUPA
2004	BUPA
2020	Burger King UK
2016	Butlins
1996	Butter Council
2020	bwin

2010	Corsodyl*
2016	Costa*
2020	Cotswold Co.*
1982	Country Manor (Alcoholic Drink)
1986	Country Manor (Cakes)
2018	Covonia*
1984	Cow & Gate Babymeals*
1982	Cracottes*
2004	Cravendale (Milk)*
2000	Crime Prevention
2003	Crimestoppers Northern Ireland**
1980	Croft Original
1982	Croft Original
1990	Croft Original*
2011	CrossCountry Trains
1999	Crown Paint**
2002	Crown Paint
2003	Crown Paint**
2000	Crown Paints*
2004	Crown Paints
1990	Crown Solo*
1999	Crown Trade**
1999	Crown Wallcoverings**
1984	Cuprinol*
2014	Cuprinol*
2007	Curanail
1999	Cussons 1001 Mousse**
1986	Cyclamon*
2009	Cycling Safety*

D

2014	Dacia*
1996	Daewoo*
1982	*Daily Mail**
2002	Dairy Council (Milk)*
2020	Dairy Milk
2000	Dairylea*
1992	Danish Bacon & Meat Council
2008	Danone Activia*
2012	Danone Activia*
1980	Danum Taps
2003	Data Protection Act
1990	Data Protection Registrar
2008	Dave*
2018	David Sheldrick Wildlife Trust*
1980	Day Nurse
1994	Daz
2006	Daz*
2008	De Beers*
1996	De Beers Diamonds*
2002	Debenhams
1980	Deep Clean*
2005	Deep River Rock – Win Big
2000	Degree
2003	Demand Broadband**
2011	Department for Transport
2012	Department for Transport*
2011	Depaul UK*

2006	Dero*
2008	Dero
1980	Dettol*
2014	Deutsche Telekom AG*
2009	Dextro Energy
2002	DfES Higher Education
2018	DFS*
2010	DH Hep (C)
1984	DHL Worldwide Carrier
2020	Diageo portfolio*
2012	Digital UK*
1998	Direct Debit
2004	Direct Line*
2016	Direct Line*
2018	Direct Line Group*
1992	Direct Line Insurance*
2008	Direct Payment*
2007	Direct Payment (Department of Work and Pensions)*
2006	Disability Rights Commission
2003	District Policing Partnerships (Northern Ireland)
2016	Dixons
1990	Dog Registration
2006	Dogs Trust
2000	Domestic Abuse*
2016	Domino's
2002	Domino's Pizza*
2009	'Don't be a Cancer Chancer'*
2014	Doritos
2011	Doro Mobile Phones
2008	Dove*
2012	Dove*
2016	Dove*
2010	Dove Deodorant*
2012	Dove Hair*
2002	Dr Beckmann Rescue*
2001	Dr Beckmann Rescue Oven Cleaner**
1980	Dream Topping
1988	Drinking & Driving
1998	Drugs Education*
1994	Dunfermline Building Society
1980	Dunlop Floor Tiles
1990	Duracell Batteries
1980	Dynatron Music Suite

E

1988	E & P Loans*
2007	E4 Skins (Channel 4)*
2011	East Midlands Trains*
2004	East of England Development Agency (Broadband)*
2000	easyJet*
2014	easyJet*
2009	Eden and Blighty*
2014	EDF Energy*
1994	Edinburgh Club*
1990	Edinburgh Zoo

2010	Ginsters
2007	Glasgow City
1986	Glasgow's Lord Provost
1986	GLC's Anti 'Paving Bill' Campaign*
2000	Glenmorangie*S
2020	Glider
1995	Glow-worm Boilers (Hepworth Heating)**
1996	Glow-worm Central Heating
2001	GoByCoach.com (National Express)**
2018	Godiva
1996	Gold Blend*
1984	Golden Wonder Instant Pot Snacks*
1988	Gold Spot
1980	Goodyear Grandprix
2012	Gordon's*
2020	Gordon's Gin*
2020	Gousto
1984	Grant's Whisky
2020	Great Western Railway
1988	Greene King IPA Bitter
1992	Green Giant
1990	Greenpeace
1988	Green Science
2014	Groupe Média TFO
2012	Gü*
2016	Guinness*
2018	Guinness*
2020	Guinness*
1990	Guinness (Draught) in Cans
1996	*Guinness Book of Records*
2018	GWR

H

1992	Haagen-Dazs*
2020	Haig Club
2009	Halifax*
2006	Halifax Bank of Scotland
1982	Halifax Building Society
1992	Halifax Building Society
1994	Halifax Building Society
2002	Halifax Building Society*
1980	Halifax Building Society Convertible Term Shares
1994	Halls Soothers*
1982	Hansa Lager
1999	Hartley's Jam**
2007	Hastings Hotels
2002	Hastings Hotels (Golfing Breaks)*
2001	Hastings Hotels (Golfing Breaks in Northern Ireland)**
2000	Health Education Board for Scotland
2012	Health Promotion Board Singapore*
2014	Health Promotion Board of Singapore
2014	Heart and Stroke Foundation of Canada*
2018	Heineken*
2020	Heineken 0.0*

1994	Heineken Export
2010	Heinz*
2008	Heinz Beanz Snap Pots
1980	Heinz Coleslaw
2020	Heinz [Seriously] Good Mayonnaise*
1984	Hellman's Mayonnaise*
2020	Help for Heroes
2016	Help to Buy
1982	Henri Winterman's Special Mild
1996	Hep30 (Building Products)
1990	Herta Frankfurters
1992	Herta Frankfurters
2008	Hewlett Packard Personal Systems Group (PSG)
2005	Hidden Treasures of Cumbria*
2005	Highlands and Islands Broadband Registration Campaign
2011	Hiscox
2007	Historic Scotland*
2006	HM Revenue & Customs (Self Assessment)*
1980	Hoechst
1992	Hofels Garlic Pearls
1984	Hofmeister*
2020	Hollyoaks
1982	Home Protection (Products)
1984	Home Protection (Products)
2006	Homebase
2012	Homebase
1990	Honda
2004	Honda*
2016	Honda Odyssey
1986	Horlicks
1994	Horlicks
2006	Horlicks
1986	Hoverspeed
1992	Hovis
1996	Hovis
2002	Hovis*
2010	Hovis*
1990	H. Samuel
2010	HSBC*
1984	Hudson Payne & Iddiols
1996	Huggies Nappies
1994	Hush Puppies

I

2018	IAG Cargo*
2012	IBM*
1996	I Can't Believe It's Not Butter!*
2008	Iceland
1992	Iceland Frozen Foods
1980	ICI Chemicals
1984	ICI Dulux Natural Whites*
1992	IFAW*
2014	IKEA
2018	IKEA*
1998	Imodium

1988	LEGO
2004	LEGO Bionicle
2014	The LEGO Movie
1984	Leicester Building Society
1996	Lenor
1986	Le Piat D'or
1990	Le Piat D'or
1996	Le Shuttle
1988	Levi's 501s*
2002	Levi Strauss Engineered Jeans (Japan)
1980	Levi Strauss UK
1992	Levi Strauss UK*
2020	Libresse
2014	Lidl
2018	Lidl*
2018	Lidl Ireland
2016	Lidl UK*
2014	Lifebuoy
2005	Lift Off
2012	Lights by TENA
1990	Lil-lets*
1996	Lil-lets
1996	Lilt
1992	Limelite*
1980	Limmits
1999	Lincoln Financial Group**
2000	Lincoln Insurance
2000	Lincoln USA
1980	Lion Bar
1988	Liquorice Allsorts
1992	Liquorice Allsorts
1980	Listerine
1988	Listerine*
2004	Listerine
1998	Littlewoods Pools
2011	Liverpool ONE
1984	Lloyds Bank*
1992	Lloyds Bank
2020	Lloyds Bank*
2010	Lloyds TSB*
1999	Local Enterprise Development Unit (NI)**
1990	London Buses Driver Recruitment
2009	London Business School*
1982	London Docklands
1984	London Docklands*
1990	London Philharmonic
1992	London Transport Fare Evasion
1986	London Weekend Television
2020	L'Oréal Paris
2020	L'Oréal Paris
2016	L'Oréal Paris Age Perfect*
2018	L'Oréal Paris True Match*
2020	L'Oréal Paris UK
1980	Lucas Aerospace*
1996	Lucky Lottery
1980	Lucozade*
1992	Lucozade

2008	Lucozade Sport*
1988	Lurpak
2000	Lurpak*
2008	Lurpak
2014	Lux*
2012	LV=*
2002	Lynx*
2011	Lynx*
2004	Lynx Pulse*
1994	Lyon's Maid Fab
1988	Lyon's Maid Favourite Centres

M

2014	Maaza
2004	M&G
1988	Maclaren Prams
2016	Macmillan Cancer Support*
2003	Magna Science Adventure Centre**
2007	Magners Irish Cider*
1999	Magnet Kitchens**
2004	Magnum
2012	Magnum Gold?!*
2009	Make Poverty History
2006	Make Poverty History (Comic Relief)
1990	Malibu
2018	Maltesers
2006	Manchester City*
1999	Manchester City Centre**
2001	Manchester City Centre**
2002	*Manchester Evening News* (Job Section)*
2003	*Manchester Evening News* (Job Section)**
2003	ManchesterIMAX**
1982	Manger's Sugar Soap*
1988	Manpower Services Commission
2011	Marie Curie Cancer Care*
2016	M&S Food
1994	Marks & Spencer
2006	Marks & Spencer*
2004	Marks & Spencer Lingerie*
1998	Marmite*
2002	Marmite*
2008	Marmite*
2011	Marmite XO
1998	Marmoleum
1988	Marshall Cavendish Discovery
1994	Marston Pedigree*
2001	Maryland Cookies**
2006	Mastercard
2008	Mastercard
2016	Mastercard
2016	Mattessons*
2014	Mattessons Fridge Raiders*
2009	Maximuscle*
1986	Mazda*
1986	Mazola*
2008	McCain

1997	North West Water (drought)**
1998	North West Water (drought)
1998	Norwich Union
2002	Norwich Union Pensions
1990	Nouvelle Toilet Paper
2000	NSPCC*
2006	NSPCC
1990	Nurofen
1986	Nursing Recruitment
2009	Nutella*
1994	Nytol

O

2004	O$_2$*
2006	O$_2$*
2010	O$_2$*
2014	O$_2$
2018	O$_2$
2020	O$_2$
2008	O$_2$ UK
1980	*Observer, The* – French Cookery School Campaign
2002	Ocean Spray*
2016	Octasa
1988	Oddbins*
2012	Odol-med3
2016	Officeworks*
1998	Olivio*
2002	Olivio/Bertolli*
2014	Olympic Delivery Authority/Transport for London*
1998	Olympus
1982	Omega Chewing Gum
1998	One2One*
2005	onlineni.net
2014	ONLY*
1992	Optrex*
2010	Oral-B
2005	Oral Cancer*
1996	Orange*
1998	Orange*
2010	Orange*
2000	Orange International
2000	Orange Just Talk*
1984	Oranjeboom
2007	Organ Donor Recruitment (Scottish Executive)*
2011	Organ Donor Register*
2007	Original Source*
1990	Otrivine
2001	Our Dynamic Earth Visitor Attraction**
2011	Ovaltine*
2016	OVO
1988	Oxo
1990	Oxo
1992	Oxo*
1998	Oxo Lamb Cubes

P

2007	P&O Cruises
2016	P&O Cruises
2007	P&O Ferries
2014	Paddy Power
1986	Paignton Zoo
2000	Pampers South Africa*
2011	Panasonic Toughbook
2014	Pancreatic Cancer Action*
1988	Paracodol*
2018	parodontax*
1984	Paul Masson California Carafes
2005	Payment Modernisation Programme
1982	Pedal Cycle Casualties*
2014	Pedigree
1998	Penguin
1994	Peperami*
2011	PepsiCo Walkers*
1994	Pepsi Max
2016	Pepsi Max*
1986	Perrier
1990	Perrier
2000	Persil*
2006	Petits Filous
2014	Petplan
1990	PG Tips*
2000	PG Tips*
1996	Philadelphia*
1994	Philadelphia
1988	Phileas Fogg
1988	Phileas Fogg
1994	Phileas Fogg
2010	Philips
2018	Philips
1980	Philips Cooktronic
1980	Philips Video
2003	Phoenix Natural Gas
2003	Phones 4u**
1998	Physical Activity Campaign (HEB Scotland)
2009	Pilgrims Choice
2007	Pilkington Activ*
1990	Pilkington Glass
1992	Pilsner
1986	Pink Lady
1984	Pirelli
1986	Pirelli
1990	Pirelli
1996	Pirelli
1994	Pizza Hut
1996	Pizza Hut
1998	Pizza Hut*
1990	Plax
2010	Plenty
1980	Plessey Communications & DataSystems
2016	Plusnet*
1998	Polaroid*

1997	Royal Mint**
1990	Royal National Institute for the Deaf
2020	Royal Navy*
1996	RSPCA
2011	Rubicon
2016	Rugby World Cup 2015
1988	Rumbelows
2012	Ryvita
2006	Ryvita Minis
2007	Ryvita Minis*

S

2004	s1jobs
1994	S4C
1988	Saab*
2004	Safer Travel at Night (GLA)*
1996	Safeway
2002	Sainsbury's* (Jamie Oliver)
2002	Sainsbury's* (Promotion)
2006	Sainsbury's
2008	Sainsbury's*
2010	Sainsbury's*
2012	Sainsbury's
2014	Sainsbury's*
2016	Sainsbury's*
2018	Sainsbury's
2008	Sainsbury's magazine
2001	Salford University**
2003	Salvation Army, The**
2014	Salvation Army, The*
1996	Samaritans
2020	Sambito S.A
2020	Samsung
1980	Sanatogen
1986	Sanatogen
1988	Sandplate*
2016	Santander*
1986	Sapur (Carpet Cleaner)
1992	Save the Children*
2016	Save the Children*
1988	Schering Greene Science
2001	Scholl Flight Socks**
2000	scoot.com*
1980	Scotcade
2005	Scotch Beef S
1984	Scotch Video Cassettes
1992	Scotrail
1992	Scottish Amicable*
2008	Scottish Government: Teacher Recruitment
2005	Scottish Power*
1998	Scottish Prison Service
2005	Scruffs Hard Wear
2002	Seafish Industry Authority
2006	Seeds of Change (Masterfoods)
1980	Seiko
2010	Self Assessment*
1992	Sellafield Visitors Centre

2001	Senokot**
2002	Senokot
2005	Senokot
2016	Sensodyne*
2014	Sensodyne Pronamel*
1999	Seven Seas Cod Liver Oil**
1980	Shake 'n' Vac
1984	Shakers Cocktails*
2012	Shangri-La Hotels & Resorts*
2009	Shell
2002	Shell Optimax
1999	Shippam's Spread**
1980	Shloer*
1986	Shredded Wheat
2020	SickKids*
1990	Silent Night Beds*
2005	Silent Night My First Bed*S
2009	Simple
2016	Sixt*
2018	SK-II*
2018	Skittles*
2018	SKODA
2002	Skoda*
1982	Skol
1992	Skol
2008	Sky
2012	Sky
1999	Slazenger (cricket bats)**
2009	Slendertone*
1980	Slumberdown Quilts
2016	Slurpee Flavour Fest
2016	Slurpee Xpandinator
2020	Smart Energy GB
1990	Smarties
1980	Smirnoff Vodka
1980	Smith's Monster Munch
1982	Smith's Square Crisps
1992	Smith's Tudor Specials
1992	Smoke Alarms
1994	Smoke Alarms*
2011	Smokefree North West
2012	Snickers*
2016	Snickers*
1996	So ...? (Fragrance)
2006	Sobieski (Vodka)
1986	Soft & Gentle
1996	Soldier Recruitment
1995	Solpadol**
1994	Solvent Abuse
1996	Solvite
1999	Solvite**
2000	Solvite*
1988	Sony
1992	Sony
2006	Sony BRAVIA
1992	Sony Camcorders
2006	Sony DVD Handycam
2006	Sony Ericsson K750i/W800i*

2004	Toyota Corolla
2014	Toyota Daihatsu
1996	Toyota RAV4
2008	Toyota Yaris
2018	Translink
2003	Translink CityBus
2007	Translink Metro
2003	Translink Smartlink
1982	Trans World Airlines
2016	Travel & Surf
2005	Travelocity.co.uk*
2006	Travelocity.co.uk*
1984	Tri-ac (Skincare)
2009	Tribute Ale
2008	Trident*
2007	Trident (Metropolitan Police)*
2004	Tritace
1980	Triumph Dolomite
2006	Tropicana Pure Premium*
2020	Truth Project*
1986	TSB*
1988	TSB*
1994	TSB
2016	TSB
2020	TUI
2004	TUI (Germany)
1982	Turkish Delight*
1986	TV Licence Evasion*
2006	TV Licensing*
2012	TV Licensing
2014	Twix
2000	Twix Denmark

U

2018	U by Kotex*
1984	UK Canned Salmon
2016	UK Government*
1986	Umbongo Tropical Juice Drink
2003	UniBond
1999	UniBond No More Nails**
2005	UniBond Sealant Range*
2005	University of Dundee*S
1998	UPS
2003	UTV Internet
1990	Uvistat*

V

1988	Varilux lenses
1994	Vauxhall Astra
1990	Vauxhall Cavalier
1996	Vauxhall Cavalier
1999	Vauxhall Network Q**
1996	Vegetarian Society
2006	Vehicle Crime Prevention (The Home Office)*
2004	Vehicle Crime Reduction (The Home Office)
2012	Velvet Toilet Tissue*

2001	Vimto**
2020	Vimto
1986	Virgin Atlantic
2008	Virgin Atlantic*
2010	Virgin Atlantic*
2012	Virgin Atlantic*
2012	Virgin Media
2018	Virgin Media*
2004	Virgin Mobile*
2004	Virgin Mobile Australia*
2004	Virgin Trains*
2006	Virgin Trains*
2010	Virgin Trains
2012	Virgin Trains*
2014	Virgin Trains
1994	Visa
2006	Visit London
2020	VitalityHealth
2012	VO5 Extreme Style*
1986	Vodafone
2016	Vodafone
2018	Vodafone
1998	Volkswagen*
2002	Volkswagen (Brand)*
2016	Volkswagen Commercial Vehicles UK*
2004	Volkswagen Diesel*
2006	Volkswagen Golf*
2006	Volkswagen Golf GTI Mk5*
2002	Volkswagen Passat*
2012	Volkswagen Passat
2020	Volvo
2020	Volvo*
2016	Volvo Cars*
2008	V-Power
1992	VW Golf*
2016	Vype
2018	Vype*

W

2020	wagamama*
1980	Waistline
2002	Waitrose*
2007	Waitrose*
2008	Waitrose*
2012	Waitrose*
2003	Wake Up To Waste (Northern Ireland)**
1992	Wales Tourist Board
2010	Walkers
2012	Walkers*
1996	Walkers Crisps*
2002	Walkers Crisps*
2016	Wall's*
1980	Wall's Cornetto
2006	Wall's Sausages
1984	Wall's Viennetta*
1996	Wall's Viennetta
1998	Wallis

Index